Disorganized Religion

Disorganized Religion

The Evangelization of Youth and Young Adults

Sheryl A. Kujawa, editor

COWLEY PUBLICATIONS
Cambridge ✦ *Boston*
Massachusetts

Library of Congress Cataloging-in-Publication Data:
Kujawa, Sheryl A., editor.
   Disorganized religion: the evangelization of youth and young adults/Sheryl A. Kujawa.
      p.   cm.
   Includes bilbliographical references.
   ISBN 1-56101-149-5 (alk. paper)
   1. Church work with youth. 2. Church work with young adults. 3. Evangelistic work. 4. Episcopal Church—Membership. 5. Anglican Communion—United States—Membership. I. Kujawa, Sheryl A.
BV4447.D574 1998
259'.23—dc21   98-17667
                                                                                    CIP

This publication was made possible through a grant from the Standing Commission on Evangelism and the Ministries with Young People Cluster of the Episcopal Church Center.

Pete Ward's essay "The 'Youth Church' Question" formerly appeared as chapter 7 in *Youthwork and the Mission of God* (London: SPCK). Used by permission of the publisher.

Cynthia Shattuck, editor; Vicki Black, copyeditor and designer
Cover photographs by Patricia Aboussie

Cowley Publications • 28 Temple Place
Boston, Massachusetts 02111
800-225-1534 • http://www.cowley.org

Table of Contents

Contributors

Ramón I. Aymerich, a native of the Isle of Pines, Cuba, is the rector of the Church of the Holy Comforter/Iglesia del Espiritu Santo in the Latin Quarter of Miami, and former chair of the National Hispanic Commission's subcommittee on youth ministries.

Dean Borgman is the Culpepper Professor of Youth Ministry at Gordon-Conwell Theological Seminary in South Hamilton, Massachusetts, and adjunct professor of youth ministry at Fuller Theological Seminary in Pasadena, California.

Edmond Lee Browning is the former Presiding Bishop of the Episcopal Church.

George Carey is the 103rd Archbishop of Canterbury.

Anna Chakko-George is a youth worker and tutor at Oxford Youth Works in Oxford, England. She is founder of the Intercultural Project, working with young women originally from the Indian subcontinent.

Steven Charleston serves as chaplain of Trinity College in Hartford, Connecticut, and is the former bishop of Alaska.

Cathleen Chittenden-Bascom serves as chaplain at Kansas State University.

Thomas K. Chu is the staff officer for ministries with young adults and in higher education at the Episcopal Church Center. He is co-author with Sheryl A. Kujawa and Anne Rowthorn of *Godworks: Youth and Young Adult Ministry Models...Evangelism at Work with Young People* (Morehouse, 1997).

Ronald H. Clingenpeel is the chaplain at Tulane and Loyola Universities in New Orleans, Louisiana, and president of the Episcopal Society for Ministry in Higher Education (ESMHE).

David E. Crean is coauthor of *The Journey to Adulthood: A Parish Program of Spiritual Formation for Young People* (LeaderResources, 1993-1997) and its offshoot, *The Adult Journey* (Leader Resources, 1993-1997). He is also the director of J2A Youth Pilgrimages.

Julia Easley is the Episcopal chaplain at the University of Iowa in Iowa City, and the director of the Agape Cafe, a student-staffed restaurant for the poor.

Catherine S. Edwards is the producer of the nationally syndicated radio talk show "Janet Parshall's America" and was formerly on the staff of *The Weekly Standard* magazine.

Ann Gordon recently retired as the executive director of the National Association of Episcopal Schools (NAES).

David Gortner is a student at Seabury-Western Theological Seminary and an intern at Canterbury Northwestern and St. Chrysostom's Church in Chicago, Illinois.

Jane S. Gould is the Episcopal chaplain at the Massachusetts Institute of Technology and the coordinator of MIT's Technology and Culture Forum. She is a leadership fellow of the W. K. Kellogg Foundation.

William R. L. Haley is the director of outreach for the Falls Church in Falls Church, Virginia, where he oversees international and inner-city ministries as well as leading Kairos, a ministry to young adults.

Timothy J. Hallett is rector of the Chapel of St. John the Divine and Episcopal chaplain at the University of Illinois, Champaign-Urbana.

Richard L. Harris is the director of Saint Augustine Ministries, Inc., in Boston, Massachusetts.

Lisa Kimball is the canon missioner for youth and congregational development for the diocese of Minnesota.

Sheryl A. Kujawa is associate professor of pastoral theology and director of congregational studies at the Episcopal Divinity School in Cambridge, Massachusetts. She is the former program director of ministries with young people at the Episcopal Church Center and coeditor of a *Resource Book for Ministries with Youth and Young Adults in the Episcopal Church* (Episcopal Church Center, 1995). She is also co-author with Thomas K. Chu and Anne Rowthorn of *Godworks: Youth and Young Adult Ministry Models...Evangelism at Work with Young People* (Morehouse, 1997).

Ann E. P. McElligott is principal and director of Christian Formation of the College of St. John the Evangelist in Morpeth, New South Wales, Australia. A canon of Christ Church Cathedral in Newcastle, she is the author of *The Catechumenal Process: Adult Initiation and Formation for Christian Life and Ministry* (Church Hymnal, 1990).

Clayton L. Morris is the liturgical officer for the Episcopal Church. With degrees in church music and theology, he has served as rector, director of music and liturgy, and organist and choirmaster in large and small congregations.

Sam Portaro is the Episcopal chaplain at the University of Chicago and author of *Brightest and Best: A Companion to the Lesser Feasts and Fasts* (Cowley, 1998), *Conflict and a Christian Life* (Morehouse, 1996), and coauthor (with Gary Peluso) of *Inquiring & Discerning Hearts: Vocation and Ministry with Young Adults on Campus* (Scholars Press, 1993).

John Robertson is an attorney in private practice in Iowa and an adjunct faculty member at Mount Mercy College in Cedar Rapids.

Edward W. Rodman is the canon missioner of the diocese of Massachusetts. He is the convener of the Episcopal Urban Caucus and serves as a consultant to the national and Massachusetts chapters of the Union of Black Episcopalians.

The late *Charles N. Rosemeyer* was the mission coordinator for the diocese of Pittsburgh.

Jacqueline Schmitt is the Episcopal chaplain at Northwestern University and the editor of *Plumbline*, a journal of ministry in higher education.

Charles Virga is rector of St. Luke's/Iglesia de San Lucas in Chelsea, Massachusetts, and cofounder of *Dreamworks,* a consulting group that provides anti-racism training and consultation on strategic planning to congregations and other groups.

Pete Ward is the Archbishop of Canterbury's advisor for youth ministry and author of a number of books in the field of youth ministry, including the recent *Youth Work and the Mission of God* (SPCK,1997). He has developed graduate courses on youth ministry and theological education at King's College in London.

Foreword

The term "disorganized religion" in reference to the evangelization of young people first appears in this collection in the article by Steven Charleston, the former bishop of the Episcopal diocese of Alaska, and current chaplain at Trinity College in Hartford, Connecticut. While Charleston's use of the term applies specifically to the reaction against organized religion among many young people, along with their subsequent religious responses, I found myself reflecting on the appropriateness of the term in characterizing the way the church needs to adapt to become more effective in our efforts in the evangelization of young people. While communicating the time-honored truths of the gospel as lived within our Christian and Anglican/Episcopal heritage, we are called to empower young people to interpret those truths within the context of their own experience and culture. The essays in this book discuss the obstacles and the challenges facing the church in creating ourselves anew in this generation.

Evangelization is not a one-time event, but a continuous, lifelong process of conversion whereby a Christian makes an ever-deepening commitment to a personal and communal relationship to Jesus Christ and to living the gospel message by working to bring about the reign of God. Young people are not unfinished Christians, but pilgrims along with their adult brothers and sisters in this lifelong process of conversion. Thus, conversion calls into question almost every aspect of our communal life.

This collection of essays is designed to be both practical and theoretical; it provides basic information, as well as constructive challenges. All the authors are engaged in some way in a ministry concerned with the evangelization of young people. In the editing process we have done our best to preserve the "voices" of the authors, and have not attempted to alter the expressions of their own experiences. Every effort was made to include diverse authors in order to stimulate the quality of the conversation.

Special support for the development of this book was provided through the Episcopal Church Center and the Standing Commission on Evangelism, which first envisioned the need for resources concerning the evangelization of young people. Thomas K. Chu and Julia Easley were involved with planning the shape of this volume, as well as the choice of authors. The clarity of the final manuscript was greatly enhanced by the wisdom and skill of John Ratti. The editorial expertise of Cynthia Shattuck and Vicki Black, as well as the gifts and skills of the rest of the staff of Cowley Publications, brought this book into fruition.

Consider these essays an invitation, an opportunity to meet some of the church's most dedicated companions to young people in their journey of faith and a way to participate in a movement toward a more faithful way of being the church in which you, too, can lend your own voice and perspective.

part one

Sharing the Good News

The Challenges We Face

George Carey

Like many others in many different parts of the world, my late teens and early twenties were crucial in the formation of my Christian faith. It was when I was seventeen that my brother Bob first invited me along to our local congregation, where he had started attending services some years before. There I, in my turn, moved from a reverent agnosticism into a living faith. That change is not something I can put a date to, but happened gradually early in 1953.

The years that followed were equally momentous. My time in the youth group gave me the grounding in the Bible study, church membership, worship, and private prayer which have stood me in good stead ever since. But it was as much what the youth leaders did as what they said that really impressed me. Here were people who were prepared to take time with me—who believed that who I was, and the questions I had, really mattered. The debt I owe to the young people I met in those days, to say nothing of the contribution of discerning, caring clergy, is incalculable.

Two years in the Royal Air Force followed and it was in Iraq that I first began to think that God might be calling me into the ordained ministry. Stuck out in the desert, without a chaplain in sight, I, and one or two others, took it in turns to lead services and speak at them. That first taste of Christian ministry excited me and kept me enthusiastic in the years that followed.

As I talk with people about work among young people, I am so often reminded of the significance of those years in my own life. More than that, those experiences underline for me the importance to our health as a church in having a strong work with and to young people. Their life and enthusiasm is something we cannot afford to be without, both now and in the future. As we look to the next millennium so we must make the evangelization of young people one of our highest priorities.

Let me offer two reflections and identify four key challenges to this work of evangelism. First, despite what some social commentators say, young people are not unspiritual. It is true that many of them have turned away from institutional forms of Christianity. In many countries, especially in the West, belief is often kept separate from the question of belonging to a congregation. Yet the quest for spiritual realities, particularly those rooted in experience, is common to all cultures. Such a quest sometimes expresses itself in mysticism or in a fascination with anything supernatural. Sometimes, too, it focuses on issues to do with justice, human rights, or concern for the environment. But what all these have in common is that they lead out of, or into, profound spiritual questions—and the church must be ready to respond to them.

Soon after I became archbishop I saw this in the lives of a thousand young Anglicans I took with me on a pilgrimage to Taizé in France. For many of them it was to be a week that profoundly affected their lives as they discovered their spiritual quest being reflected in the lives of their contemporaries from other parts of Europe and, indeed, from the rest of the world. Some time after that I attended the Greenbelt Festival in England, an annual event that brings together some twenty-five thousand young people. To sense the depth of their spiritual hunger was both enormously encouraging and humbling. No one who experienced those events could have gone away from them unimpressed by the seriousness with which they approached their spiritual pilgrimage.

My second reflection is that the Anglican tradition in particular endows us with opportunities for reaching out to young people. Both its commitment to education at every level and long history of social involvement provide us with the chance to build relationships with young people in natural, nonthreatening situations. As many have pointed out, a pilgrimage to faith often begins with friendship, and we must never underestimate the value of the kinds of opportunities we have for forming such friendships.

I think, for instance, of the visit I paid to Christian College in Madras, which over the years has provided education for many of the leaders of that society, whatever their own religious background. In June of 1996 I saw a remarkable project in Maputo, the capital city of Mozambique, inaugurated by Dinis Sengulane in the aftermath of the civil war that has afflicted that country for so many years. Adults are encouraged to hand in their weapons, including, as we saw, rifles, bazookas, and mines, and to exchange them for useful tools such as sewing machines. Children also bring in their toy guns and are given a nonmilitary toy in exchange; then they are invited to join a workshop where they can make toys of their own. In a quite different context, I think of the network of support for orphans established by Alexis Billindabagado in response to the genocide in Rwanda. Such examples of care that provide natural links with young people can be multiplied many times over around the Anglican Communion and represent a living tradition of service of which we can, with justice, be proud.

If those are my reflections, then what of the challenges facing us in evangelism with young people? First, the challenge of worship. All around the world the youth scene is characterized by a ferment of experimentation. In liturgy this is expressing itself in the development of many different styles of alternative worship services that show just how creative this age group can be—and how unwise it is to believe the media caricature of "Raves in the Nave"! The challenge here is to foster such experimentation with flexibility and accountability while at the same time finding ways to help the members of those services remain a part of the church and so allow their vitality and new insights to benefit us all.

I have already mentioned my experiences at Taizé and Greenbelt, but these are by no means unique. Norfolk is known as one of the more conservative areas of England, yet I attended a quite remarkable event for young people at St. Nicholas, Great Yarmouth. The church building itself is the largest parish church in England and, as we entered it that evening, we found ourselves in the midst of a kaleidoscope of colors and sounds. Within the building there were, among other things, three bouncy castles, a nonalcoholic cocktail bar, and two stages on which bands were playing alternately. Yet in the center of the church and much in use was a candlelit area for reflection and prayer, and the organizers had planned that a celebration of the eucharist should be the high point of the evening. When we came to it there was no doubt that it was, and the sense of reverence was almost tangible.

Second, we have the challenge of financial resources. While no one can quantify in monetary terms the huge amount of voluntary time and effort that goes into the care of young people, nevertheless the lack of financial investment in this area is a worrying feature of our life at many different levels. Youth work is unlikely to flourish if people do not commit money to it, and if more people are not employed to make this a full-time commitment. It is often a salutary exercise to look at your budget—whether as a congregation, a diocese, or a province—and to ask yourself to what extent youth work can be seen to be a priority within it.

Third, we have the question of training. Historically, in England and elsewhere, much of our youth work has been done by those with little or no specialized training, and there is still a temptation to avoid treating this question of training with the seriousness it deserves. I would not wish for one moment to belittle the achievements of those who have worked faithfully over the years, but the changing world we are in requires us to approach all our youth work with a new degree of professionalism. Too often youth workers have been undervalued and their skills have gone unrecognized or left underdeveloped. I therefore welcome everything that is being done, particularly in the United States, to enhance further the status of youth workers, both paid and voluntary. I also welcome the way in which courses are developing, frequently on an ecumenical basis, to train people in this field. Such developments are vital if we are going to see young people being trained up as disciples of Christ.

Finally, evangelism. I began with the story of the development of my own Christian faith. The late teens and early twenties are still a crucial period for many people in their spiritual pilgrimage and, as in my own case, it is often their peers who help them on that journey. But young people with little or no experience of church life will only listen to the message of the faith if they are welcomed into our churches and made to feel that they belong. We must recall that the church is always "one generation away from extinction." If all church members, young and old alike, do not hand on the incomparable riches of Christ, then we shall be failing our Lord. As bishops are reminded at their consecration, we are called upon, as a church, to proclaim the faith "afresh in each generation." My hope is that we will set as our goal to do precisely that—so that many thousands of young people may come to find, as I did over forty years ago, the excitement, challenge, and satisfaction of a living relationship with God.

Three years ago I visited the diocese of Sabah in what has since become part of the province of South East Asia. Heavy rain had been falling and our journey from the coastal city of Kota Kinabalu to Teleupid in the interior was fairly hazardous at points. But when we reached there we were greeted by hundreds of young people, many of whom were preparing themselves to serve for a period of two years as evangelists. Our service was interrupted by a tropical rainstorm, the like of which I have rarely seen, but it seemed nothing could dampen their commitment and enthusiasm. I left that place convinced that God was going to do a great work through them and vividly reminded how much we need that enthusiasm in all of our churches. Their examples reminded me that we must never underestimate all the good things God has in store for us through the ministry of young people, and that we need to seize every opportunity we can to further that ministry throughout the church.

The Church Will Be Changed—and That is Good

Lisa Kimball

The challenge raised by evangelism with youth and young adults is formidable. It is not because young adults present a problem that we cannot solve, or have needs for which we cannot develop a program, but because they bring gifts that we, the traditional church, may not be willing to receive. From where I stand, youth evangelism is not about numbers or techniques, but about our soul as a church. "Welcome!" is understood as "Come, join me at the table—if you look and sound and act just like me."

Are we, the established church, those who have made it in, ready to be transformed by a living evangelism that will transform the way we do business on this earth? Are you and I honestly willing to take young people seriously, to listen to them, to admit that God is indeed already at work in their lives, and to be changed by the encounter? I hope so.

Gallup youth surveys consistently show that about ninety-five percent of teenagers in the United States say they believe in God. On the other hand, Barna Research Group polls find that only thirty-four percent of them say that religion is "very important" in their lives, compared to over fifty percent of adults. "Religion is breaking out everywhere," says journalist and commentator Bill Moyers. "Millions of Americans have taken public their search for a clearer understanding of the core principles of belief and how they can be applied to the daily experience of life. Public confidence in both organized religion and the clergy has been renewed."[1]

In an interview around the October 1996 release of his PBS television series called *Genesis: A Living Conversation,* Moyers claimed that overall church attendance in recent years has held steady and in some groups, such as teenagers, it has actually increased. "People seem to want to talk about God," he said. It is true that recent novels, music releases, newspaper articles, and magazine covers reflect a new attention to religious matters. All over the country newspapers are introducing feature sections under the umbrella of "faith and values." The search is on, and in our post-Christian world teenagers are leaving the mainline churches. They are embarking on their spiritual journeys without us. If they do come through our doors and into our programs we are still playing catch-up and too often try to pour this new wine into old wineskins. I am not convinced that increased attendance, good as that seems, is equivalent to more young people becoming mature Christians. In a consumer-minded culture teenagers, like the rest of us, shop around. They will keep moving on until the church truly meets them where they are. More often than not, as a minority population stirred from deep within to find the gospel, young people view us, the aging churchgoers, with deep skepticism and suspicion.

Many young people bump into Christianity—on television, in the streets, by hearsay—as law and judgment long before they experience it as loving relationships, reconciliation, and wholeness. What they think they hear is either that Jesus is just for the wimps, or that Jesus would condemn them outright if he really knew what was going on in their lives. They do not want to go somewhere (and who does?) where they know that they are going to fail. They have little interest in something that appears to deny or trivialize their experience. For them the church teeters on the verge of hypocrisy and irrelevance.

If a teenager lives with his mother in a one-bedroom apartment, has never known his father, and is struggling to stay in school, he is not likely to walk into the beautiful, rich people's church. The Census Bureau reports that children made up nearly half of the chronically poor in 1992 and 1993, living in families that stayed below the poverty line ($14,763 for a family of four) in every month of those years.[2] Poor adolescents and young adults are twice as likely as middle-class people their own age to have a physical or mental disability.[3] They are three times more likely to drop out of high school: in 1989 almost half of the sixteen- to nineteen-year-olds had jobs, and by far the majority worked because they had to. Today the estimates of older adolescents in the work force range from fifty to sixty percent. The cycle of poverty continues. To whom is your church reaching out?

Friends matter more than anything else to young people. They are profoundly loyal. These friendships can lead to sex. About three-quarters of eighteen- and nineteen-year-old girls are sexually active, regardless of their race or their ethnic background, while almost a third of all teenagers have had sexual intercourse. In 1992 there were 505,419 live births to girls between the ages of fifteen and nineteen. Teenagers with the poorest academic skills and the least economic means are the most likely to have babies as teenagers, while every day an estimated 1,140 teenagers have abortions. If teenagers are having sex—or even considering it—they *know* that the church does not want them. It is that plain. So they do not go to church because they do not want to lie. Deception suits neither their desire for honesty nor their intuitive understanding of God.

Where is the church when they are longing to hear an alternative voice?

If they drink on Saturday nights—and most of them do—they *know* that their elders would not approve. And so they hide. More than half the seventh- through twelfth-graders nationwide drink alcohol and about forty percent drink weekly. On average, teenagers start drinking at about the age of thirteen. If we, as the adult church, cannot get through a family reunion without alcohol, if we cannot get through a vestry retreat without alcohol, if we do not tell the truth about who is and who isn't in recovery, it is no wonder that we are not in a position to help young people with issues as serious as alcohol and other addictions.

If young people have questions about life and how it works, the tragedy is that the last place many of them would go for advice is the church. Somehow we have sold them a bag of goods: they think they have to know what we believe and they have to agree with it before they are going to be welcome in our midst. Twenty percent of six- through seventeen-year-olds report that they have not had at least a ten-minute conversation with their parents, or parent, in the last month; it is estimated that the average American family spends just twelve minutes a week in significant conversation with its teenagers.

It is also estimated that there are 135,000 guns in U. S. schools on any one day. Violence is the leading cause of death among teens and young adults in the United States; one young person is killed every ninety-eight minutes. The murder rate for teenage boys more than doubled between 1985 and 1991. Approximately five thousand teenagers commit suicide each year, and three and four times that number attempt it. Gay and lesbian young people who are searching for their sexual identity are two or three times more likely to attempt suicide.[4] One parent, an active lay leader in the church, was unable even within the safety of parish life to tell the truth about her son's "accident." She insisted that he had fallen out of a third-story window. In fact, he tried to kill himself. Young adults are asking why, if we believe in a loving and forgiving God, are we so afraid to tell the truth? What happens in your parish at coffee hour? Are you talking about real issues? Are you hearing people's real hurts? Or are you being polite?

Young adults are searching for meaning. They are asking questions. They may even want answers. At the same time, we must recognize that we are missing something if young people—with their energy, their searching, their truth-telling, their willingness to try new things—are not in our midst. We cannot sit around and expect young adults to find us. It is not enough to put out our "Welcome" signs and wait. It is pretty clear that they are not coming in droves, and if they do show up very few become fully incorporated into parish life. More often than not, if young adults are brave enough to venture into church on a Sunday morning, they are quickly recruited to help with the youth group, to sing in the choir, or to serve on the outreach commission. We view them as fresh batteries, coming in to recharge tired leadership. We typically overlook their spiritual needs or the circumstances of their lives.

To established parishioners, young adults often come across as irresponsible and self-centered, preoccupied with their own lives and unwilling to make sacrifices. Older parishioners become resentful when young adults are reluctant to take on responsibilities or show up late for a meeting, but the life rhythms of young adults are not well-suited to those of a typical church congregation. Sunday morning is the best time to sleep in, especially when they are not in their own beds. If they are awake, they may have to go to work. The last thing that they can tell you a week ahead of time is that they will be there for sure at ten o'clock on Sunday morning. Neither school nor entry-level work positions are known for giving people much room to negotiate their schedules. Few young adults have the financial means to choose not to work an hourly job in favor of a church event or the retreat that everyone is pressing them to attend, so they rarely come. They certainly rarely pledge. And the frustration builds on both sides.

The nature of evangelism that will make sense to young adults calls for the radical reorientation of congregational life. We must learn to invite in new and unencumbered ways. We must learn to "be church" in ways and at times that fit with young adults' lives. Our theology is incarnational. Our baptismal covenant challenges us to seek and serve Christ in all persons, loving our neighbor as ourselves. Does that not include the unchurched young adult? We are not about the business of bringing Christ to the other; rather, we must listen for Christ already at work in the other and be prepared to name and honor what we hear. It is time to get out from under our conventional definitions of the church to discover the sacred altars in everyday life. Let's trust that God is big enough to handle even the smokiest sports bar or the toughest ethical dilemma.

For the last fifteen years I have been involved in youth ministry in ever-widening circles. As networks of youth and youth ministers we have worked hard and watched youth ministries grow in size and substance. We have faced hard issues head on: institutional racism, multicultural ministry development, economic justice, human sexuality. We have attempted to offer gospel-based strategies that lead young people and our church toward a vision of the inclusive reign of God. We have taken the baptismal covenant seriously and accepted God's help all the way. I believe we have been pretty successful. A generation of young adults whom I admire has graduated from high school and moved confidently into independent, faithful adulthood.

*But...*most of the young people we have worked with originally came to us through the church itself. We did not have to look very far to find them. What about the millions behind them who are unchurched and in pain? What about the young people whose parents are not active in our churches, or in any other religious tradition? Are we ready to welcome them too?

The young men and women who have been active in Episcopal youth ministries during the last fifteen years are already asking hard questions. They are going to challenge the comfort of our status quo by asking us, even those of us who have worked and walked with them, "Why are there no black people in this congregation?" "Why do we spend $50,000 for a new organ but not do anything about the violence in our neighborhood?" "Why is the church not talking about human sexuality, except to argue, label, and judge?" They are the young adults who make the connections between their Christianity and the world they live in. They hang out with friends at coffee shops, at work, at school, in the mall, on the Internet. They are looking for mentors and friends who take the gospel seriously and connect it with justice. They will work hard to change the system if the system is leaving somebody out, or if the system is unwilling to hear the voice of the oppressed. They are giving us the clues that we need for effective evangelism with their peers.

If, however, these committed Christian young adults meet complete resistance, they will probably give up and take their energy and their vision somewhere else. Loyal they are, fiercely denominational they are not. We, the established church, have everything to gain (and very little to lose) if we enter into evangelism open to our own transformation.

How can we do this? We need to show up, we need to listen, and we need to tell the truth.

We need to show up in the lives of youth and young adults by going where they hang out: in schools, on the streets and in the malls, in fast-food joints, dance halls, and coffee shops, in video arcades and parking lots, at sports events, in hospitals, in prisons and shelters, on college campuses. We need to find out more about them: read and digest information and statistics abut them, become "bilingual," learn to understand their language. Tell them, by our interest and not just by our physical presence, that they do not have to be perfect little adults in order to be noticed. They are worthy just the way God created them.

Then we need to listen, closely. We need to be available, to listen with our full attention. Listen to what is behind their vernacular or body language or hairstyle. Assume that God is at work in their lives and find those points of contact. Listen to the questions. We must learn to believe them when they tell us what they need or what they fear, to encourage their dreams and hopes. We need to make connections between their lives and the gospel, between their lives and the sacraments of our church. If they have been close to death or pushed to the limits with risky behavior, they might be ready to understand dying to ourselves in order to know new life in Jesus Christ. We must help young adults with discernment on questions of vocation as meaningful and appropriate work, being prepared to move them from an apparently secular context toward a theological framework and ultimately to baptism, when appropriate.

Once we are perceived as authentic, we have earned the right to tell our truth. We can then express our confidence in God, our own understanding of Jesus, and how our baptism influences our life. We can introduce scripture into the conversation and invite people to join us in reflecting on what the gospel means for our lives. We can raise questions about choices young people are making, help them imagine alternatives, identify necessary resources for effecting constructive change, and offer encouragement along the way. It is not our job to defend the faith; God will handle that. When we do not know the answer, we can offer to work with them to find it.

Above all, we must keep our promises. We must take their faith journeys seriously, negotiating a level of commitment that is both realistic and challenging while resisting the temptation to take them into formal church settings before they are ready or inviting them to worship services they would find alienating. Why not gather instead with a small group of friends for conversation and whatever activity suits them at a coffee shop, a movie theater, an art gallery, a pool hall, or a park? Worship together in that location and at times that meet their needs. Build up a constituency that will have some strength when it engages the formal church structures, and prepare the congregation to welcome these newcomers. We may need to translate or run interference at times, but we must always keep our focus on the gospel. Then we can try taking some risks: holding Saturday night worship service at a local community center, creating a young adult residence, initiating an intergenerational job fair, asking young adults to build a parish web site and teach folks how to use the Internet, starting a community service program for young adults.

If we in the church begin to tell the truth about our own brokenness, if we begin to see that in areas of human sexuality, alcohol use, racism, environmental degradation, and economic injustice we have contributed to the problems that are frightening and keeping young people outside, then we will indeed be open to healing and renewal and growth. As long as worship is boring and we pretend it is not, as long as it is not all right to talk about things that matter, and as long as the good news of Jesus Christ is buried underneath "We've always done it that way!" then young people will go elsewhere to find meaning and authentic community. I am not at all sure we can continue to shut out a generation of youth that is seeking the truth of Jesus Christ, without losing our souls in the process.

I know I have not given up. We have much that is good to offer young people today and they are hungry to receive it. Let's be something young adults can believe in. Let's accept the challenge they present, and trust that together we will grow deeper in our knowledge and love of Jesus Christ.

Endnotes

1. *USA Weekend* (October 11-13, 1996), published by a division of Gannett Company, Arlington, Virginia.

2. Associated Press News Service (August 19, 1996); *Youthworker Update* 11, no. 2 (October 1996), CCM Communications, Inc., Mt. Morris, Illinois.

3. The statistics in the following paragraphs are provided by the Children's Defense Fund, 25 E Street NW, Washington, D. C. 20001.

4. United States Department of Health and Human Services, *Report of the Secretary's Task Force on Youth Suicide* (1989).

Good News for Young Adults

Thomas K. Chu

In examining the area of evangelism with young adults, we realize not only that we have refined our ideas about human and faith development to include young adulthood as a discrete area of study, but also that the context for our ministry has shifted within the span of our lifetime. It is not difficult to see that young adults are absent from our congregations, our ministries, and our decision-making bodies in proportion to the general population, and the anxiety this raises about the church's future is part of the motivation for this study. In this essay I will raise some of the generational and developmental issues facing young adults and explore the scope of our ministry and mission to people between the ages of eighteen and thirty.

The term "Generation X" was invented by author Douglas Coupland for his work of fiction *Generation X* in 1991. Although he probably did not intend for it to become the code word it is today, for many people the term implies a group of young adults without focus, hope, or credibility. The field of generational studies itself is based on the premise that groups of people sharing the same cultural and social context over a span of years are shaped by it to such an extent that one can differentiate their preferences and behavior. Although some would seek to discredit generational studies research on the basis of its marketing orientation, it provides insights that are helpful to our work. Young people in the so-called Generation X, or 13th (U. S.–born) Generation, many of whom are adults today, were born roughly between 1961 and 1981. As a group, "13ers" have been shaped by common social and cultural experiences:

- *Television and other electronic media.* Not only do they spend more and more time in a passive posture, 13ers see the world as fast-paced, complex, and entertaining while being weak on the fundamentals.
- *Unstable families.* Fathers are often absent, and mothers are usually working outside the home.
- *Collapsing institutions.* At almost every turn, institutions such as health care, criminal justice, religion, education, and government services are failing.

◡∴ *Receding expectations.* Fewer expect that the continually escalating cost of college education will actually result in a full-time, well-paying job. The available positions are more likely to be marginal and part-time with few benefits, with the result that many people in their early twenties live with their parents.

What does this combination of factors result in but a deep cynicism that is in some ways well founded? Bombarded by advertising from every direction, and aware of the cycles of "planned obsolescence" of products and services, even children suspect they are being manipulated by the market. One can safely assume that those in leadership positions—politicians, CEOs—promote primarily their own self-interest over and above any sense of the "common good." It seems that the lessons to be learned by young adults from those in authority today are that people with wealth and power should consolidate their positions, and continue to do so. Knowledge becomes a commodity to be bought and sold, to turn the criminal justice system to one's own side, to avoid paying taxes, to benefit "me and mine."

In our own lives, we are distracted by a combination of "busy-ness" and consumerism. Some are working harder and longer hours to buy things they do not need, while others are working just as hard to meet their basic human needs for housing, food, and health care. In either case, many are overwhelmed yet at the same time have little to show for their fatigue. Given this reality, what suffers? Our health, time, and space for family nurture, opportunities for community engagement, and true leisure. In such an environment it is easy to be cynical, and to write off any commitment to others or to the "common good" as a veiled act of enlightened self-interest.

Where do the different parts of any community come together and share a sense of participation and responsibility? Although the common ground of town meeting, coffee shop, bodega, and general store still exists in some places today, it is mostly gone. Publicly shared spaces of main streets and parks have been supplanted and displaced by private shopping malls and atriums. Contemporary daily existence does not have room for much more than an occasional greeting from a retailer or service provider. As architects and planners try to combat this alienation, we are presented with yet more privatized expressions of nearly public space such as widely acclaimed developments in Seaside, Florida, and the Disney Corporation's new town of Celebration, USA.

In *Common Fire: Lives of Commitment in a Complex World*, Laurent A. Parks Daloz and his colleagues outline the shape of what they call the "new commons," where common ground is electronic, alienated, anonymous, and fleeting.[1] Even when we are with many strangers in a crowded restaurant or a packed elevator, we are alone together, or together alone. Yet not all of the changes that our culture has experienced have been negative. The increase and ease of communication and international travel means a greater, if not a deeper, sense of interdependence as a planetary community. Boundaries have shifted and blurred between work and home, secular and religious, social and natural environments, male and female, "we" and "they."

How do young adults cope with these changing contours? Some respond by compartmentalizing their personal lives and corporate lives, maintaining parallel and often competing value systems, suspending discernment and judgment when necessary. For example, Paul is a successful financial analyst for a Fortune 500 company whose policies and goals are geared toward profit at the expense of the environment, but on weekends he gives his time to the Nature Conservancy. Michelle faces discrimination on the job yet says very little about it, even to her colleagues. No one seems interested—and besides, there is a difference between ethics and "the real world." These are incomplete and fragmented ways of dealing with the world, but they are a reality for more people than we would like to think, even for ourselves as people concerned and struggling with issues of faith. Hypocrisy in our current atmosphere of cynicism is easy to detect.

Layered upon this reality is the paradox of the world getting larger and smaller at the same time, becoming more complex, with ever more communications and information competing for attention. This complexity does not invite easy and pat answers to questions, but rather indicates the need for a keener recognition of diversity and ambiguity, a greater capacity for connection, and more creative, reflective, and strategic responses to suffering and difficult problems in the world.

How do we address these realities as bearers of the good news of the gospel? In what ways can we be available to young adults who are both cynical and questioning?

First of all, each of us has opportunities in our daily work to demonstrate the presence of Jesus Christ. It is incumbent on us to offer our stories and make invitations to others—and not only for their sake. For our own well-being we also need to have good friends along the way for study, discussion, mutual challenge, and support.

Next, consider becoming a "threshold person" who can offer relationships to young adults that span the generation gap. In your life and work, take care to challenge, support, and inspire young adults. Be someone who can discuss ambiguity and complexity with integrity, and help young adults move beyond cynicism to a healthy skepticism, with greater awareness and more questioning and dialogue.

This can only be done by embodying commitment oneself. The etymology of commitment—from the Latin *cum* (with) and *mittere* (send)—implies a relationship rather than merely a personal choice; one is drawn out or led by a force beyond oneself. By whom are we sent? For what mission or purpose are we sent? What keeps us focused? In ministering to young adults, foster a sense of vocation (from Latin *vocare*—to be called) and be clear about your own calling in relation not only to your work and profession, but to the wider world and to all of creation. We can "teach the ropes" or help a young adult "climb the corporate ladder," but we are challenged to convey the vision and good news of what the world *can* become, a world that is reconciled to God and to itself.

Knowing that our "new commons" may demand new skills to fulfill new tasks, we may find ourselves learning to be good company for the journey rather than "teaching the ropes." So much of our institutional learning has revolved around the "banking theory" of education: placing material inside someone's head to be drawn out when the time for exams comes around, just as money in a bank account is drawn out with a check. Teacher and philosopher Paolo Freire condemns this approach in favor of "dialogical" education, where the human person, by virtue of being, has a "vocation to be a subject," not an object.[2]

Sharon Parks, in her landmark work *The Critical Years: Young Adults and the Search for Meaning, Faith and Commitment,* expands the well-known faith development work of James Fowler in *Stages of Faith.* Where Fowler offers six stages of faith development, Parks makes the apt observation that there is a unique stage of questioning in the young adult years, which includes what she calls "probing commitment," a self-aware search for inner authority to discern truth and a "fragile inner-dependence" not connoting weakness, but the fragility of trial and exploration.[3] For those of us extending hospitality and acting as evangelists along the way, an invitation is implied at this stage to relationship and sharing, to questioning and listening, to openness and engagement. In such a relationship of clarifying values and commitment, faith is embodied as an activity that Parks calls *meaning-making.*

She offers a helpful metaphor of faith as meaning-making in H. Richard Niebuhr's phrase "shipwreck, gladness, and amazement." In the experience of dealing with a disaster or threat to one's sense of self, God, and the world, one enters a cycle of "shipwreck," or shattering of reality, then "gladness," or relief that one has survived, then "amazement," or a deepening of faith.[4] Rather than a linear understanding of faith development, Niebuhr implies something more like a spiral or a helix. One scriptural story that might illuminate this point is that of the shipwreck told in Acts 27. It is often at these critical junctures of reality being shattered or significantly challenged that young adults seek connections with other persons or communities of faith.

On the corporate level, how do we prepare our congregations to be receptive and welcoming to young adults? The relational work of individual evangelists must be continued in the context of a celebrating community. One of the greatest gifts of our liturgical tradition is the intactness and richness of images, symbols, stories, ritual, and song that we have inherited. In a world that is immersed in commercial and disposable visual and symbolic language, there is a great potential for the symbolic action that is enacted through liturgical celebrations.

However, we can no longer take for granted that even those who received traditional Sunday school instruction in their childhood years will understand the meaning of so many layers of tradition. As an example, the symbols of water and the Spirit in baptism refer to many images and stories that few besides regular churchgoers recognize and recall. In a way, every eucharist needs to be an instructed eucharist, and perhaps our liturgical gestures need to be less streamlined and abbreviated but bolder and more public. It is imperative that our liturgy not become a living museum for students of only English culture and music.

Furthermore, our observances, programs, public ministry, and outreach constantly need to reach in two directions, offering ways to make meaning out of living. This can only be done in relationship. For the sake of our own integrity and wholeness, it cannot mean a vision of faith communities as places merely for pause and refreshment. As educator Maria Harris tells us in *Proclaim Jubilee!*, spirituality not only is withdrawing, turning inward, and attending to God and one's inner self, but must also be deeply involved with and engaged in the world.[5] In terms of scope, we can and should recast our modern concept of the parish to see it as a geographic and social area of responsibility for ministry rather than a church building.

What good news does the Episcopal Church have to share with young adults today? Our tradition honors the intellect and individual discernment in surroundings of communal relationships and ritual celebration. The good news, however, is not only embodied in the sayings and teachings of Jesus Christ, but is also rooted in the Hebrew scriptures and the prophetic tradition, one in which God chooses sides and calls people to account.

Luke's gospel tells the story of Jesus' return to the synagogue at Nazareth, where he read from the scroll of Isaiah:

> The Spirit of the Lord is upon me,
>   because he has anointed me
>   to bring good news to the poor.
> He has sent me to proclaim release to the captives

and recovery of sight to the blind,
  to let the oppressed go free,
    to proclaim the year of the Lord's favor. (Luke 4:18-19)

The passage from Isaiah continues:

to provide for those who mourn in Zion—
  to give them a garland instead of ashes,
the oil of gladness instead of mourning,
  the mantle of praise instead of a faint spirit.
They will be called oaks of righteousness,
  the planting of the LORD, to display his glory. (Isaiah 61:3)

At the end of the reading, Jesus rolled up the scroll and sat down, as was the custom, and then said to the congregation, "Today this scripture has been fulfilled in your hearing" (Luke 4:21). Perhaps as contemporary Christians we forget the urgency of this good news. Good news is not like today's lukewarm "human-interest news" relegated to the last segment of the evening news, but the kind of news worthy of sending a herald to tell others about it. God's choice of the poor, the imprisoned, the blind, the oppressed "to display his glory," is surely good news. Now is the time "to proclaim the year of the Lord's favor." When the church has achieved this wholeness, Maria Harris tells us, it can bring together the hallowing of time, gathering the people, probing the word, breaking the bread, and repairing the world.[6] Or as the prophet Micah exhorts us, we are "to do justice, and to love kindness, and to walk humbly with [our] God" (6:8).

All of these statements are radically integrative, and our vision, interpretation, and strategies need to reflect this. Yes, there are political, economic, social, psychological, and spiritual ramifications to embracing good news for ourselves and for others. We are called to create or reform inclusive communities that do justice, extend love, and practice mercy, that proclaim the good news by what they do as well as by what they preach—lively communities that "do what they say and say what they do." We are also called to extend hospitality to all, which means extending our boundaries. As we saw in the words from the prophet Isaiah, God chooses precisely those who are traditionally outside the bounds to hear the gospel. This extension of hospitality may alter our sense of time and space, of what is comfortable and customary, of who is "in" and who is "out."

Our preaching and teaching are to encourage dialogue and develop compassion, as well as to offer insights that acknowledge the complexities of the world. Celebrating and probing the word should give comfort but also challenge us to action, to our common vocation of *repairing the world*. We need to make space and time for pause, reflection, and assessment. The "year of the Lord's favor" in

Luke 4 refers to the Jubilee tradition of letting the land lie fallow; in the same way, our personal lands need time for pause, reflection, and assessment. More than any other institution in our society, the church must understand the necessity of pause and sabbath time, and learn to make better use of it.

Finally, we need to be aware of our changing social context. Just as Jesus knew the audience who was listening to his teaching and addressed each listener in a way that each would understand, we too need to be sensitive and adaptable to a social context that is increasingly multicultural, formed and informed by technology and science, and globally connected. This may affect our style and idiom, but not the content of the gospel we proclaim.

In all of these suggestions lies the basic premise of applying the specialized knowledge of young adults and their needs to what is the primary vocation of the church: to reconcile people with God and each other. When evangelists are doing their work of invitation and formation and communities of faith are doing the work they are called to do, when teachers and mentors are true partners along the way, God's will for justice, love, and mercy be done.

Endnotes

1. Laurent A. Daloz, et al., *Common Fire: Lives of Commitment in a Complex World* (Boston: Beacon Press, 1996), 3.

2. Paolo Freire, *Pedagogy of the Oppressed* (New York: Continuum Press, 1989), 58-59.

3. Sharon Parks, *The Critical Years: Young Adults and the Search for Meaning, Faith, and Commitment* (New York: HarperCollins, 1986), 84-88.

4. *Ibid.*, 24-27.

5. Maria Harris, *Proclaim Jubilee!: A Spirituality for the Twenty-First Century* (Louisville: Westminster/John Knox Press, 1996), 75.

6. *Ibid.*, 33.

Ministry for the Meantime
Evangelism as Marketing or Ministry? Sam Portaro

The faith of most young adults is a "work in progress." For that reason, I propose to play with several dimensions of the key word in my title. The word *meantime* offers rich material for reflection, and reflection is probably the best place to begin and end any consideration of evangelism among young adults. For where we have failed to proclaim the gospel among this constituency, it is for lack of solid, thoughtful reflection. And where we have reached them with that gospel, it is the result of an insightful and sensitive reflection upon the realities of young adulthood.

At the outset, it helps to consider that much of what passes for evangelism is actually marketing. When this is the case, we can uncover clues as to why such evangelism fails young adults—and, for that matter, nearly everyone from the baby boomer generation to the present. By now it is no secret that my post-World War II generation now identified as "boomers" was intentionally targeted by every major marketer in America. We were literally sold a bill of goods by manufacturers and retailers who courted our favor and lusted after our buying power. Many of us eventually wised up and even fought back. But given the subtle and pervasive influences of our indoctrination into this mind-set, we are at best "recovering consumers," as our habits evidence.

Given these realities, we have learned to be more critical of marketing ploys and skeptical of advertising claims. We are a hard sell. So are our children. They, even more than we, have honed a sharply critical attitude toward the marketplace. More than one of the "zines"—those print and electronic journals that more reliably chart the pulse of the present generation of young adults than their slick, marketing-driven counterparts filled with denim ads—have published articles and devoted whole issues to the wiles of the modern marketplace. The Madison Avenue sobriquet for "Generation X" flashed briefly on the scene and faded quickly. The label was quickly disavowed by many thoughtful young adults who saw it for what it was: a name imposed by media and marketers attempting to corral a whole generation into a neat and manageable niche. These young adults have been far more successful than their parents, who still respond to a name and a label given them by someone else. This generational difference has profound theological implications.

The baby boomer generation, given a name it did not choose for itself, actually grew into that name and adopted the lifestyle it describes. Even though my generation remains critical of this consumerist lifestyle, vacillating between love and hate, we cannot deny our complicity in the systems and habits that powerful retail marketing has created for us. This marketing system deployed every technology—radio, television, and all print media—in a vast educational enterprise that shaped the attitudes and habits of this generation. The method behind this madness bears striking similarity to another pedagogy.

Many baby boomers were among the last wave of Americans to receive a name at baptism, the name "Christian." We did not choose that name for ourselves, but actually grew into fairly decent approximations of it. Evidence of this is found in our opposition to the Vietnam War and our engagement in the struggle for a more just society even while we remained critical of Christian institutions and vacillated between love and hate in our relationship with them. When we reached young adulthood we mounted a rebellion unprecedented in its social force, adopting an attitude of suspicion of anyone over thirty (it became our rallying slogan), and attacking every vestige of parentalism, paternalism, and authority.

The boomers were critical of all institutional authority and favored open confrontation in the social sphere, mobilizing and demonstrating for social and political change. As we matured, so did our suspicion. While less extreme or violent, our opposition remains and continues to be expressed in a collective passive aggression, apathy, and occasionally antipathy. This passive resistance is, at least in part, responsible for the sharp decline in voter participation, a lack of engagement with or support for traditional political process. It is also apparent in the precipitous decline in church membership: the most obvious gap in the pew is not created by missing eighteen- to thirty-year-olds, but their parents' generation. While some of the boomers may have "come back when they got married" (the vain hope of those who chose not to pursue them), we certainly did not return in any quantity approaching that of previous generations. Moreover, because of my generation's antipathy toward authoritarianism, the boomers who did return did not embrace uncritically the traditions of a hierarchical church. Thus our children, the successor generation, has pretty much evaded baptismal naming. Some escaped baptism because their parents' ambivalence toward such practices spared them the imposition of the sacrament, others because their parents abandoned institutional Christianity and its traditions altogether.

If the end or goal of our evangelism is baptism, we must consider whether marketing is an effective means to that end. More importantly, we must seriously consider whether that end is appropriate to Jesus' own expectations of and instructions to his successors. If the intent of evangelism is to win more members for the institutional church through baptism and inspire their "brand loyalty," then marketing is probably as appropriate an approach as any. But we must also recognize that such evangelism pits us against some pretty stiff competition, not only within the sphere of religious options available in this pluralistic society, but also within the even larger array of pagan options available in the marketplace, where even the purchase of perfumes with names like "Eternity" has spiritual connotations.

If by evangelism we mean instead "an incarnate and dynamic expression of God's love for the world and each person in it that is so compelling it invites a response," then our evangelism will not look like marketing so much as it will become a ministry, a way of being *with* people in the world. This is precisely what is meant by our emphasis upon the Incarnation: For God so loved the world, and those in it, that God became one of us for no greater purpose than to *be* with us in a way that is accessible to us. If this is what we mean by evangelism, then we can benefit from a deeper consideration of what it means to be a young adult and to be, as young adults are, in the meantime.

∴ mean *(n)* **The middle point or state between two extremes.**
Young adult, as the words imply, is a status poised between youth and adulthood, a transitional period in human development. All aspects of the life of young adults are in flux. As they traverse the territory between youth and adulthood, they will invariably evidence aspects of each of these two extremes. This leads to an understandable confusion and ambiguity that is insufficiently appreciated at both extremes of the spectrum. The young adult's youthful, less mature peers tend to be scornful of his/her emergent expressions of adulthood; and the adult, more mature peers and associates tend to be scornful of the young adult's residual expressions of youth. The same is often true of the institutions around them.

Youth-oriented institutions cannot accommodate the young adult's desire to be and act like an adult, even to try on adult behaviors. (This explains why hard divisions exist between high school and college, and between college and graduate study—instances and contexts where age alone would suggest affinities that experience itself vehemently resists and denies.) But adult-oriented institutions cannot tolerate the young adult's struggle to shed youthful behaviors, especially behaviors that manifest themselves as playful or irresponsible. Few structures exist, really, to support the young adult in this transition, even to the point of offering sympathy.

For several decades the church offered some institutional assistance in the form of campus ministries. These communities allowed young adults on residential campuses to live a little more comfortably in the nether world of young adulthood by providing a safe space for spiritual inquiry and for practicing leadership (and making mistakes) in a forgiving setting. But this experience was limited only to those who were fortunate to attend a residential college or university; now that experience is further limited to those fortunate enough to attend a college or university where the church retains these resources for them.

More commonly, young adults are, in their earlier years, assigned to the youth ministry of the parish and, in their later years, are allowed to drift aimlessly—against the hope that the anchoring influences of marriage and children will reorient them to the church. While there are marvelously creative and courageous exceptions, the saddest phenomenon of all is the parish "young adult group," often dominated by a hodgepodge of singles and childless marrieds ranging from the late teens through the late forties. What is missing is an evangel that welcomes the young adult person, whose life is a roiling mass of change, with a spiritual and institutional setting sufficient in grace to accommodate the tornado.

⌣ meantime   (*n*)   **Intervening time or occasion.**

Young adult spirituality is a "time out," a time apart from whatever the norms of religious and spiritual observance may have pertained in a person's youth. For the young adult reared in a specific religious setting like Christianity, this may mean taking leave of the denomination or communion, trying a wider variety of Christian traditions, or non-Christian ones, or even none at all. For an increasing number of young adults reared outside any specific religion, this "time out" may mean experimentation with religion in any of its many guises, including very traditional forms of Christianity. Or it may express itself in a passive or rabid antipathy toward anything vaguely religious—which is to say, any institutional expression of religion—whether that antipathy is based in personal experience or not. It is neither helpful nor wholly accurate to brand this experimentation or antipathy as "rebellion"; it is probably more helpful and accurate to accept it as an expression of personhood appropriate to the maturational process.

After all, one of the transitions of young adulthood is the change from the dependence of youth to the interdependence of mature adulthood. In that transition we may experience the need to exert a fierce independence. The ferocity of this independence may vary from person to person, but it represents the energy necessary to extricate oneself from dependence. The closer and more entangled and constricting one's dependencies, the greater the effort necessary to break away. It ought not to surprise us that youth reared in highly disciplined, even restrictive, religions may go to extremes to free themselves from these dependencies. But the opposite is also true—youth reared in passive, even permissive, environments where religion is at best an elective may go to extremes to distance themselves from this environment, ending in highly controlled, rigorously disciplined religious settings.

Evangelism that seeks to perpetuate the dependency or denigrate the newfound refuge will likely fail. It will fail, in part, because it fails to understand the young adult's experience, the need to establish one's autonomy as a prerequisite to assuming responsibility for oneself. But it will also fail because it succumbs to the temptation to compete, pitting itself as a rival and demanding that the young adult choose—when what the young adult really wants and needs is freedom *not to choose,* room to explore and experience, to grow in relationship to the point of trust—which is another way of saying to grow in faith.

What is needed is far more difficult and demanding. What is needed is an evangelism that is willing to be with the young adult, to be present to that person and walk with that person on the way. It is an evangelism suggested by Jesus' walk on the road to Emmaus with two disciples who had just come from Jerusalem and the events of Easter (Luke 24:13-35; Mark 16:12-13). The disciples in question, Cleopas and his companion (possibly his spouse), were dazed and confused. They had just left Jerusalem, a place of tremendous activity and swirling stories, of myriad interpretations of crazy events that included execution and reports of resurrection. They were on their way home to Emmaus; more specifically, they were on their way home to the place they called their own. But before they could get there, they stumbled along, lost in rapt conversation about what they had seen and heard. They were having difficulty making any kind of meaning out of it for themselves when they became aware of another in their company.

The stranger apparently walked with them for some distance before they even noticed him. Gradually they drew him into their conversation. He gently reminded them of the story of God's people as he patiently outlined once more the history behind what they had seen and heard. A trust grew among them, to the extent that upon reaching Emmaus, they invited the stranger to enter (presumably) their home and dine with them. At the table, as he broke the bread, the *meaning* became clear and though for some time they had been in their own house, in that brief moment they found themselves strangely, marvelously, and spiritually, at home.

∽ **mean** (*vi*)   **To intend or design for some purpose.**

Those disciples, like their contemporary counterparts, were seeking *meaning*, seeking to find some ultimate purpose in their lives, for their lives. This is the primary work of young adulthood, assuming responsibility for the meaning of one's life, a life that heretofore has been defined and interpreted by others. Parents and friends impose meaning upon our lives, for good or for ill. The fortunate among us grow up loved and cherished, with a sense of self-worth balanced by humility. But even the best parents and the most supportive environment can be undermined by the powerful and even demonic forces loose among us.

A loving family can lose a child or young adult to the wellspring of peer affections represented in a gang or a zealous religious cult—or just the pervasive messages of a retail marketing culture that defines the standards of beauty, style, achievement, and worth. Powerful cultural messages that degrade and demean a person's race or sexuality or gender or abilities can overwhelm and undermine the most affirmative childhood. Perhaps worse still are those powerful and corrosive messages that tyrannize the insecurities and doubts of vulnerable children, youth, and young—and even mature—adults. These are the images that limit beauty to a narrow, unattainable standard and place more value on a particular brand of athletic footwear than on a human life. These are the myriad forces that surround the young adult struggling to establish and enrich the sense of self, challenged to define what that self means: "What does it mean to be who I am, where I am, now?"

As the African proverb maintains, it takes a village to assist a child through this process. Indeed, it takes the concerted efforts of a whole community of "whole" people a whole lifetime to sustain us in this journey. It takes more than a caring pastor, a dedicated campus chaplain, a devoted Sunday school teacher, or a single creative program. It takes an intentional commitment to be present to one another, to accompany one another, all along the way.

This companioning, which seems to have been the hallmark of Jesus' own ministry, runs counter to our competitiveness and our temptation to egotism. It challenges us to commit to relationship, to genuine sharing. This is what it means to be a true mentor, to accompany another in a process of mutual growth and discovery. But mutuality itself is a challenge; it admits no distinction of inferior or superior.

∽ **mean** (*adj*)   **Poor or inferior in grade or quality. Having little worth or consequence.**

The realities of young adulthood—its transitional nature and its ambiguity—do not endear it to institutional religion, which values stability and certainty. Only lately has the larger culture begun to appreciate the flexibility and ambiguity as something other than liabilities. The corporate business culture, like the religious culture, tended (and still does in some sectors) to relegate young adults to positions of little responsibility and to punish them severely for instability. In business, married men, for example, were sometimes hired and promoted over single men on the assumption that marriage evidenced stability. Women were once confined to the secretarial pool and perpetual youth in language that referred to them collectively as "the girls."

Such attitudes—and they persist even if their guises have changed—lend to the "meantime" of young adulthood the specter of this pervasive judgment that sees them and their status as somehow inferior. Even so seemingly innocent an expression as "young adults are the church of the future" denies the value and importance of young adults to the present life and leadership of the church. Until we address this insidious ageism—which is actually as difficult to dislodge as our racism and sexism, since it crosses both realms—we consign whole generations to a meaner, lower status and deny them their contribution. Every life of every person at every stage of maturation makes a significant contribution to the life of the whole. Does our evangelism incarnate that gospel and proclaim it?

◡ **mean** *(adj)* Vicious; ill-tempered.
While times and practices have certainly changed, these are still mean times for many young adults. American society denies them youth but withholds adulthood, thus protracting their sojourn "in the meantime." Their childhood is often assaulted by premature demands for mature behavior, asking them to shoulder the responsibilities of self-discipline before they are ready. They may be required to assimilate the wrenching emotional impact of divorce, to make moral decisions and shape essential disciplines without parental direction, and are pressed to achieve beyond their years. Yet they are simultaneously barred from adulthood by an inflation of academic credentialing that makes an undergraduate degree equivalent to yesterday's high school diploma, lengthening their financial dependency upon parents or saddling them with a crippling load of debt.

They undertake the demanding transition from youth to adulthood in an economic marketplace that continually increases the standard for success while it grows increasingly competitive. Those fortunate enough to find jobs are often underemployed, which once again holds them at arm's length from adult responsibility and access to adult society. Low wages and scarcity of jobs send many young adults home to their parents as the only means of economic survival. Furthermore, those whose education and experience are wasted in menial jobs and those who are compelled to live at home, either out of their own financial need or the needs of their aging parents, see themselves made the butt of jokes each evening on television. While there are plenty of exceptions, this is still the reality for many—and these are the young adults privileged by race and/or means, those who complete high school and college or even beyond. The reality is magnified to tragic proportions for those without such privilege, as the literature on poverty and the lengthening litanies of desperation's violence in the daily news reveal.

Evangelism that places a premium on conviction and commitment, on involvement and participation, on the contribution of talents and treasures, cannot reach young adults because they cannot meet its demands. Such evangelism denies them the necessary ambiguity and room for exploration that might lead one day to commitment. This kind of evangelism also denies them the time out and the place apart necessary to establish their own sense of self and asks them to give time, energy, and money they do not have. That's not good news; that's bad news. Worse, it's mean; it makes the "meantime" even meaner.

◡ mean *(adj)* Difficult; troublesome; dangerous.

Is it any wonder, then, that young adults seem to the church difficult and troublesome? People meanly treated can hardly be expected to behave differently. People who are dismissed by the church as worthless or useless are always a little difficult to deal with. Is that a harsh indictment of the church—of our church? Perhaps. But before we get defensive and argumentative (which is to say, difficult and troublesome), ask what kind of evangel our church proclaims to young adults.

Are they greeted like an alien species and treated as ornaments scattered decoratively around the worship space? (Tokenism is not confined to racism.) If they grew up in the parish, are they still addressed by their childhood nicknames? Worse, are they treated and referred to as "kids"? Are they offered opportunities to explore their own spiritual questions and to socialize with their peers, or are they assigned to lead the youth program and wait tables at the parish pancake supper?

Are young adults accepted as seekers whose questions offer us continual opportunity to confess the living faith that is in us, or are they and their inquiries feared as dangerous and intrusive? Are they welcomed as full, participating members? Are they accorded full consideration for positions of leadership and responsibility? Are they offered opportunities and challenges appropriate to their gifts? Are they appreciated and thanked for their questions and their contributions?

Most important (and this principle pertains to children and youth, as well as young adults), are they attended and accompanied in their journey by a sensitive, patient, caring company of believers—the congregation—or are they expected to tag along, tolerated so long as they "behave"? Any person or congregation that undertakes to make the journey as companion and friend to young adults knows the rewards of such caring evangelism.

↶ mean   (v)   To be of specified importance.

The "meantime" of young adulthood is, then, a time of specific importance, a necessary and even desirable time, a time that means something. To the extent that the church appreciates and even celebrates specific gifts of young adulthood, it evidences an evangel with integrity, an evangel consonant with the ministry of Jesus and his gospel.

In his lifetime, Jesus was frequently portrayed as surrounded by a rich variety of people. He welcomed and, in dramatic fashion, included people of every age, gender, creed, and race within his embrace, often in blatant defiance of the established norm for his time and culture. Until he comes again, Jesus is supposedly represented by a body of believers bearing his name, a church whose likeness is to be, in every way, like his in order that the world might see and know God. Until he comes again, such a ministry is what is demanded of us—for the meantime.

Building a Successful Youth Ministry

Charles N. Rosemeyer

"Effective, holistic, outreach-oriented youth ministry in every congregation!" That was the dream in 1989 when I accepted a position to help congregations throughout the Pittsburgh area develop youth ministry programs for junior and senior high students. However, at first it did not go as well as I had hoped. To my dismay I discovered that some congregations, even with effective full-time staff, seemed unable to develop such a program, although others with only part-time or volunteer staff were able to do a very effective job. I decided to try to find out why this was true and what could be done to help bring about stable youth ministry in every congregation in the diocese. My research to determine what produces effective youth ministry began with local congregations, and then progressed to other congregations around the country. Eventually this quest led me to over three hundred fifty youth ministry programs across the country in order to discover the critical questions that must be addressed in a congregation that wishes to foster an effective youth ministry.

The chief problem I found was that over half of the youth ministry programs I studied start and stop every year. The leaders change. The program changes. They have no plan, no training, no set program, and no evaluation process. Little or no support is received from the congregation in the form of education or leadership development for young people or adults. In well over half the congregations, only a small fraction of the young people who are baptized are still attending by the age of eighteen. Little evangelism of any kind takes place with adults, let alone with young people.

After a year of collecting data on youth ministry programs, I began to see a consistent pattern in what congregations with and without well-established, effective youth ministries did. To my surprise these characteristics were mainly philosophical and organizational, and only to a lesser degree were they programmatic in nature. Successful program formats seem to abound in great variety. Some were focused on multimedia, some on speakers, some on worship, some on drama. Some programs were led by young people, some by adults, and some by both groups. Some programs always met in a church building, while others chose different settings. In other words, the *what* and the *how* of the youth ministry program was less important to its effectiveness than *why* the program existed in the first place. In effect, youth ministry is much like building a house. The foundation, although far less noticeable than the exterior, is essential to the long life of the house. Any number of different houses could be built on a solid foundation, but if there is a poor foundation, no matter how attractive the house, it will not last.

✌ Essential Elements
In the course of my research I discerned five essential elements in effective youth ministry programs:

  ✌ A youth ministry program must have a *mission statement* with clear goals and objectives.

  ✌ A youth ministry program should run *the same activities* for several years based on the goals and objectives of the mission statement.

  ✌ A youth ministry program must be *evaluated* often and adjusted to meet the evolving needs of young people.

  ✌ A youth ministry program should *train* its core young people into peer leaders.

  ✌ A congregation that wants an effective youth ministry program must have an effective *Christian education program for all ages,* especially adults.

I would like now to consider each element in turn.

Mission statement
Effective youth ministries all have clear mission statements. More importantly, they have clear goals and objectives that are translated into a consistent program plan so that even if staff or volunteers leave, the structure of the program basically remains the same. Furthermore, the youth ministry mission statement and the congregation's mission statement must be compatible. In most of the cases I observed, the youth ministry's mission statement was developed from the congregation's and both were heading in the same direction.

Ineffective youth ministries I studied were just the opposite—neither they nor the affiliated congregation had real focus or direction. Planning was done with a calendar in one hand and a program wish-list in the other. Events were held, but no one knew what they hoped to accomplish, or why. While sometimes a congregation might be fortunate in hiring a person of exceptional skill who was able to develop a youth ministry program despite the lack of direction, the congregation would often find itself, usually after several years, in conflict with the youth ministry program. The latter, which had grown large enough to put pressure on the congregation to change in some way, was moving in a direction that the congregation did not want to go.

Many congregations work at thirty percent efficiency. That is, thirty percent of their members attend worship each week and thirty percent of that group participates in Christian education. When the youth ministry program begins to exceed this ratio, it puts pressure on the congregation to change. Rooms, money, times of events, and so on may need adjusting to make room for the dynamic, expanding youth program. It is often easier for a congregation to find a way to "kill" the youth ministry than to change, so the parish may cut the budget, reduce the staff, or limit availability of the physical plant. Subconscious though it might be, the congregation usually finds a way to return the youth program to a size with which they are comfortable.

Continuity

As I mentioned earlier, almost half the youth ministries in the survey shut down every year only to reopen as soon as a new "warm body" could be found and a new program format could be established. However, in the successful youth ministry programs the same program format has been used for seven years or more. All people, not just young people, are uncomfortable with change—especially change in which they have not played a part. For example, imagine if each year the rector of a congregation left and a whole new style of worship and program were instituted. The adults would never stay in the congregation. Neither do young people. This need for stability is also a significant reason for suggesting that the goals of the youth ministry program be based on the mission statement, goals, and objectives of the congregation, so that programs for youth are grounded by the focus of the entire congregation. Once the program format is developed it should be continually adjusted, but not dramatically changed, each year.

Evaluation

Evaluation was a regular part of the ministry within congregations producing effective, growing youth ministries. The more seriously the leadership took evaluation, the better the program. Successful youth ministries had a passion for excellence and were unwilling to stop improving. The program format was changed slowly, based on the evaluation. From the outside, the program never seemed to change—it just got better.

Relationships first

A major point that stood out clearly in the research findings was that effective youth ministry programs should be driven by relationships first and program second. In the healthy youth ministry programs there was a one-to-five ratio of leaders to young people. In these instances, the program reached at least forty percent of the youth on their rolls. More often than not they were in contact with almost all the youth in the congregation, and their friends. This ratio held no matter what the size of the program. On the other hand, in less effective youth ministry programs the ratio slipped to one adult leader to three young people, and they were reaching less than forty percent of the young people on their rolls. Thus, in a successful youth ministry, if a congregation had two leaders they would average ten young people per meeting; three leaders would mean an average of fifteen young people per meeting.

Adult education

My research suggests that strong adult education programs, though at first seemingly unrelated to youth ministry, had a definite impact on the youth ministry program in congregations. If a congregation had an effective adult education program—one reaching more than forty percent of its adult members—then it generally could support an effective youth ministry program. This was true for two reasons. First, participation in most junior and senior high ministries will fall off to the same level of involvement as the adults in the Christian education program.[1]

Second, youth ministry is driven by relationships first and program second, yet most congregations simply do not have enough trained, mature Christian adults to run a program for all the youth in their community. Typically, ten to twenty percent of a congregation will consist of young people of junior and senior high school age; a congregation of two hundred fifty people may have between twenty-five and fifty young people of high school age. Thus, the leadership team for youth ministry should be five to ten people simply to reach young people on the church rolls, and more if they want to reach out to unchurched youth. A congregation can only have that many potential leaders if it has an effective adult education ministry that is constantly training new leaders. So it was not uncommon to see congregations with effective youth ministry programs having fifty to sixty percent of their adults participating in some form of Christian education.

For example, in 1985 at a three-hundred-member congregation in Pittsburgh, a new minister began an extensive program to build up the adult education program. After five years almost half the congregation was involved in small groups, seminars, and/or Christian education. When the congregation suggested they hire a youth leader, the pastor encouraged them to begin a class for potential volunteer youth leaders. The day the youth leader started the class he had twenty-five potential volunteers and no kids. Just over a year later, the congregation was working with one hundred twenty-five on a weekly basis.

✅ Further Recommendations
In addition to the five essential elements I have just described, I would like to make four suggestions that I found important to the success of a youth program.
- ✅ A youth ministry program should provide *regular training* for its staff and volunteer leaders at least three times a year.
- ✅ A youth worker should *balance* his or her time among program, administration, pastoral work with young people, and developing leadership.
- ✅ A balanced program should have *three levels:* evangelism, nurture, and discipleship.
- ✅ If evangelism and outreach are goals, the youth ministry should have a *name* that will appeal to young people.

Training leaders
First, regular training of staff and volunteer leaders is crucial.[2] Ask any teacher or parent of an adolescent what they need to know to cope successfully with today's adolescent, and the list will go on and on. Without training, leadership dies. Again, as was so often the case, the youth ministry programs that were reaching large numbers of young people were providing more training than those who were not as successful. Most adults have a limited amount of disposable time. When offered a chance to be the best, most effective leader possible, people will gladly give up the time. However, most volunteers find it hard to give any time for mediocre training. Training can be done in theology, psychology, leadership, small groups, Bible, religion, or denominational issues. As long as the training is good and helps people do a better job, the actual type of training may vary.

Balancing time
How a youth ministry utilized their time was significant. Most effective youth leaders balanced their time between program, administration, contact work with young people, and developing leadership. In congregations that had successful youth ministries, staff spent one-quarter of their time together with volunteers in training and planning, while an equal amount of time was spent simply being around teenagers. One-quarter of the time was spent on administration and planning the program, and one-quarter was spent actually running the program. Staff persons who spent twenty-five percent of their time with volunteer leaders,

training and encouraging them, had a much higher success rate than those who spent less time with leaders and more time with kids. Relationships between staff and volunteer leaders proved to be key, and, as with leader/teenager ratio, a one-to-five ratio was apparent. The vast majority of ineffective youth ministry programs spent most of their time either doing program or planning program. In these instances, very little time was spent with leaders or with young people outside of the actual program time.

Throughout the congregations surveyed, solid planning with youth leaders was deemed an essential element for good, well-planned, and well-executed programs. In effective youth ministry programs the amount of time a volunteer was willing to spend, although a concern, did not appear to be a major factor. When the quality of the training and planning time was beneficial, volunteers were usually willing to make the sacrifice necessary to attend.

The contrast between quality versus quantity in training and planning time also applies to the content of youth ministry programs. If a congregation can only muster one good activity a month or three good programs a year, research indicates that might be enough. The Search Institute, an organization in Minneapolis devoted to research on youth, found that fifty mediocre programs a year will not produce spiritual growth, but a minimum of fifteen to twenty hours per year of well-planned programming can.[3] The best advice for those congregations with limited resources is to do fewer activities if need be, but do whatever they do well.

Evangelism, nurture, and discipleship

How a youth ministry program is designed has a large impact on its ability to do evangelism and then minister to those young people who participate. Ministries patterned on a three-level approach of evangelism, nurture, and discipleship have the greatest capacity to grow and be effective. In these models, the first level is strictly devoted to evangelism or outreach. The next level, nurturing, focuses on introductory Bible studies and issues of the Christian faith—taking those young people who have made or are considering a commitment to Christ, deeper in their new faith. The third level is discipleship, developing more mature Christian young people into peer leaders.

This third level proved to be a major component in pushing a youth ministry program into a totally different category of effectiveness. The ratio of one adult leader to five young people attending an evangelism meeting did not hold true in this youth ministry model, for often two adult leaders would be running a meeting with fifty or sixty young people attending regularly. However, when the number of "adult leaders" was added to the number of "core young people" (those being discipled), then multiplied by five, the answer proved to be the average number of people attending a weekly outreach meeting. For example, two leaders could disciple or train ten core youth leaders. These youth then served as junior leaders in the outreach program. Each of the ten core youth leaders reached an average of five friends, producing a program of sixty young people.

Ministries patterned similar to Young Life, a parachurch organization that does evangelism with young people, can be effective tools. They use a three-level approach to youth ministry as well: evangelism, nurture, and leadership development. The first level, which is open to everyone, is called "club." It consists of both secular and Christian contemporary music, a skit or game, and a short talk on one of the basic elements of the Christian faith. The second level, which is open to those who want to really learn about the Christian faith or are ready to make a commitment, is called "campaigners." It consists of an introductory Bible study coupled with deeper discussions of the Christian faith. The last level focuses on leadership development, fashioning mature Christian young people into peer leaders.

Naming the program

The majority of successful youth ministry programs I studied had a unique *name* for their program. If the primary purpose of the program was evangelism and outreach, the names were very generic such as Oakland Club, Cross Trainers, FX, or just CLUB. On the other hand, programs that had a name like Grace Episcopal Church Youth Group generally attracted only young people from that congregation. The name was clearly important because it represented who was welcome.

↵ Putting It All Together

What then is the connection between youth ministry in a congregation and evangelism? I don't believe it is possible to have one effectively without the other. For a congregation to minister to all the young people it baptizes, it will need a variety of approaches. The key is to make sure that a solid foundation of prayer and planning has gone into the entire programmatic effort so that, as Jesus said in Luke 14:28-29, if you plan to build a tower you have the resources to finish the job you have started. Putting time and energy into the front end of ministry planning will help you complete what you want to accomplish. Making use of a three-level program plan is one approach that is both flexible and effective.

- ↵ Level 1: Evangelism—educating young people about the Christian faith and encouraging them to make a decision regarding their response to it.
- ↵ Level 2: Nurture—helping young people to be grounded in the basics of the Christian faith and life.

◇ Level 3: Discipleship and Leadership Development—training young people to apply their faith on a daily basis, and to develop and use their gifts in ministry to others.

With these three levels in mind, let's walk through the development of a congregational youth ministry program. The key to the whole program is to start with a *solid foundation of prayer and planning*. The cornerstone to that foundation is a *mission statement* with clear goals and objectives. That mission must be consistent with the mission, goals, and objectives of the congregation. Once the foundation is laid, it is time to plan a *three-level program* outline and schedule for a year (based on the mission, goals, and objectives developed). This can be done on one level at a time or on all three levels simultaneously. Examples of each method follow.

Example 1: Three consecutive levels
September/October—Discipleship and Leadership Development

If evangelism is the mission of the congregation and the youth ministry program, training is necessary for the adult leaders and the youth who are in positions of leadership. A training series might take place one Saturday and the following four Tuesday evenings, for example.

November/December—Evangelism

Pre-evangelism events may be scheduled in November to get to know new youth and to build relationships. December would include an intentional evangelistic thrust by means of a special event or weekend retreat. Almost any program may be used (with ingredients such as games, food, concert, and so on), but be sure to include a direct presentation of the gospel by either a guest speaker or an articulate leader.

January/February—Nurture

February would be used for nurturing the new young people who were reached in December and helping them to grow in their faith. Bible study, topical discussions, or seminars are all relevant here. The cycle could then be started over again.

Example 2: Three concurrent levels
Nurture

Sunday morning during the Christian education program could be for nurture, doing Bible and/or topical studies. However, change the name of the program to something appealing to young people, such as Breakfast Club or AIM.

Evangelism

An evening meeting (Sunday or weeknight) can be the evangelism or outreach time. The meeting should be fun, and can include games, music, food, and so on. It should always include a speaker and/or discussion around the basic elements of the gospel, focusing on the following four areas: 1) Who is Jesus Christ and how does he relate to me? 2) How does sin separate me from God and others? 3) What has Jesus Christ done to bring me back into relationship with God? 4) How do I make a commitment to God and live a Christian life?

Leadership Development/Discipleship

Training should be provided for the staff and all volunteers, including the young people. This training can cover a wide variety of areas, from theology, Bible study, and current topics to developing a clear job description for each person in the leadership team. The training can be done weekly, biweekly, or monthly. The more the better, but be realistic and then hold those involved accountable.

These formats can be adjusted, based on the needs of the young people in a congregation. At the same time, the overall program should be kept in place for a number of years, or at least until the mission, goals, and objectives of the congregation are changed. *Consistency* is an important element in attracting young people to congregational life. As a program is being developed have young people *design a name* that means something to them and expresses their ownership of the program. Remember, the name is not for you but for those young people you hope to attract.

Finally, it should be emphasized that a congregation desiring an effective youth ministry program must have an effective *Christian education program for all ages,* especially adults. This has consistently proven to be the key to a long-term effective youth ministry program. A congregation cannot take its young people further without the support of caring and committed adults. Youth leaders are advised to do everything possible to encourage opportunities for adult education in their congregation.

Ultimately, of course, the evangelism of young people in any youth ministry program—the changing of lives through the gospel—is God's job. Our job is to present the opportunities of the gospel in the best, most appropriate, and most effective way possible.

Endnotes

1. Peter Benson, *Effective Christian Education: A National Study of Protestant Congregations.* A Summary Report of Faith, Loyalty, and Congregational Life (Minneapolis: Search Institute, 1990), 50.

2. *Ibid.,* 63.

3. *Ibid.,* 53-54.

The Kairos Ministry at Falls Church
William R. L. Haley and Catherine S. Edwards

Douglas Coupland, the defining novelist for baby busters, writes in his book *Life After God,* "You are the first generation to grow up without religion." It is not hard to find examples of this in everyday conversations. Gary Davis, president of New England Evangelistic Development, Inc., recounted a conversation that he recently had with a teenager. Gary mentioned his work with Leighton Ford, Billy Graham's brother-in-law. "Who?" the teenager asked. "Leighton Ford." "No, the other guy." Gary went on to ask him, "Does the name Jesus Christ mean anything to you?" "Isn't he supposed to be God or something?" was the reply.

Generation X is the first to grow up in a post-Christian American culture. We can hear a story like that and be appalled at the lack of knowledge in this new generation, or we can look excitedly to the future opportunity to communicate Christ anew to a group of people who will hear about the true biblical message of Jesus for the first time. It is a matter of whether or not we see the challenges represented in reaching Generation X as obstacles or opportunities.

After Coupland's *Generation X,* the bestseller *13th Gen* by Neil Howe and Williams Strauss, and an increasing number of articles in the popular press, many of us are familiar with the common stereotypes of twelve- to thirty-two-year-olds in the United States. Most often we are defined negatively, even down to the names for our generation. Slacker generation, lazy generation, MTV generation, whining generation, even the name baby busters—all of these connote a generation without much promise. Admittedly, some of our common characteristics are not all that cheery. But if we look at some general characteristics from a different angle, we may be looking at a most exciting future for the Christian church in the twenty-first century.

Kevin Ford, a noted Christian author on issues facing ministry to baby busters, says of us, "We don't like to think too much—it doesn't do much good. We tend to think in images (MTV) and stories rather than logical progressions." While this is not absolutely true for each individual, statistics like the drop in SAT test scores underline this growing trend. It has been observed that while access to information has increased drastically in the last twenty years, the ability to retain that information and actual knowledge is decreasing, in part because of information overload. Books, televisions, newspapers, magazines, the Internet, CD-ROM, music, and music videos have exploded in the last five to ten years. As young Americans we are tired of trying to take it all in. It is as if we were trying to pull a semitrailer with an old Volkswagon van on the information superhighway.

The distrust of logic is the postmodernist shift away from the assumption that truth can be obtained primarily through reason and fact. The church has largely bought into the modernist way of thinking about how to find and express truth. For example, in the debates over creation versus evolution, we sought to do battle on the field of science, which came along with the assumption that science alone could answer these questions. But when presented with facts and logic, a buster may well respond with Kurt Cobain and Nirvana, "Oh well, whatever, never mind." While not abandoning reason as a way to communicate the gospel, we must learn to adapt our ways of thinking in order to reach young adults who may not think the way we do. We can use our logic to figure out ways to be more creative in our presentation of the truth in Jesus Christ.

We might look at this generation as a tremendous opportunity to explore more diverse ways to communicate the action of a creative God in this world. One of the primary ways to attempt this is to integrate the use of story in our preaching and church life. While the Bible is a book of propositional truth, it is certainly also a book of stories: a great story set on the stage of creation, with conflict in the fall, resolved in redemption, and room for a sequel set in the age to the come. The Bible obviously is a book with many stories within it: the pilgrimages of God's family, from Adam and Eve to Abraham, Isaac, and Jacob, from Moses and David, Ruth and Esther, Jeremiah and Isaiah to Jesus, Paul, and Timothy.

Leighton Ford writes persuasively in his book *The Power of Story* that we must use narrative to communicate the gospel in this age. The story of history, he writes, is God's Story colliding into each of our individual stories—thus providing a larger story of which we become an integral part. This story will appeal to those who feel their lives are insignificant, with no place in the larger purpose of history. It answers the busters' question of "What's the point?" As Richard Peace, a professor at Fuller Theological Seminary and expert on reaching this youth culture, writes, "Busters live without much hope...and give the appearance of being a generation that is clinically depressed." Many authors, both Christian and secular, have noted that young adults seem to be living out the practical implication of nihilism and the loss of purpose. You don't have to look any further than grunge music, which one author has described as "the sound of homes breaking."

This generation of young adults has experienced the divorce of their parents more than any other age group in American history. The U. S. Bureau of the Census reports that there has been a two hundred percent growth in single-parent households since 1970, from four million to eight million homes. Estimates are that almost half of all children are likely to experience their parents' divorce during childhood, and that sixty percent of busters will divorce. Commitment does not characterize this generation, because they have helplessly watched their primary model of commitment blow apart, leaving a wake of emotional damage. Brian, a twenty-two-year-old Christian from a divorced home in California, passionately told me, "Your folks' divorce infuses every aspect of your life." We have yet to see fully the long-term effects of divorce, since this trend accelerated in the 1970s and peaked in the late 1980s, the developmental years of Generation X. As the commentator David Watson observed, "Today we live in an age not only of personal insignificance, but also of great loneliness."

Along with the search for meaning, Generation X is on the search for intimacy. Without moorings in the family, they look to friends. Not belonging at home, they look to belong in community. Once again, the Christian church and message of Christ rings with resounding encouragement as we seek to see this generation's loneliness as an opportunity for outreach. Through Jesus, we can be called sons and daughters of God the Father, who is everything that our earthly parents were not. As children of the same Father, we enter into relationship with a new community, brothers and sisters in Christ, "the family of faith" (Galatians 6:10). With Jesus as our Lord, our friend (John 15:15), and the "firstborn within a large family" (Romans 8:29), the Christian message offers hope for new relationships and even reconciliation of our broken families and fractured relationships. There is no greater context for God's hopeful encouragement than to enjoy belonging to a new family and community under Christ.

It has been well observed that while Generation X and the culture at large is exhibiting an increased interest in spirituality, many are actively rejecting the traditional Christian church as a viable expression of spiritual reality. Given that there is an anti-Christian bias in the most influential institutions of our culture (the media, government, and education), this fact is not surprising. While some young adults might not actively dislike Christianity and the institutional church, many are certainly distrustful of it. This distrust is compounded by negative experiences with individual Christians or with churches that are not sensitive to how young adults understand teachings and principles. Thus, the gospel is confused with institutional religion, and what busters know of the institutional church smacks of irrelevant traditions, legalism, authority, and prudishness. In an ironic twist, Generation X plays the part of the prophet in pointing out and judging the weaknesses of the church on our own terms and demanding authenticity and change.

✌ Reaching Generation X: Obstacle or Opportunity?

The Falls Church, located in northern Virginia, is one church that sees great potential in this generation. The congregation hired a director of outreach to help develop a ministry to twenty-somethings living inside the Washington, D. C., beltway. While there was already a large number of twenty-year-olds at the church, they did not have a place for fellowship. Ministries with children and high school age youth was very solid, the men's ministry was effective, and large numbers were involved in ministry to women. Young adults, however, did not have a solid ministry that dealt specifically with their needs. Because our generation hungers for intimacy, fellowship, and spiritual truth we realized there was a need to form a ministry that would facilitate growth in these areas.

So we did, and we named it "Kairos." The Greek word *kairos* means a unique moment in time, a predestined era, a watershed epoch. Os Guinness describes *kairos* this way in *The American Hour:* "It is the hour which is the God-given moment of destiny, not to be shrunk from but seized with decisiveness, the flood of opportunity and demand in which the unseen waters of the future surge down to the present." Our generation inherits a *kairos* moment. Kairos exists to challenge and enable us to take advantage of this time when we can feel history being written. It is not a ministry that panders to the negative stereotypes of our generation, but rather endeavors to build on our strengths. It is too easy for all people, and our generation particularly, to turn our eyes inward and look at ourselves. Kairos challenges us to raise our eyes upward, to God and to our moment in human history.

In order to minister to any group of people, there has to be an understanding of their needs. Many twenty-somethings in the metropolitan area of Washington, D. C., lead frenetic lives, work long hours for low pay, and, unlike the generation before them, do not expect job security. The young people who inhabit the halls of Congress, the meeting rooms in the West Wing of the White House, the press galleries, and the boardrooms of Fortune 500 companies have come to Washington to make a difference. They are America's rising stars. Many come with several academic degrees—Arlington, Virginia, for example, has the highest number of degrees per person of any American city. Not only do they have degrees, they have drive. Young Washingtonians break the stereotypes of "slacker." That's how they got to Washington in the first place.

Unfortunately, the people these young professionals work for also see their potential and passion, and exploit them for all they're worth. This town is where young energy gets burned for the sake of someone else's agenda, and because Washington is a city of power and political prestige, many twenty-somethings come here to change the world by rubbing shoulders with the powerful. They come to the Falls Church idealistic but overburdened, drinking deeply from the fountain of the Beltway and still thirsty, seeking to heal the world while broken, working hard for someone else, and crying out for trustworthy relationships where they do not have to perform.

So the ministry of Kairos has been tailored to meet their needs. The letter to the Ephesians picks up many of the themes that Kairos is about: community, unity, diversity, servanthood, growth, truth, love, and fullness. Paul tells us that God made people with different gifts,

> to equip the saints for the work of ministry, for building up the body of Christ, until all of us come to the unity of the faith and of the knowledge of the Son of God, to maturity, to the measure of the full stature of Christ....Speaking the truth in love, we must grow up in every way into him who is the head, into Christ, from whom the whole body, joined and knit together by every ligament with which it is equipped, as each part is working properly, promotes the body's growth in building itself up in love. (Ephesians 4:12-16)

Kairos targets people from the Beltway who are as young as college students up to folks in their early thirties, though there is, of course, no clear boundary that excludes those of different ages. We aim to be of diverse marital status, education, class, gender, and race, with the goal of realizing biblical community. Our leadership team mirrors the ministry as a whole; we have men and women, singles, and young marrieds on the team. We try to achieve a balanced ministry in the context of community that is a natural place for evangelism and discipleship, where young adults find Christ and grow in Christ. As a three-legged stool stands firmly, Kairos rests on three pillars. Kairos is a place to be, to be together, and to be a servant.

A place to be

As young Washingtonians, we all struggle with the balance of being and doing. The temptations of the Washington area are not unlike many other places—to perform, achieve, and succeed at the cost of being human. Made in the image of God, we were created to enjoy beauty, experience emotions, appreciate the arts, expand intellectually, think critically, and, ultimately, grow spiritually. In that Christ is the way that we are redeemed to experience life as it was intended, it is through growing in him that we can "have life and have it abundantly." So we desire a place simply to be in Christ, and know him who desires that "our joy would be made full." Kairos provides that place to explore our humanness, redeemed through Christ. Through Kairos, young adults in the Washington metropolitan area have great opportunities to enjoy life and relish what it is to be human, made in the image of God.

A place to be together

Relationships are among the highest priorities of our generation. Not coincidentally, they are also one of God's highest priorities, relationship with Christ and relationship with one another. Through Bible study and worship we provide the opportunity to grow in our relationship with God. Further, at Kairos we nourish meaningful relationships with each other that are accountable, encouraging, and challenging. As a group we have gone skiing, hiking, biking, and dancing. Bimonthly film forums provide the chance to hang out and discuss movies like *Dead Man Walking, Romero,* and *The Shawshank Redemption.* We have taken advantage of what Washington has to offer in the arts and have visited museums and galleries together. Conferences and retreats provide further opportunity to be together outside of our usual harried environments. Kairos shoots for the goal of experiencing in flesh the true community we are as believers and reflect the diversity of the family in the kingdom of God.

A place to be a servant

To be a Christian is to be a servant, for Christ served and has called us to follow in his footsteps. Those around us need ministry as well—in our churches, offices, schools, and homes, even as we ourselves need the ministry of those around us. Our group offers free child care on "parent's night out," giving young parents some time on their own and ourselves the joy of being surrogate parents for an evening. Beyond reaching out to our own parish family, inner-city Washington has many opportunities for service, including mentoring programs. Since many of us are single or newly married and do not yet have children, we can serve Christ more fully than those with such commitments. We seek to be Christ as he himself was, a servant.

Building on the foundation of Christ and the scriptures, we hope to achieve "Ephesians 4 maturity" through unity and ministry in the context of diversity. We are very conscious of the challenges of walking the balance between intimacy (relationships that are deep and safe) and exclusivity (cliques that keep newcomers away), and yet strive to go the middle way. Among young adults in our area schedules are so tight that we implemented a structure that allows for a sense of commitment without heavy obligations. In a month's time, young adults have the opportunity to participate at varying levels of commitment in a monthly rotation of Bible study, prayer, and worship peppered liberally with opportunities for fun and fellowship.

The Kairos ministry revolves around scripture. We sponsor Bible study three Tuesday nights a month in small groups, starting our studies with the Acts of the Apostles—the story of beginning a ministry and forming a community in a non-Christian society, courageously embracing a radical lifestyle. On one Tuesday night a month we worship together in a nontraditional way that is reverent, deep, and passionate, with teaching and opportunities for personal testimony and witness. We call these gatherings "Kairos *Alive!*" Each month we highlight a major biblical theme that would appeal to this generation of young adults, such as hope, justice, compassion, redemption, reconciliation, community, individuality, and love. For example, when we took a night to focus on creation, we began with praise songs that focused on God as Creator, then viewed a slide show that corresponded to a reading of Genesis 1, followed by more praise. Then Leslie, an artist, spent about fifteen minutes displaying her paintings, illustrating that men and women, created in the image of a Creator, are to be creators themselves. I spoke about the need to live in wonder in light of creation, and after a time for personal testimonies we closed with a Celtic evening liturgy.

In order to be effective ministers to this generation, we who seek to minister to them must not stray from the centrality of the scriptures or the confession of Christ as Savior and Lord, which is where true relevance lies for this generation, as it does for any generation. Young adults represent great hope for our church, our country, our world, and, ultimately, for the kingdom of God. In order to recognize this promise, we must look with new eyes on this much-maligned generation.

part two

Identity and Culture

The Episcopal Church Welcomes You?
Evangelizing Students and Young Adults
Jacqueline Schmitt and David Gortner

One of the positive sides of the reduction in church funding for campus ministries is that many of us now engage in direct appeals to congregations, alumni, parents, and friends of our chaplaincies. The good side of what some regard as the difficult task of asking people for money is that we get to tell our story to new audiences, and, given that most of our campus ministries have something worthwhile going on, that is an easy story to tell.

We often take students with us on these parish visits, for they are bright and shining examples of young adulthood: engaged in a vocational and educational search, members of our campus congregation, articulate about why church is important. In many ways, these students are the easy ones. They are committed, embarked on a spiritual journey. They have found a place in the church, either with us or in their home congregations, where they have been nurtured, recognized, and raised up as leaders. They are the best and the brightest. They fit the old cliché of "the future leaders of the church."

Yet when we go on these visits students often receive quizzical looks from parishioners and clergy who either react as though these young adults have come from another planet, or assume that today's college experience is much like theirs of a generation or more ago. The students are confused or annoyed by these reactions. No, they don't come to Canterbury Club to find dates. Yes, they really do come to church every week.

We risk making light of these reactions by exaggerating them, but we do so to make a point: young adults are startling visitors to many of our congregations. They *are* different from the rest of the congregation of children and older adults, because they are in a different phase of the life cycle. People deal with different issues during the young adult years than during the formative years of infancy and childhood and during the mature years of adulthood and old age. They are not, however, of another species—any more than are the teenagers of the church who attend parish youth groups. Adults who want to reach out to students and young adults in their congregations can do so by remembering, perhaps in a deeper and more thoughtful way, the struggles, joys, and challenges of what it was like to be in their late teens and early twenties. The circumstances may have changed, but what it means to be human, to come to adulthood, to make decisions on career, intimacy, faith, and commitment, remains very much the same.

At Canterbury Northwestern we have begun to look at these questions of faith development and incorporation, questions of how to do evangelism among students and young adults, in light of the development of the campus ministry at Northwestern University and the young adult ministry in a congregation in the diocese of Chicago. Our concern for ministry with young adults grew out of years of experience, both inside and outside the church. In a variety of contexts we noticed the talent, enthusiasm, and creative energy of young adults; we also noticed insecurity, a lack of specific direction, and frustration with the difficulty of finding a niche in society. We could see the enthusiasm and idealism in their eyes, and hear their hesitance in the mild vocal tension and frequent raising of pitch at the end of sentences that turns each one into a tentative question. We also observed the low numbers of young adults involved in organized religion in contrast with the high degree of enthusiasm of young adults who did seek connection with a church and were given places of responsibility.

Real evangelism, spreading the good news of Jesus Christ, is a two-way street. As we seek to understand the faith development of young adults, we learn new things about how God works through human experience: how the resilience of the human creature, nurtured by the love of God, comes through as each person learns how to live with the rapidly changing challenges and demands of life. What the church brings to this dialogue is the wisdom of the tradition, the stories told over the centuries of how women and men of faith have lived in, cared for, and changed, for good and ill, the world God has made. We bring the good news of hope for new life in Jesus Christ, a perspective on what is truly important in life, a space for reflection and contemplation, and a community of fellowship and prayer.

As a denomination, the Episcopal Church has moved sluggishly on the development of evangelism for the unchurched and on Christian education for young people in the church. While other denominations have begun in the last forty years to recognize adolescence as a unique period of life and have made some coherent efforts at ministry for adolescents, the Episcopal Church has not channeled the amount of resources comparable to other denominations into these efforts. A strong body of literature and networking continues to develop around ministry and Christian education for adolescents, but our outreach efforts with unchurched adolescents remains sporadic.

Regarding ministry to college students, the Episcopal Church has done well, providing ministry for undergraduates in a manner comparable to other mainline Protestant churches. Earlier in our history, the establishment of Episcopal colleges and, later, college chaplaincy programs received strong financial and emotional backing. However, with the cultural appeal of Christianity on the wane, ongoing tension between state universities and religious student programs, a shift in support from campus ministry to the civil rights movement, and consistently diminishing financial and emotional support from dioceses and local congregations, much of our campus ministry has ended up on the fringe, allowing evangelical and parachurch organizations willing to invest more time and resources to supersede us. Congregations in towns with colleges or universities may welcome college students as visitors or temporary guests, but they rarely offer programs or outreach specifically directed at incorporating college students into their ongoing life.

There is much discussion in mainline churches about "the graying of the church." In the Episcopal Church, we are concerned about an aging population that is not being replaced with "new blood." But our evangelistic invitation is often, in reality, less inclusive: "The Episcopal Church Welcomes You" *if* you are in your thirties and forties, are raising a family, and have enough income and energy to pledge and take over all the tasks of running the congregation so we seniors can take a well-deserved rest. That is perhaps a flippant response to a serious and heartfelt yearning by many parishioners to have people of all ages in the pews and in positions of congregational leadership. Yet as some clergy and lay leaders admit, we simply do not seem to know what to do or how to approach the problem of evangelism—even to "our own" who do not meet our criteria. This uncertainty can be seen most dramatically in the marked age gap in lists of members and attendees at almost any parish in the United States (and, for that matter, Canada and Western Europe): consistently the age group least represented in church is between the ages of eighteen and thirty-five.

Early adulthood is a period of life that is only beginning to be investigated by educators, developmental psychologists, and people concerned with ministry. Roughly extending from the end of adolescence into the early- to mid-thirties, this period of life is characterized by:

- a period of wandering or nomadism, combined with a yearning for community;
- a period of strong ideological attachments (normlessness);
- a period of isolation and testing;
- a time of trying out a career path;
- a period of high anxiety;

❧ a period of high creative energy and output;

❧ a time of emotional intensity;

❧ a time to learn how to juggle life's demands;

❧ a period of searching for meaning.[1]

Psychologist Daniel Levinson provides the following excellent summary of young adulthood:

> Most of us simultaneously undertake the burdens of parenthood and of forming an occupation. We incur heavy financial obligations when our earning power is still relatively low. We must make crucial choices regarding marriage, family, work, and life-style before we have the maturity or life experience to choose wisely. Early adulthood is the era in which we are most buffeted by our own passions and ambitions from within and by the demands of family, community, and society from without. Under reasonably favorable conditions, the rewards of living in this era [of life] are enormous, but the costs often equal or even exceed the benefits.[2]

News media and marketing surveys, both past and present, have described people in their early adult years as deeply spiritual but suspicious or skeptical of organized religion, as intensely valuing autonomy and adventure but desiring community. While recent media studies have particularly focused our attention on "Generation X" as an aberrant group of drifters, earlier media reports from the 1960s and even from the 1920s indicate that the same patterns existed in prior generations as they traversed the challenging terrain of early adulthood.

More recent psychological studies, along with statistics from insurance companies and employment agencies, point out a somewhat disturbing picture. A majority of the major psychiatric and psychological disorders (such as schizophrenia, major depression, panic disorder and other anxiety-related problems, and several of the major personality disorders) emerge with full force during the years of early adulthood.[3] Both men and women in this age group show a lack of job stability, with college graduates in their mid-twenties holding an average of two jobs within a two-year period.[4] The frequency of driving accidents also remains high through the early- and mid-twenties, as higher insurance rates for this age group demonstrate. The multiple stresses in finding one's niche in society can certainly take a heavy toll.

On the brighter side, young adults retain the remarkably speedy cognitive powers and energy of adolescence, combining them with their fledgling expertise in various areas of their lives to make sophisticated decisions and plans. Some of the most innovative new businesses in this decade have been formed by young adults in their early- to mid-twenties, and these young entrepreneurs are reinventing the entire milieu of office culture. The highest level of creative output in many artistic and professional disciplines is during the ages between twenty-five and thirty-five.[5] Young adults are more likely to emphasize the importance of relationships and personal development than many older adults, are often more amenable to change, and, in general, seek to attach their vocation and lifestyle to a particular "script" of meaning.

Our own narrative and interviews with young adults support the themes of early adulthood stated above. We were primarily interested in learning how young adults characterized their religious and spiritual life with regard to meaning, purpose, and depth. Ten young adults were interviewed individually, in depth, while twenty more were interviewed less formally, often in group settings. Over half of these young adults are active church members. We asked a variety of questions during a one- to two-hour interview, including:

- ✌ Where do you invest the most energy in your life? In what areas do you invest the least energy?
- ✌ What have been some of the "intense" experiences that you carry with you—either positive or negative—within the last two years?
- ✌ How do you make sense of things when they are not going well? What do you do to cope?
- ✌ When have you felt really connected to the human race, the world, the universe, or some large group greater than yourself? When have you felt really alone?

Among the thirty young adults interviewed, the theme of nomadism repeatedly came up, as they expressed the need to wander and explore in order to get to a point of stability. None of the thirty young adults had held a full-time job with a single company for over two years. Many were long-term temporary workers, some were graduate students with assistantships, some were in transition from one corporation to another, and some pieced together several part-time jobs to get by.

One waitress in California related her story of an unexpected breakup with her long-term boyfriend after she changed careers from marketing and management to waitressing. "I really needed to work in a completely different setting. My boyfriend and I discussed it. He left for work the next morning, saying that he really didn't want to live his life with a waitress. By two o'clock that afternoon, I was gone." After about two weeks of wandering, she ended up in a desert town in southwest Texas. She said that for the first two weeks there the isolation was so intense that "I would watch the sunset each night and cry. Just sob my eyes out." In another interview, a lawyer said that his graduate training took him and his (now ex-) wife through North Carolina and Kansas for a period of four years before he finally ended up in Chicago.

The young adults interviewed also demonstrated a wide range of ideological commitment in their search for meaning. A woman in the Wiccan community spoke with near-evangelical enthusiasm and ardor about her beliefs, her community of faith, and her experience of nature as divine. A man studying neuroscience delighted in explaining all of the miracle stories of the Bible in terms of natural events, but did not seem to doubt that they had actually occurred.

Emotional intensity is high during early adulthood and expresses itself through work, among intimate relationships and sexuality, and in various leisure activities. One man we interviewed in Kansas who was in his early thirties left the Roman Catholic priesthood because of his conviction that he needed to explore sexuality and long-term companionship. He was full of eagerness and vision for his quest, to the extent that his friends perceived him as enthusiastic, passionate, and somewhat volatile. In Washington, a woman was still dealing with the emotional fallout from college, where her three closest friends were all murdered. Emotional intensity in early adulthood stems from a variety of sources and may simply be a mirror of the intensity of life experiences among young adults.

In juggling life's demands, young adults make a strong bid for personal control. People in their early- and mid-twenties are more likely to claim vast personal control over the events in their lives, while people in their later twenties and thirties begin to recognize the potency of external factors—and even chance—on the courses of their lives.[6] But the search for meaning remains one of the most salient and widespread themes, a serious search for how to make sense of good, evil, sin, suffering, and justice.

Traditionally, our society has held up a model of stable adulthood. According to this notion of stability, once someone is past childhood (or, more recently, adolescence), behavior, personality, and roles become set and consistent until old age. The church has typically accepted this traditional understanding of adulthood, and then looked askance at young adults who did not fit this pattern of stability. As a consequence, ministry for young adults is a quite recent phenomenon, particularly once people graduate from college or vocational training. As a form of ministry it remains in its infancy, undeveloped in theory, often undifferentiated from youth ministry, and completely inconsistent throughout the church. Financial and emotional support for ministry for young adults is scant. Sadly, people in this period of life often make their final drift away from the church, and only about half of them return when they have children. While young adults invest energy in a quest for meaning or spiritual reality, they often view the church dimly or with scorn.

Loren Mead and the Alban Institute have demonstrated to the mainline Protestant churches the need to renew their vision. Not only have the mainline churches steadily declined in overall population since the 1950s, this decline runs contrary to the growth of the general population. Parallel patterns are exhibited in most industrial and postindustrial societies. Perhaps the most disturbing feature of Mead's research is the evidence that mainline Protestants not only withdraw from evangelization efforts to those who are unchurched, they also lose much of their emerging core membership due to a *laissez-faire* approach to ministry among youth, college students, and young adults. Mead found that over fifty percent of church members "lapse" for an extended period in their lives; twenty to thirty percent return to their original denomination; and about thirty percent never return to church at all. Hence, in the absence of outreach as new generations emerge, the number of active members in churches is decreasing, while the number of people growing up in our society without any connection to the central myths and stories of Christianity is rising.[7]

Mainline churches have adopted a policy of "permissive parenting," assuming that a period of lapsing or drifting away from the tradition was necessary for growth and maturity. This *laissez-faire* message perhaps even encourages these seekers to leave and work through their angst—and come back when they "have it all figured out." While that may or may not be true, the assumption that follows—"and they will return when they are settled and have children"—has turned out to be false. Mainline traditions are slowly awakening to the need to provide active, viable, and relevant ministries to people throughout the lifespan.

Part of the problem is the church's lack of attention and resulting ignorance of cultural change. Tex Sample has shown that culture is fundamental in multiple areas of our development, from speech patterns to posture, from food eaten to ways of processing information.[8] Out of the unique development that occurs in each culture emerges a unique way of viewing the world. The Episcopal Church and its deep love of ancient tradition faces a cohort of young adults reared in a culture of "electronic orality," with spiritual values arising out of experience, experimentation and exploration, emotional expressiveness, and an orientation toward process and journey.

Some excellent attempts at young adult ministry have been made in the Episcopal Church, locally and regionally; and a central desk at the national office has helped to raise consciousness within the church about this type of ministry. Unfortunately, our investment of resources and energy once again lags behind other denominations. The evangelical tradition tailors its ministry to young adults through generational "pigeon-holing," designing programs that focus on the most salient features of the current generation as reported by the media. The Roman Catholic Church, having adopted a developmental and evolutionary view of life, has begun to create programs for young adults that attempt to deal with the unique challenges of that period of life. The Mormons have a well-established process of enculturation into their church that carries youth and young adults through well-defined and age-specific roles. In comparison to the efforts of the Episcopal Church in young adult ministry, the efforts of these other traditions are more cohesive, vibrant, and consistent. Within the other mainline denominations, approaches remain sporadic, experimental, and with tentative emotional and financial investment.

We have some data to back up our assumptions about the effect this lack of effort on the part of the Episcopal Church toward teenagers and young adults will have. Three years ago, analysis of the Cooperative Institutional Research Program Freshman Survey (a thirty-year-old study of the backgrounds and attitudes of entering college students across the United States) showed some disturbing trends among young Episcopalians:

> The data historically have shown that freshmen from an Episcopal background are more than twice as likely to abandon their parents' religion as the average freshman.

> If you compare the number of students who list their own religious preference as being different from that of their parents, you discover that Episcopal students are leaving the church of their families in higher percentages than any other Christian denomination.

> The snapshot of the Episcopalians in this survey (two percent of the student body nationally) reveals a picture of our young adults as bright, self-motivated and self-assured, altruistic, engaged in the world, and affluent. They are better educated, better prepared, and better off than many of their contemporaries....The results speak of families and church communities that have given these young people all that they can to prepare them for their college experience. Yet the data also seem to indicate that while this attention ensures adequate preparation for college, it seems to leave our students shallowly rooted in their own faith.[9]

Students and young adults may not be from another planet, but they may be going to another planet—or church, or social group—instead of having anything to do with the mainline churches. At an ecumenical consultation on ministries in higher education in the northeastern states Kortright Davis, professor of systematic theology at the Howard University Divinity School, put the challenge this way:

> The church which was founded by a band of young people, and whose pioneer died at a very early age, is now completely dominated, controlled and defined

by those who can no longer claim to be such. Qualification for entry into the Kingdom was described as being similar to being young, but we have overturned such a criterion by insisting that the young must imitate the old. The future of campus ministry is inextricably bound up with the future of the church, and I do not see how either will have a future unless we are rescued by the younger generations, however much we kick and scream about holding onto power and traditions of our authority. Let campus ministries become more subversive of the growing gerontocracy in the church. Let them infiltrate all the pews, pulpits and vestry rooms with younger blood, fresh commitments, unspoilt religious habits and new visions of God's beautiful world.[10]

To meet this challenge will require work, prayer, and persistence. It is, in a pure sense, *mission* work. One of our students here at Northwestern joined the Peace Corps in June. The Corps sent her reams of information about her new country (Cameroon): geography, language, religion, custom, dress, food, climate, everything. The student took an extra quarter or two of French before she left. She had to put all her personal papers and affairs in order. She rounded up all of her friends and had us recite the daily office into a tape recorder so that she would continue to pray with and for us, and us for her. She got rid of everything she would not need for the journey, and after only a week's orientation in Washington, D. C., flew to Cameroon to be immersed in teaching English as a third language (after Cameroonian and French) to people preparing for college or work in international business in Europe and North America. For as much good as she would do in teaching English, she knew that her life would be far more deeply affected by this sincere encounter with another culture.

Her experience can be a model for our mission of evangelism with young adults. Prepare ourselves as deeply as we can in the culture, development, needs, and yearnings of young adults. Strip ourselves of the baggage we do not need: false assumptions, predetermined expectations, worn-out excuses, established rules. Convince ourselves that we can succeed. Be open to being changed by the young people we meet and the way God speaks to us through them. And most of all, remember that what we have to give is what people truly need to bring wholeness and hope into their lives.[11]

Endnotes

1. For a discussion of these challenges see the following sources: Daniel J. Levinson, et al., *Seasons of a Man's Life* (New York: Alfred A. Knopf, 1978), 40-49; Erik H. Erikson, *Psychological Issues,* monograph, 1, no. 1 (1959), 95; James E. Marcia, "Ego Identity Status: Relationship to Change in Self-Esteem, 'General Adjustment' and Authoritarianism," *Journal*

of Personality 35 (1967): 128-33; George E. Vaillant, "Adult Development: Reality or Fantasy?" unpublished paper, Cape Cod Summer Symposia Series, Orleans, Massachusetts (July 1993); W. W. Meissner, "Developmental Psychopathology of Adult Disorders," in volume 5 of *The Course of Life: Early Adulthood,* ed. George H. Pollock and Stanley Greenspan (Madison, Conn.: International Universities Press, 1993); W. Dennis, "Creative Productivity Between the Ages of 20 and 80," *Journal of Gerontology* 21 (1966): 1-8; David T. Gortner, "On the Question of Change and Development in the Personality and Identity Formation of Young Adults," unpublished master's thesis (Wake Forest University, 1994), 42-44; A. M. Juhnsz, "A Role-Based Approach to Adult Development: The Triple-Helix Model," *International Journal of Human Development* 29 (1989): 301-15; L. J. Montgomery, *Young Adults: A Call to Dialogue* (New York: Libra Press, 1980), 8-10.

2. Daniel J. Levinson, "A Theory of Life Structure Development in Adulthood," in *Higher Stages of Human Development,* ed. C. N. Alexander and E. J. Langer (New York: Oxford University Press, 1990), 40.

3. *Diagnostic and Statistic Manual of Mental Disorders,* 3rd edition (Washington, D. C.: American Psychiatric Association, 1987).

4. Gortner, "Question of Change," 42-44.

5. See J. A. Blackburn and D. E. Papalia, "The Study of Adult Cognition from a Piagetian Perspective," in *Intellectual Development,* ed. R. J. Sternberg and C.A. Berg (New York: Cambridge University Press, 1992); John Simons, "The Youth Movement," *U. S. News and World Report* (September 23, 1996), 65-69; and W. Dennis, "Creative Productivity Between the Ages of 20 and 80," 6-8.

6. Gortner, "Question of Change," 56-58, 69-71, 77-78.

7. Loren Mead, *Transforming Congregations for the Future* (Washington, D. C.: The Alban Institute, 1994).

8. Tex Sample, *Hard-Living People and Mainstream Christians* (Nashville: Abingdon, 1993).

9. William S. Korn and Giles L. Asbury, "Where Have All the Young Ones Gone…," *Plumbline* 22, no. 2 (July 1994), 16-20.

10. Kortright Davis, "In Search of a Vision: The Church's Mission to the Campus," *Plumbline* 23, no. 1 (June 1995), 18.

11. The research reported in this chapter was underwritten by a generous grant from the Episcopal Church Foundation. The full version of the Canterbury Northwestern Project in Young Adult Ministry forms the basis for a proposal to Seabury-Western Theological Seminary for curriculum in college and young adult ministry to prepare clergy and lay leaders for this ministry in the church.

Evangelism Among African-American Youth

Edward W. Rodman

Any discussion of evangelism must start with the rather obvious but important observation that in both the animal kingdom and the kingdom of God it is sheep that make sheep, not shepherds. The most effective evangelism is done at the peer level among the converted who, in their commitment to Jesus and their enthusiasm for the faith, are able to convince those with whom they come in contact that following Jesus is the way, the truth, and the life. In my thirty years of experience in the ministry I am increasingly convinced that there is no magic formula for authentic evangelism anymore than there is for the related areas of stewardship and social ministry. In fact, each relates to the other at a fundamental level of understanding of the breadth of the gospel and the depth of the commitment that is required to live fully into a life of faith.

I am also convinced that our baptismal covenant prescribes the areas of responsibility that aware Christians assume in the name of Jesus to be his hands, heart, eyes, and ears in the world. This responsibility is no small one. It is the ultimate expression of ministry to which we all have been called regardless of our order—lay or ordained. I also believe that the basic elements of effective witness in the name of Jesus are true for all generations, young and old. Their application or emphasis may change—either because of the context in which the ministry must be exercised or because of the age group and its capacity to respond to the demands of the gospel realistically within their own peer groups—but the challenge remains the same.

My primary task is to talk about the evangelization of African-American youth and their needs in the context of the church today. My experience, however, is not unique, and as I have come to know my peers and those older than myself throughout the black church, I have heard countless testimonies to the priority that was given to youth ministries in the segregated black church and to the vital role that clergy and lay people played in instilling in us high moral standards and a great appreciation for learning and the importance of higher education. Most especially, they held great expectations for our success in a world that would be changing as a result of our efforts at desegregation. Certainly more than once, when the going has gotten tough throughout the years, I can remember those mentors, within both the church and the segregated public school system, whose sacrifice and faith in us provided the inspiration necessary to keep my eye on the prize. I hope that I have been able to keep faith with them. Unfortunately, it goes without saying that to a very large extent this intra-community network of nurture and support has all but disappeared within the urban public educational system, and is much more difficult to maintain in the urban black church of today, whose membership has become middle class and no longer lives in the neighborhood.

Certainly, I do not wish to appear romantic about my experience or those of others who would testify to the same positive environment of nurture and support, but rather to contrast it with circumstances as they exist for today's youth of color, especially in the public schools, but even sadly enough, within many of our churches. Those values and experiences were not unique to a given time or place, but in fact I believe are fundamental to the Christian understanding of community and the collective responsibility we all have for the nurture and encouragement of our young people. ("It takes a whole village to raise a child.") Somehow we have lost sight of this focus and must reclaim it and respond with the energy and sense of priority that our young people deserve from us.

My initial job as a deacon and then assistant minister was at St. Paul's Church, New Haven, Connecticut, where I began in July 1967, just in time for the New Haven riots. My first official service as a minister was to perform the funeral of a young black marine who had been the youth leader at St. Paul's prior to my arrival. He had been killed in combat in Vietnam, and needless to say, this was a very sobering initiation, not only into the ministry, but into the whole world of urban youth and their families. Now the unique thing about St. Paul's was that it was a predominantly white church that had made a very serious commitment to the inner city of New Haven, and at the time that I arrived had a ten-percent black membership.

During the previous year the rector and the vestry of St. Paul's had decided to hire a bright young white seminarian from Yale Divinity School to inaugurate a youth ministry program for urban black teenagers. Being an enterprising young man and following the wisdom of the day, he had consulted the fledgling youth group at St. Paul's and ascertained the major need this ministry could meet. They had determined that Sunday evenings were a "dead" time in New Haven and there was "nothing" wholesome for young blacks to do, so they had decided to start a so-called youth lounge, which really meant a Sunday evening dance. Beginning in February 1967 with a nucleus of about twenty-five young people and three adults, the lounge had started on a promising note with high hopes. The seminarian who started the program was the most relieved person I believe I have ever seen in my life when, as he was leaving, he introduced me as the new youth minister and quickly got out of town.

To my surprise, at the time of my arrival the clergy, vestry, and members of the church were still supportive of the basic idea of a youth lounge, but were scared to death at the potential for disaster that such large numbers presented, both for the physical property of the church and its parish house, where the dance was held. There was also concern for the growing racial tension within the community that in retrospect, we now know was leading to the August riot.[1] Since none of this had been fully explained to me before I arrived, shock may be too mild a term to describe my first sight of the gathering throng on my initial Sunday evening. As fate would have it, on my first night of duty two fights did break out which, to my great relief, were expertly handled by the male members of the St. Paul's youth group who were the hosts of the lounge.

Indeed, throughout the evening I was impressed with the level of organization the handful of young men and women from St. Paul's had developed to handle this unique situation, to keep things reasonably in order, and to continue to make the case for the value of this ministry. For this I was indeed thankful to God, for at least there was a nucleus of intelligent, committed young people to work with. Later that evening I was also able to begin to meet some of their parents and other young adult members of the congregation who had volunteered to function as chaperones, and who worked with and supported the young people in carrying off the dance. While this did not reduce the level of panic that I was feeling, it at least kept it from getting out of hand. The other clergy and wardens of the parish merely smiled and wished me good luck as they all left town on vacation, leaving me in charge of the church and preparing for the funeral of the former youth leader.

Needless to say, nothing in my seminary training, other than my field work experience, had prepared me for this particular aspect of ministry. Fortunately, my background in civil rights had given me a deep appreciation for the importance of discipline and organization, and a positive belief in the capacity of young people to find their own order and direction if left alone to do so, and then appropriately supported. Certainly my own decision to become an Episcopalian was influenced by the openness of the church to recreational activities, including dancing, and as such, upon reflection, I was able to approach the task with the "comforting" realization that here was a wonderful opportunity to put my beliefs into practice. Armed with that philosophical approach, we quickly moved to expand the base of the responsible youth leadership group by involving non-Episcopalians. There was minor resistance to this move by the "old-timers" within the original St. Paul's youth group, for the obvious reasons. They, however, understood their own need for peer support and quickly identified fifteen more young people who could provide the appropriate leadership.

The second task was to see if any of the parents were willing to take some responsibility for the sponsorship of this activity on an equal basis with the church. This took about six months to work through, but in fact a group of about twenty parents, most of whom were not members of the church, did agree to constitute a working parents group, and were recognized by the clergy and vestry of St. Paul's as co-sponsors. They eventually took the responsibility for managing the program from the church, and I established a relationship of accountability with them.

This was a vital step for two reasons. First, it assured the congregation that they were not alone out on a limb in this risky venture, and that at least some of the parents of the young people who were benefiting from the program were sufficiently appreciative of the church's good will to share in the responsibility of trying to maintain the program. Both the young people and the parents group that worked with me and the young adult group of the church (which we organized into a house church meeting on Friday evenings to prepare ourselves spiritually for the Sunday evening event) were clear that young people needed their own space and the recognition of an institution such as the church to give credibility to their right to have a good time in safety and in peace. Second, it was made clear from the beginning of my ministry there that I did not expect to attract new members to St. Paul's through this ministry, although certainly we never indicated that people were not welcome to join, and in fact in the long run some did. We simply wanted to make it clear that we were not inviting them out of self-interest, but out of genuine concern for the community and the young people. This was hard for many to believe for a long time.

Once this infrastructure was put in place the "teen lounge" was able to continue for two years with only minor trouble. It was ultimately disbanded (banned would be a better word) by the New Haven police who, in their anxiety over the upcoming Bobby Seale trial and the general unrest threatening the city, felt compelled to close down the lounge for public safety reasons. Needless to say this did not sit well with the young people, and because the police decided not to announce their decision publicly, we were put in the position of having to tell the young people on a Sunday evening that the lounge had been closed. The mini-riot that followed in downtown New Haven that night was a mild statement by the young people of their humanity and their reaction to the disrespect that had been shown them by a police department whose racism was well-documented. While none of us was pleased with this conclusion to such a unique ministry, it was merely another sign of the times, both in terms of the fear (even in those days) of the society toward young blacks, and the pulling away from recognizing their particular needs.

Over the two years that the lounge continued, many amazing and significant things occurred within and among the various subgroups of young people we were able to organize and encourage in various ways. We had a wonderful basketball team for the young men and an exciting young women's precision drill team that won many awards. We had two very successful dance groups, with some of the young women beginning to study ballet with the New Haven Dance School next door to the church. The cast and many of the crew members of the Broadway play *Pearly Victorious* came to New Haven on three separate occasions to provide workshops on acting and stage production. A modern jazz workshop was developed to study and perform both contemporary and classical music. Indeed, on Sunday evenings, to break the monotony of rock and roll, each and all of these activities were featured from time to time, both to encourage participation from other young people and for them to show off to their peers. We also had discussions on black consciousness and history to supplement the lack of such material in the public school. We were able to refer many young people to tutoring situations and to encourage some to go to college.

These young people had a wide variety of interests and talents, but they lacked an accepting environment in which they were free to express those interests and gifts. They also needed caring adults who would listen to them and respond, not by telling them what to do, but by encouraging and enabling them to do what they felt they could do. Providing such an environment for them was the most fulfilling and gratifying part of that whole experience. As we got to know the young people individually and in small groups, we also learned that issues of child abuse, single-parent households, illiteracy, experimentation with drugs and alcohol, and teenage pregnancy were all urgent concerns, and if ignored, would fester and ultimately lead to dropping out of school, crime, social dysfunction, or prison.

Thus, as we begin to focus on evangelism among adolescents, especially African-American youth, we must always adhere to the fundamentals if we are to be faithful to the full gospel that we are called to impart. Evangelism is no substitute for good education, good health, positive recreation, or vocational counseling. Older adults and youth all have a responsibility to serve Christ in their situations, to proclaim the gospel, and to be faithful in worship and study. All age groups are called to a life of prayer founded on the law of love and based on the principles of forgiveness. People who do that provide the basic models for faithful witness that have to be the foundation of any Christian life.

There is a saying going around these days that runs: "In our grandparents' day religion was an experience. In our parents' day religion was a duty. In our day religion is a luxury. In our children's day religion is a nuisance." For our grandparents the church and the Christian community was the focus of life and provided the primary context for understanding who they were and whose they were. It provided a means of survival in a hostile and confusing world and provided hope when, for many in communities of color in this country, there was little hope. Those of us who grew up in the church remember the strong commitment that our parents had to the church and the stern requirements laid upon us to attend Sunday school, to participate in youth activities, and to try to live Christian lives as best we could in difficult times. Many of us, I am sure, were aware that our parents did this because their parents had inculcated it in them, and for many of them it was a struggle, because competing demands of work and social advancement made participation in the church important but not primary.

It was thus that my generation, born after the Depression, came to understand religion as a luxury. It may have been important in our formation and we may look back on it nostalgically, but in terms of our participation in organized religion, we can take it or leave it. This stance is a result of the increasing complexity of our culture and the slowness of traditional and mainline religious institutions to adapt to the complex and diverse world in which the old values have yet to find new expressions that are relevant and compelling in our lives. For this reason religion has become a nuisance in the eyes of many of our children. In the final analysis, the behavior of young people in any culture is merely a reflection of what they have been taught through the example and attitudes of those who came before them. Our children's tendency to see religion as a nuisance also makes the challenge of inculcating in them a sense of responsibility toward converting others more difficult than it has been for many generations, requiring greater creativity on the part of those of us in the church.

To discuss evangelism among youth of color in a single essay is a daunting task, and at a minimum requires the exploration of three preliminary concerns and the articulation of three primary points of reference. First we must talk about perseverance and commitment, the importance of social analysis, and the significance of providing alternatives. We are then in a position to focus on the engagement of youth, their enrichment, and their empowerment. What follows will be my effort to make this case as the foundation for evangelism among youth of color, and African-American youth in particular.

ᴠ Commitment and Perseverance

I believe there are many reasons why we lose, or fail to attract, adolescents and young adults to the church. Certainly any church that has made the commitment to this group has reaped the benefits of their presence, but that commitment is sorely tested by the need to have appropriate facilities, the right type of adult leadership, and the capacity to sustain the engagement, enrichment, and empowerment of youth over the long haul. It is totally unrealistic to expect a congregation and its clergy leadership to believe that young people will come to the church simply because it is there. It is also unrealistic to believe that there are magic formulas and quick fixes that will entrap young people in the web of the church family and hold their interest if they do not sense that they are important to the life of the church and if they are not are given the opportunity, space, and resources to participate and make a difference.

The traditional responsibilities and roles of youth—being acolytes, singing in the choir, and providing support services for adult activities—are no longer adequate. They come from a time when religion was a duty and it was a privilege to serve. Given the many opportunities that young people have in our society to do other things, to expect that those traditional roles and models will be compelling is, on the face of it, ludicrous.

This is not to say that those roles are not important or that young people should not take part in those activities. Seeing adults as acolytes and doing the support chores of maintaining the community provides the appropriate models for young people to understand that this type of service to the church and to the community are consistent parts of the Christian life at all ages, and are not relegated to youth or, even worse, seen as a series of hurdles that must be jumped over before they are accepted into the community.

Creative efforts at reinterpreting rites of Christian initiation are vital if we are to model the inclusive concept of the Christian community for the modern age. Therefore, I would think that groups such as intergenerational inquirers' classes would be significant venues for Christian education and formation, and should be seen as an opportunity for both young people and adults to learn about the importance of Christianity and its application to our lives. This type of flexibility is an example of the kind of commitment that the clergy and lay leadership of the church must be willing to make in changing its instruction and way of doing things if we are to be successful in sustaining youth presence. Beyond that, however, lies the vital role of social analysis and of understanding how we must be positioned to attract young people.

✌ Social Analysis

Understanding the type of world in which African-American young people live is integral to attracting them in the first place. The twenty-first century that these young people will inherit will be dramatically different from the world that those of us who grew up in the 1950s and 1960s ever anticipated. The economy, the demands of increased technology, and the profit-driven job market, when coupled with the high cost of education and low entry-level wages that are available even to college graduates entering the job market today, have marked the transition generation known as "Generation X" as the group that seems to be lost in contemporary America. It is precisely that group of young adults who should provide the energy and the leadership for evangelism among youth. But if they themselves are lost, view the church as a luxury or a nuisance, and have not found how their faith can make a difference in their lives, it is unreasonable to expect that we can skip over them and have any impact on their younger siblings who live with the boredom and hopelessness that marks a consumer-oriented culture epitomized by the modern mall. At the same time, it is also true that within Generation X, as in every generation, there are serious young people who are seeking an alternative to the chaotic cultural scene. The importance of providing alternatives looms large as a prerequisite for their engagement.

Ethnic ministry in the Episcopal Church has always been rooted in the segregated nature of housing and community development, and this church is not particularly well-versed in the art of diversity or multicultural ministry. Our lack of experience, when coupled with our insensitivity to this concern as a priority in preparation for ministry, leaves us vulnerable to the ministry of good intentions. Today, the problem is made far more complex by the threat of drugs, the breakdown of support for public education, and desegregation that has led to the elimination or diminution of many strong African-American institutions. At the same time, the oversimplification of race relations perpetuated in the debates of the 1960s and early 1970s has been superseded by a more honest recognition of the great diversity within all ethnic groups. The fact of the matter is that there never was an "African-American community"—nor Hispanic or Asian-American communities—but a whole range of nationalities and subcultures within these groups, and the tensions that exist *within* them are often greater than the tensions between ethnic groups in general. We see this clearly with gangs: Dominicans are more likely to fight Puerto Ricans, and Cape Verdians to fight Jamaicans, than Hispanics to fight Asians, who themselves are trying to keep peace between the Vietnamese and the Cambodians.

This same dynamic exists within the church. Within the African-American community we are attempting to develop a concept known as Afro-Anglicanism, which is designed to encompass the variety of cultural expressions that have emerged within the African Diaspora among those who have become Anglicans. Thus one can see an Afro-Caribbean Church, an Afro-American Church, and an African-American Church (the latter being made up of first-generation African immigrants to this country), each seeking its own cultural, spiritual, and ecclesiastical identity. In some places these differences are being overcome; in others, they are a major problem. I suspect the same is true among Hispanics and Asians.

This situation requires, I believe, a total rethinking of what we mean by cultural and racial identity, as well as what we mean by Christian formation. While oneness in Christ is the goal, we live in a society in which racial and ethnic identity is one means of survival. We must therefore focus on the need to establish strong and positive identities among African-American youth because we understand that their backgrounds are distinctively different after the great migrations from the American South, the Caribbean, and Central America throughout most of this century. This further complicates the identity question, which must be worked out in a culturally diverse urban environment.

The issue of cultural and racial identity is especially pronounced for young people who come from racially mixed marriages or are adopted by white families. Indeed, there are some actively working to create a whole new category of racial identity in this country that they would call "American." While this speaks to the ideal it is at best premature, and at worse harmful to the young person of color who has to exist within a racist society in which categories are based on external features rather than the content of their character. However, young African-Americans who come from broken homes, who are the children of children, who are second-generation immigrants, or whose parents themselves do not know who they are, all need help in this area, and there are precious few places where it can be found. Clearly, if there is one place where the church can make a difference, it is working with young people in developing a positive self-image and helping them to overcome the self-hatred and negativism that can result when one is subjected to the ravages of poverty, class, and racial discrimination.

Critical to this endeavor is an environment that accepts and reflects the young people themselves, both in physical appearance and in cultural norms. Many middle-class African-Americans are very uncomfortable with poor children and find it difficult to relate to them in any meaningful way other than attempting to make them over into someone else. There are also many predominantly white congregations that may find themselves in a culturally diverse or racially mixed neighborhood and have difficulty reaching out, especially to the youth. It is this reality that continues to fuel the membership roles of predominantly African-American churches and makes the Pentecostal Church an attractive option for so many poor immigrants. The Roman Catholic Church addresses this problem by maintaining national churches, that is, ethnic churches that respond to the cultural formation needs of Roman Catholic immigrants seeking entry into the American mainstream. The Episcopal Church has done this with some success with middle-class blacks and West Indians. While many valiant attempts have been made by inner city churches to address this matrix of problems, there are very few who can maintain that they have had real success. Indeed, those churches that have succeeded have done so by bridging the generation gap and learning the language—Pentecostal, Muslim, and free church communities that are unencumbered by tradition and arrogance.

✓ Engagement

The first step in engaging young people is to model the values that we have discussed to this point. Among those values must be saying "yes" to the future and to the hope that the gospel provides, rather than being judgmental and saying "no" to those things that distract us from that quest. Drugs and violence have always been a reality in the world. The fact that younger and younger people are engaged in them is but a byproduct of the disintegrating culture that has lost a sense of value and meaning. If we model accepting responsibility for our actions and acknowledge our failure to bring about the kind of positive change that will make a difference in people's lives and give them hope, then we may have a little more credibility in reaching out to young people and enlisting them in the effort.

At a minimum, the value of respecting the dignity of every human person is central to our task and critical to engaging young people. All around them they have many examples of a lack of respect for who they are and what they represent, as well as a lack of appreciation for the means of survival they have developed in the face of a hostile environment. There is not one young person in the history of the world who asked to be born, or who can escape his or her biology or the natural exuberance of youth. They deserve special care and concern, not blame or lack of understanding. Admitting that we do not have all of the answers and respecting their intelligence and creativity would go a long way in bridging the gulf that currently exists in our society between the races, as well as between the generations.

Second, if we do not understand their context, language, and values, then, like any other missionary in any other time and place, we will be irrelevant to them. Or, we will be put in the position of trying to summon up greater magic or power to convince them of the truth of our God and the paucity of their culture. Such missionary activity is the bane of our contemporary world. We are currently reaping the whirlwind of that bastardization of Christianity, whose effects provide many of the root causes of our contemporary world crisis. It fuels the unrelenting quest for identity and power that inevitably results when people realize that they have been robbed of their culture and selfhood by an imperialist Christianity that was more committed to European cultural norms than to the gospel imperatives of justice and peace. If we cannot acknowledge this reality and approach rap culture with an understanding of its existence as a countercultural reaction, then we will have missed the point.

A very wise drug counselor who had been asked to address the religious leaders of Boston once noted that "if you are going to engage young people in the community as it currently exists, you must understand that there are only three types of people on the street—namely, buyers, sellers, and the police—and it is often difficult to distinguish among them. Anyone else is a threat." The refusal of the church to hear those words, to understand the nature of the context in which young people have to exist and the role of gangs in providing youth a community as an alternative to abusive and destructive family life, lies at the foundation of the inability of the church to engage and make a difference among youth at risk.

◡: Enrichment

Any program of enrichment that is faith-based must first be rooted in the belief that young people possess problem-solving skills, though they may have been either attacking the wrong problems or misapplying their skills. Certainly any young person who can remember ten verses of a complicated rap lyric is capable of learning Shakespeare. The issue is not their capacity, but their motivation. Certainly the young person who has the skill to lead a gang or to survive gang pressure and continue to function effectively in the chaotic public education system has mastered certain principles of survival that are of great use to adults who have not figured out what to do in the face of downsizing and job change. The potential, therefore, for intergenerational learning and adaptation is rich, but the context must be established in which that learning and the sharing of knowledge and insights about life must be focused and maintained. Thus, the development of leadership styles and experience in exercising leadership become critical to the enrichment process and to the building of community among young people in the church. To do this effectively requires talking about real issues—sexuality, HIV/AIDS, the importance of family and marriage, parenting skills—all of which are fundamental to enabling adolescents and young adults who have responsibilities thrust upon them at earlier and earlier ages to make critical decisions regarding their development and maturation.

This same context then offers a unique opportunity to introduce practices of spiritual development and theological reflection as new and different tools not only to expose young people to a different way of approaching life, but also as a valuable means to understanding themselves and what Christ would have them do in their world. Too often we see this form of Christian formation and its application as secondary to first capturing young people and giving them the basics of reading, writing, arithmetic, and reasoning—rather than understanding that the reverse is true. For example, if young people can begin to capture the wisdom of Jesus and the power of the gospel and what it can do for them in their lives and for their brothers and sisters and friends, then the utilization of these other skills in furthering this self-awareness becomes important as a means to an end instead of an end in itself.

While contemporary educational institutions may not be able to apply this catechetical method, it is at the heart of Christian formation. Simply building upon the strength of that tradition can provide exactly the kind of alternative approach that we were speaking about earlier. Indeed, that the church can provide this alternative approach to understanding the world and learning about meaning in life is not a weakness to be hidden but a strength to be celebrated. It is precisely in times of chaos, change, and crisis that those gifts should be called upon and brought to the fore. For if and when this approach is taken, we will begin to have the kind of enrichment that makes evangelism real and can produce hope, enthusiasm, and the energy to encourage young people to go out and recruit other young people to join and become involved in this new way.

Critical to this approach, however, is the willingness to give youth both the responsibility and the authority to carry out these programs and to develop initiatives of engagement with social problems, whether they be in school, in the family, or in the community. In this way, the application of their learnings and understandings can be tested in the fire of real life. Simply to create safe spaces and to provide alternative learnings and values and problem-solving skills without applying them merely prolongs the day when the test of their faith will have to be made in the real world. And this real world is one in which their decision-making is either informed by their morality and sense of self, or crumbles in the face of the many temptations that abound around them and all of us. This approach, then, sets the stage for the final step, which is empowerment.

✧ Empowerment

When we talk about meeting the needs of these youth within the Episcopal Church, we are forced to turn to the traditional African-American congregations who still continue to maintain a presence on the urban scene. Certainly when I was coming along, being a black Episcopalian was not considered a contradiction; some were among the most highly respected individuals in the community, just as Thurgood Marshall, Colin Powell, and Bishop Barbara Harris are today. Integral to the identity formation of any person is providing role models with whom he or she can relate and in whose emulation a positive self-image can emerge. It is vital that prominent African-American Episcopalians who have been able to maintain a sense of commitment to their roots but who have also been able to succeed in the broader community must be provided opportunities to interact with young people.

Beyond this critical exposure, which was pivotal in my own adolescence, comes the critical task of providing ongoing structures—summer camp or conference experiences, for example—where this can happen in depth. It is also important to maintain an ongoing weekly youth gathering that can pick up on these basic themes and provide the underpinning of black history and cultural achievements in literature and music, as well as peer group discussion. This rudimentary outline must be augmented by caring adults and some parents if it is to have credibility within the church and the community, thereby convincing the young people and their families that they are a priority for the church.

The key to empowerment, therefore, is understanding that young people have already demonstrated that they have the power and creativity to create their own environment and to develop a subculture that works well for them. The fact that this subculture has all the materialism and violence of the larger culture out of which it has developed goes without saying. The existence of racism, sexism, and other forms of oppression have taught young people that, apart from suicide, their only alternative is to distrust a culture that can hurt them because of who and what they are. The refusal of youth to conform is in fact a strength, but it must be translated and transformed into an understanding of how that strength and insight must be used in the service of others and in the name of Christ. This cannot be done by coercing young people into a passive state that accepts rote learning from an authority figure. It can only be engaged and enriched by a secure faith that is based on empowerment, and encourages young people to reimagine their future—to transform their world view in such a way that they can begin to move in the direction of that future. A faith that, most importantly, gives them the skills and the strength to get there.

Empowerment thus becomes the new context in which young people find themselves, and are able to express their faith with conviction and relevance in the environment in which they have to live and breathe and have their being. This is the kind of problem that I believe St. Paul was speaking to when he said that we must be renewed "by the transforming of our minds." It is this transformation that enables us to see the truth of the gospel and its application in our world in new and exciting ways, and gives meaning to life and hope for the future. When this becomes the reality I believe that young people can overcome racism, identify their own prejudices and self-limiting behaviors, and not only modify and change them in reference to others and themselves, but also begin to model the behaviors that build community and lead to solidarity and action for the common good. This is where service projects become so important. Young people have the energy and the enthusiasm to believe they can make a difference when they are properly focused and have the appropriate support and resources to do so.

Empowerment also means, in this context, helping young people come to terms with *who* they are and *whose* they are, affirming their roots and coming to a better understanding not only of what it means to be a Christian, but what it means to be a Christian in a particular time and place. Cornell West, the author of *Race Matters,* recently spoke to a group of young people who were about to embark on a learning and service trip to South Africa. In the course of the talk he observed, "The heart of the task of any culture is to properly understand its history, develop a sense of compassion that is based on an understanding of that history, which in turn can develop a vision for the future. Once that vision is shared by all, then the commitment to make the sacrifices necessary to fulfill that vision becomes possible and progress can continue." What West implied but did not explicitly suggest was that the exclusion of the story of the oppression of people of color in our history is at the root of many of the cultural divisions among us. By not giving a proper place to all at the table, we encourage building community on principles of exclusion rather than inclusion, and render notions of compassion passé—that is, believing that we can outrun the bear and allow our neighbor to be sacrificed.

Further, as we suggested earlier, the lack of vision for a future in which principles of compassion, inclusion, and justice are central to the mix renders belief in a disciplined approach to life tenuous at best and self-defeating at worst. The principle of "eat, drink, and be merry, for tomorrow we may die" is not a new one, but it has certainly gotten a new lease on life in contemporary America. The counter to hedonism is not to say "no," but, as St. Paul suggested, to understand that we become new people in Christ and can put away our childish practices. Such an empowered faith can give young people the confidence that making such a choice is positive—and freeing.

Finally, if empowerment is to have meaning, it has to give us not only the skills and capacity to influence our environment and future, but also an understanding of the way in which this newfound power must be actualized and how it makes sacrifices necessary. The first of four steps in the process that we all must constantly keep in mind is to gain access to the means of life and health—food, clothing, shelter, education. The second step is to have the capacity to sustain that access. Any analysis that overlooks the fact that it is the struggle between access and sustainability that informs all of our current conflict misses the point. A future that is built on inclusion and compassion must have the ability to gain access and to sustain the environment and the economy in such a way that all can progress. It means some having less so that all can have more. As this future is realized, then the third principle of equity, treating each other according to the Golden Rule and with respect and dignity, becomes possible. If we are struggling merely to survive, then we do not respect our enemies and we certainly have no reason to treat others like ourselves. And if the vision of a world of dignity and respect begins to become compelling, then the final concept of justice can begin to have some meaning. For a society without justice will have no peace—equity will never be fully realized—and the culture and economy of that society cannot be sustained because it will increasingly exclude and make access to the means of survival more difficult rather than less. The genius of the gospel is that it suggests a better vision, a better world, and a better way to get there. Thus, engaged young people who are enriched and empowered to work for such a world and in the name of such a vision will have the means of grace and the hope of glory.

◡ Conclusion

In the final analysis, I am quite aware that the picture of the kind of evangelism that I have painted in this article is difficult if not impossible to obtain. I am also aware that the call to justice, equity, sustainability, and access is an age-old call that has never been fully realized. I believe that in honestly expressing and exposing this paradox, acknowledging the mistakes of the past and the cultural captivity of religion to young people, we open the way to giving credibility to our proclamation of the gospel and provide a way for them to participate in that most critical task. Young people of color are no different from any other children of God. We are all called to be faithful witnesses, not successful apostles of church growth. For when the words of that very insightful drug counselor can be heard, marked, and inwardly digested, we can begin to remove our own egos and desire for power, and can then model a little more humility and a little more confidence in Christ's power in our own lives. It is at this point that the youth and people of all color may come to have a deeper respect for our principles and a greater willingness to participate with us in the building of God's kingdom.

Endnotes

1. I might add that, because of the network of youth, community leaders, and police we developed to support the continuation of the program, we were able to avoid a riot following the death of Dr. Martin Luther King, Jr., and were given the responsibility of conducting the community Commemorative Service on the New Haven Green.

Iconoclasm

Shattering "Ethnic Minority" Youth Work   *Anna Chakko-George*

The situation of Asian girls growing up in Britain, and by extension in other western nations, represents a unique challenge for the church. Girls socialized in one culture at home encounter another in the wider community. Tensions, misunderstandings, and frustrations are commonplace, and yet this situation is rich in intercultural and inter-religious contact and communication. Young people from different cultural and ethnic groups are growing up together in many of our cities and towns. Cross-cultural friendships are commonplace. The church needs to respond both to the problems faced by these young people as well as to the richness which their friendships represent. As a context for sensitive mission and evangelism those involved in youth ministry need to take seriously the question of how to engage appropriately with these mixed groups while remaining faithful to the gospel.

In this essay I shall examine the needs of young people from minority ethnic groups, beginning with a case study of Asian teenagers in Britain that focuses on questions of identity and assimilation. Next, I will look at the traditional response of "ethnic minority"[1] youth work in order to critique the extent to which those needs are being addressed. I will go on to propose an alternative model for youth work, using a pilot conference called "Iconoclast" as a case study. Finally, the strengths and weaknesses of that model will be examined to shed further light on the needs of young people from minority ethnic groups and on appropriate ways to meet them.

✌ A Case Study

School A has a large percentage of Asian girls, almost all of whom are Asian Muslims. They tend to stick in all-Asian groups. Racism is evident both in institutional policies and in the relationship between the Asian girls and the rest of the school. The work with Asian Muslim girls in this school exposed the fact that they are consciously (as well as subconsciously) struggling to find some resolution to this question of identity. They are wrestling with the question, "Where do I as a second generation Pakistani Muslim girl fit into 'British' society? I'm not English, I'm not Pakistani, so what am I?" On the one hand, they feel a strong allegiance to their faith and culture in terms of the identity it gives them. On the other hand, their desire to express another part of themselves, and to enjoy the same freedom as their peers, means they rebel in various ways against parental pressure to conform to Asian culture.

By contrast, the few white girls who are part of their group of friends do not appear to be asking any questions as a result of their friendships with girls from this very different cultural background. They do not ask themselves, "What does it mean when we talk about Britain as a multicultural society?" or, "Will understanding who *she* is help me understand differently who *I* am?" The white teenagers' interests tend to dominate the conversation in terms of music, dance, film, careers, men, and clothes. The Muslim teenagers' strong religious and (closely tied) cultural differences, against a backdrop of institutionalized racism, make their struggle for identity an essential part of their existence and result in a sense of separateness. The white girls, since the power base is theirs, do not have the same need to work out their identity in the light of their culturally mixed friendships. Separateness is recognized but understood as being an "Asian problem—they're the ones who are different." Yet in many ways this "Asian problem" becomes a strength in their struggle for identity, for selfhood, and against assimilation.

School B has far fewer Asian girls, predominantly Asian Christians, dispersed in culturally mixed groups. Racism in the school is most often experienced as colorblindness, although this itself is a thin and peeling veneer. Generally speaking, these teenagers belong to culturally mixed friendship groups to a much greater extent than the Asian girls at School A. While this may seem to be a much healthier, more positive state of affairs, a closer look at the group suggests that the Asian girls at School B are denied much opportunity to express their cultural identity. Most of them are from Christian family backgrounds and are not involved in the conscious "thinking through" of their identity that was true of the Asian Muslim girls at School A. There is not the same sense of struggle; "fitting in" is second nature. They value integration at any cost, even the loss of their identity. It is more important to belong in the mainstream than to have recognition for their own culture, which is not necessarily that of their parents. They seem almost reluctant to acknowledge their "Asian-ness," let alone explore it for themselves. It is important to ask why Asian young people are choosing this kind of cultural oblivion—is it free choice or tactical survival, given the uneven playing field?

Coming from a Christian background may have made it easier for many of these Asian girls to "fit in" with Western society since their Christianity has taught and allowed them to separate religion from culture. Their parents or grandparents were converted to Christianity from another religion, and, very probably, were taught to leave anything that had cultural ties with their old faith behind. Their old faith was seen as part of their "culture," and consequently was considered to be clearly separate from and irreconcilable with their new Christian faith. So they can go into school with the parts of themselves that fit, and leave the parts that do not—their Asian culture and, ironically, their Christianity—at home. This cleavage cannot be the wholeness promised in Christ. The desire to get on, fit in, and somehow belong to the mainstream of society means that these young women have chosen to accept an identity given to them by the dominant culture over and above self-worth and cultural integrity. The cost of integration has been assimilation, and with it the danger of an irreversible loss of cultural wholeness.

Perhaps the danger for the Asian Muslim girls, on the other hand, is that a resolution of the struggle may be found in allegiance to their inherited faith and cultural identity at the expense of fully participating in the society of which they are legally a part. Or it may be found in the rejection of the whole Asian culture and a wholehearted embrace of Western culture at the expense of their roots and their history.

From this case study of Asian girls, it is evident that there is a specific need for youth work that supports all young people of color in their cultural identity, which is not one prescribed by the dominant culture. This sense of identity should not have to be bought at the price of cultural integrity, nor of full and equal participation in society. Hence there is also the need for youth work that promotes the opportunity of these young men and women to express this cultural identity in society as well, which means challenging institutional prejudice and racism.

Traditional "Ethnic Minority" Youth Work

Most statutory bodies now recognize the inequality of opportunity that exists in most areas of civic life for people from minority ethnic groups, and have adopted policies that seek to address this inequity in their practice. Racism is becoming widely recognized as one of the key issues to be covered in informal education or youth work practice. Consequently, many urban youth service agencies, both statutory and voluntary, have an "ethnic minorities" team, worker, or project. For example, the Oxfordshire County Council Youth Service has an ethnic minorities team, which has recently been renamed The Asian and African Caribbean Youth Project. Their Annual Report 1996 states: "The purpose of our work is to involve black young people in youth provision which allows them to explore issues that affect and surround them including culture, tradition, identity and positive images."[2]

The need for culturally specific ministry and evangelism is also crucially important. Historical inequalities, daily experiences of discrimination, verbal and physical attacks, struggles with cultural identity, negative self-images created by racial stereotyping and prejudice—all are part of the experience of young people of color. Culturally specific youth ministry must underpin any work in this context that seeks to be holistic, addressing the social as well as the spiritual needs of black young people. Failure to recognize and provide for cultural differences institutionalizes racism; white cultural dominance becomes structural, part of the setup of the youth ministry. "Colorblind" ministries are intellectually impaired ministries, for if cultural difference is made illegitimate, then the ability to own, explore, and express one's cultural identity is lost. "Colorblind" ministries are also *prophetically impaired* ministries—they are unable to declare God's will against injustice, oppression, and inequality, since they can neither see beyond nor speak into a situation of which they are intrinsically a part.

This failure to perceive injustice and therefore effect change is evidenced in many areas where such "Colorblind" policies are in practice, a fact noted in a recent report on the achievements of pupils from minority ethnic groups in schools in the United Kingdom:

> Failure to address ethnic diversity has proved counter-productive at the school level. Where schools have adopted "Colorblind" policies, for example, inequalities of opportunity have been seen to continue. In contrast, research has begun to examine the benefits of addressing diversity as an important and changing part of school life.[3]

Remarkably, the emphasis in the church's activity—often in attempting to address issues of racism—has been on ignoring ethnicity for the sake of unity. Recognizing cultural difference and the need for culturally specific ministry, let alone addressing it, is a rare and endangered practice in the arena of Christian youth ministry. It is necessary for those engaged in youth ministry, if not for the church as a whole, to learn from models in the secular youth work field. This is not to encourage an imitating or copying mentality (one which sadly is already too common in church culture and youth ministry), but to engage with and critique such models in order to better our practice as youth ministers.

Several months ago I found myself in the midst of a situation of racial conflict at the local school where I am the intercultural youth worker. I had gotten to know an Asian girl—I shall call her Susan—and her group of friends. The four other girls in this group are all black. Susan and her group were threatening to fight an Irish boy—I shall call him Ryan—who had allegedly called Susan "a Paki bitch." This, the girls informed me, was the latest in a stream of racist behavior toward Susan and others. The atmosphere had reached fever pitch, with a large group of girls on one side and an even larger group of white (many of them Irish) boys about two feet away on the other, venting anger, hurling abuse, and threatening to erupt into a physical fight at any moment. I was asked to intervene by one of the Asian girls present. I suggested that it would be easier to resolve the situation if we could ascertain exactly what had gone on by talking to the two individuals concerned.

I started by talking to Ryan on his own, away from the group. He was very upset, almost tearful, and adamant that he was not "a racist." He explained that although some of his friends often used racist language and had shouted racist names at the girls, he did not participate. He did not want to point the finger at one of his friends, but neither did he want to be accused of racism. He agreed to apologize for anything he may have said or done that might have unintentionally caused offense.

I then talked to Susan, explaining what Ryan had told me. I asked her if she could be sure that the insult had come from Ryan, and not another member of his group. She could not be certain, and although it did not take away the fact that one of the group had thrown the insult, she agreed to accept an apology from Ryan.

After the apology had been made, I got into a conversation with Susan and her group of friends. It was one of those groundbreaking dialogues in which my relationship with the girls suddenly went much deeper as we talked honestly and at length about our experiences of racism, and the girls shared feelings they were unable to express to others in school. One of them said, "But you know what it's like—sometimes you can't take it anymore, you just want to fight back." I went on to explain that fighting back is important, but that sometimes physical fighting does not help to get the message across—it simply reinforces the stereotype and feeds prejudice.

I was extremely pleased with what I felt was a great piece of youth work. I had prevented a fight in a constructive way. I had managed to talk to both parties about how they were feeling and how they saw the situation. Ryan had apologized to Susan and Susan seemed to accept his apology. I had opened up discussion with the girls on a real level that deepened our relationship, and we had explored issues of race, culture, and identity. An excellent example of what my role as intercultural project worker is all about—*and,* all in the space of a forty-five minute school lunch break!

Since that day Susan and her group have never talked to me again.

On reflection I can see part of the reason for this. On one level the girls may have seen my actions in preventing a fight as aligning myself with the teachers and school authorities. Fights are one of the highlights of school breaks, and I had effectively stolen their thunder. Underlying this, though, is a more serious message. The girls, all of whom are from minority ethnic groups, saw the fight as a way of making themselves heard and their feelings acknowledged in a white arena. Talking to me about their feelings and frustrations was fine, perhaps even valuable, but because of my own intervention in the conflict those feelings remained hidden from their white peers. For me the conversation was so much more valuable than a fight, but to the girls it may have been ultimately worthless.

As this episode shows, such a model of youth work marginalizes the very people it seeks to serve. Restricting the exploration of questions involving culture and ethnicity to ethnic minorities themselves simply reinforces the racist perception that the dominant white world view is the "norm," and that words or phrases like "ethnic" and "cultural background" only apply to *"them."* This traditional structure of "ethnic minority" youth work also marginalizes the youth worker. Most youth work agencies operate under a particular framework in terms of youth work practice. Staff discussions and critique of youth work practice will center on this framework and its generic application. Therefore the "ethnic minorities" project worker has to undertake the necessary "translation" of this thinking (into the context of Asian, black, Chinese) as a solitary activity. This leads to a sense of isolation, both of the work and of the worker.

Finally, this model marginalizes the thinking that lies behind it. The lessons that should be learned and applied by *all* young people in today's multicultural society remain on the sidelines, out of the "mainstream"—important research for specialists in the field but seemingly irrelevant for general youth work practice. Therefore the traditional model of "ethnic minority" youth work aims to provide a service which addresses specific cultures and needs, but at the same time it isolates those needs and cultures from the mainstream of social concern and activity. It also ignores the need for whites to understand and address "culture" and "ethnicity" and to recognize the contributions people of color can make to this understanding. Racism is tackled at a number of levels, but it remains institutionalized as long as these challenges are characterized only as "minority" concerns instead of the concerns of all.

What then might be a suitable model for such a youth ministry, given that a "Colorblind" model is at best inappropriate and at worst racist, and that the traditional model of "ethnic minority" youth work is inadequate and shortsighted?

✔ Multicultural Youth Work: The Iconoclast Conference

"I decided many years ago to invent myself. I had obviously been invented by someone else—by a whole society—and I didn't like their invention."[4] These words by Maya Angelou describe the basic motivation behind the shaping of the Iconoclast conference. In February 1996 I invited a group of young women whom I knew through youth work in a local school to comprise a working party called

Iconoclast for two days, exploring their own cultural identity and their collective experience of living in a multicultural society. The girls were "representatives" from Asian, European, and African-Caribbean backgrounds. Each group had a facilitator from its own "race." Work was undertaken individually, in race-specific groups, and as a whole group. Here I would like to focus on a series of three sessions from the Iconoclast conference as an example of a methodology of multicultural youth work that offers an alternative to the traditional model. The three sessions are entitled "I Am," "Hearing Other Voices," and "Am I Receiving You?"

I Am

In this session, the young people met in their individual race groups with their facilitator and tape recorded thirty minutes of conversation. Each facilitator had the same list of six topics, ranging from food to parents to what it meant to be Asian, white, or black (depending on the group). Every five minutes the facilitator would give the group a new topic to talk about.

I facilitated the Asian group. For that group, just the opportunity to talk together about their "Asian-ness" was a new experience. Interestingly, the Asian girl who was always at the center of things in every conversation at school said little over the weekend. The exception to this was when the girls divided into their race groups: it was only when she was in the company of Asians alone, and not in front of her other friends, that she felt able to talk openly of her "Asian-ness." As the Asian girls started talking they became more and more excited and positive about their culture, even while being honest about its bad points. They began to own their experience as part of their identity, moving from unease and embarrassment to self-esteem and pride.

Hearing Other Voices

In this session, the three groups listened to the recording of another group: the Asian group heard that of the black girls; the black group heard that of the white girls; and the white group heard that of the Asian girls. While listening, everyone in each group had to write on a large piece of paper their comments and questions.

The young people's ability to engage with the material, and the tremendous impact it had on them in different ways, were related to the fact that they had just done the same exercise themselves. If they had not talked about the same subjects themselves beforehand, they would have heard the tapes very differently. The exercise highlighted the fact that each group had a different perspective on the same topics, and that those differences and perspectives were in some way related to culture and ethnic identity.

Am I Receiving You?

In this session, the three groups came back together as a large group to reflect on the tape they had listened to. Feedback was taken in turns. The group being discussed could not respond until the feedback was over, and then had to be heard without interruption. After each had had a chance to speak, discussion was open to all. Obviously, this session needed strong chairing! Some rules were made clear at the outset: each person spoke for him or herself, for example, and not for the whole race group; each person had the right to be heard, however extreme the opinion.

This session got very heated, largely because of the honesty with which perceptions were aired and questions were asked and answered. For example, some of the white girls asked quite genuinely, clearly feeling affronted but certainly intending no malice, "If you think of India as home and you like it so much, why don't you just go back home to India?"

For the black girls the exercise provided something of a revelation, since they had been brought up to believe that Asians were "dirty," "strange people with strange ways," and to be avoided. It was in this session that the black girls and the Asian girls were able to share and explore their discovery of a lot of common ground, including behavior expected at home, experience of church, respect for elders, attitudes to food, and experience of racism. The black girls discovered that in fact their own experience identified closely with that of the Asian girls, both in terms of their felt oppression and their tensions and struggles with their inherited culture. Hence this revelation was twofold; it was both a discovery of commonality of experience and values, and the discovery that their racial prejudice was something they had been "taught" by their parents. As a result, they began to form an alliance. The white girls suddenly found themselves isolated, and received the most direct confrontation for their views.

The white girls were now on unfamiliar territory. They were still in the majority in terms of numbers, but quickly sensed that they had become the minority—not the victims of oppression but a part of the culture responsible for it. They found it difficult to acclimatize to this shift in the power base, which increased as the Asian and black voices of the oppressed found common ground. Although they came from a variety of different backgrounds—Italian, English, and so on—they understood their identity as "white," with little or no reference to their particular cultural heritage. Yet unlike those in the other groups, these girls struggled to identify what it meant to be "white" in any positive sense, and to associate feelings with their racial identity or describe what it felt like to be "white."

The weekend highlighted for the young women the point that friendship in their culturally mixed groups need not, and in fact should not, take place only on the level of the lowest common cultural denominator. They discovered that although many of them had known each other for years and were close friends, they still knew very little about each other. Or more accurately, the Asian girls and the black girls knew much more about their white friends' lives than vice versa. Allowing their friendships to be based and governed according to a "white" agenda was limiting the potential richness of their relationships. They also began to realize that whenever they allowed such a thing to happen, they reinforced the oppression of those from "minority" cultures, which as often as not meant themselves.

For the Asian girls in particular the conference allowed them to glimpse wholeness in their relationships, and to own a part of their identity which had hitherto been considered unacceptable. For some of the black girls it was their first significant contact with Asian girls, and for all of them the experience challenged their prejudice and gave new understanding to their relationships in society. The black girls saw no separation between their understanding of their identity and their understanding of and struggle for justice, which was in different ways an education for the Asian girls and the white girls. The conference was an eye-opener for the white girls, allowing them to glimpse not only different cultures, but also the hurt and injustice their friends lived with on a daily basis. Moreover, these girls had never before consciously reflected on their culture as being one of many cultures, as opposed to "the norm."

The experience of Maia, one of the Asian girls at the Iconoclast conference, is useful as a way of measuring the conference's success as a methodology for intercultural youth work practice. Maia's home life revolves around her responsibilities as a young woman in Punjabi Indian culture. She is expected to share the duties of housework with her mother. Learning to cook and to look after the home are important preparation for her arranged marriage, which will be a matter of course in a few years. Her school life is also a large part of her social life (apart from her visits to family with family). She is the only nonwhite member of her friendship group, and conversation inevitably takes place on a white agenda in terms of boys, music, fashion, and so on. Most of her friends have never been to her house more than once—some never.

Maia is embarrassed about those parts of her life that are distinctively Asian when she is with her friends at school, and yet enjoys them when in conversation with other Asians or at home. She would like school better if there were more Asian people there, and enjoys going to visit her cousin in Birmingham for this reason. The presence of a larger Asian population there means that being Asian feels "more normal, more acceptable" there. For example, Maia would not be caught dead wearing an Indian suit to the shops in Oxford, but often does so when out in Birmingham without feeling self-conscious!

Maia's family speak Punjabi at home and attend an Asian church. They watch British television programs as well as Indian films and the Asian cable channel. Maia likes Indian food, and can make perfect chapattis—and she loves chips! Her life is one of constant negotiation between two worlds, two cultures, both of which ring true in parts. At school she feels she cannot participate in conversations about boyfriends; at home she is unable to reveal her own thoughts on men, her ambitions, and so on.

Maia found the Iconoclast conference an emancipating experience. All that she did not feel able to talk about with her friends at school, and all that she could not express in her life at home, she found herself able to bring out in the safe space the conference provided. Remarkably, Maia went from being one of the more reserved members of the group at school to one of the most vocal and participative at Iconoclast. The best part of the conference for Maia was being able to talk about Asian issues, her home life, and her family background with pride rather than embarrassment.

On returning to school, however, Maia reverted back to her old ways of relating—reticent in conversations about anything Asian, and laughing at herself out of embarrassment at her "Asian-ness" before anyone else might laugh at her. The Iconoclast conference is something she will always remember as a good experience, but its lessons have made little difference to her everyday reality. The freedom of the weekend lent her courage to speak, but school meant a different way of relating.

The Iconoclast conference can only be a first step toward challenging world-views and changing habits of relating in everyday life. Clearly, there is a need for repeated forums to challenge and opportunities for change to be effected. The conference provides the ingredients for a methodology of intercultural youth work which needs conscious and consistent application in a relational ministry over an extended period of time. New ways of relating that reflect the values of another Kingdom are not easily propagated.

✌ Identity: The Theological Task

At present, Asian young people appear to have two options. The first may be described as "cultural schizophrenia," where they live in two worlds according to two different mindsets and ethical frameworks. That way they never resolve who they are in order to live in integrity with their selfhood. The second is a kind of "cultural amnesia," whereby they become so assimilated into Western culture that they forget their own story and history. With that they never discover their "self," their *actual* as opposed to their *assumed* identity.

There must be a third way, a creative identity in keeping with history and future, with inherited East and encountered West, born out of the struggle and not as anesthetic to its pain. This third way must not be that of their parents' generation, for that would mean becoming culturally "fossilized." Culture evolves from generation to generation—what has meaning for and gives meaning to their parents' generation must change in order to be meaningful for their generation. Being true to their Asian identity cannot necessitate clinging to the static cultural form of an inherited tradition, which in its "homeland" is living and evolving all the time. The point remains true for those young people from other minority ethnic groups.

What I mean by "actual" identity is neither inherited culture nor legal stamp or passport; nor is it an identity prescribed by those from the dominant (or another) culture. Rather, by "actual" I mean our identity as purposed by and in God. Hence the question of identity choices poses a theological challenge. As a model for youth ministry, a paradigm shift in focus and in methodology of practice is necessary, since exploration and discovery of this understanding must be addressed as a theological task.

Spiritual identity should make sense of our cultural identity, not destroy it. Redemption through Christ is part of the creative activity of the Trinity; salvation comes through God's gift of rebirth. Ephrem the Syrian, in one of his hymns, describes the creative nature of Christ's redemptive activity seen in the accounts of Jesus' miracles of healing and bringing the dead back to life:

> He is the Son of the Creator
> Who came to restore the whole creation.
> He renewed the sky since fools worshipped
> all the luminaries. He renewed the earth
> that had grown old because of Adam. A new creation
> came to be by his spittle, and the All-sufficient
> set straight bodies and minds.[5]

So if the third way for young people from minority ethnic groups is to be a redemptive one, one which brings selfhood and wholeness as opposed to either separateness or assimilation, then the gospel for them may be some new creative activity of God as opposed to any existing social option. As Jesus said: "No one sews a patch of new cloth on an old garment, for the patch will pull away from the garment, making the tear worse" (Matthew 9:16, NIV).

Yet God's creative activity brings about something new out of what already is—it is characterized by restoration, by transformation, by renewal, and by regeneration. Perhaps just as Christ, incarnate in history, offers the chance to be born again, what is needed here is a cultural renaissance, born out of our history and not in spite of it. The fact of the Incarnation shows that God, though wholly "other," does not understand himself as separate from creation. God acts in history and with creation. God cooperates with creation in order to transform and redeem it. Christ reveals himself within our culture—we do not have to attempt the impossible: the attainment of a faith divorced from any culture. Our faith itself has wholeness and meaning and purpose when it becomes incarnate in our culture.

The "good news" for the Asian girls may be the discovery of the third way as their spiritual identity in Christ, which in its full sense would also mean discovering their selfhood and with it their social identity in their ambiguous, multicultural world. However, if the search for the third way is a theological task, it must be an indigenous pursuit. The journey of these young women into a faith that speaks into their lives with integrity must be embarked on with integrity, through making sense of God from their particular cultural perspective. What is needed is a situational theology, one that speaks out of their lives and experience in order for the universal gospel to be relevant to them. It must be a theology that arises out of their generational and multicultural context, one that leads them to ask, "Can I truly grasp the truth of the Incarnation if I am trying to be someone else?"

The challenge for the church is to enable all young people of color to begin the task of theologizing—not as a hobby or activity, but as part of their journey to faith. The Christian faith which they make their own must make sense *in* their unique place of cultural tension, in order for the gospel it embraces to make sense *of* their lives. So wrestling with their understanding of God must somehow be addressed simultaneously with grappling with issues of culture, equality, and identity—in fact the whole gamut of concerns that affect their understanding of self. This understanding will remain broken and inadequate as long as they give their allegiance to a culture that does not ring true to their whole selves. Cultural diversity is God-given and therefore something to be celebrated and embraced. It is the security of identity in Christ which means that positive embracing of one's own identity need not preclude celebration of another's. Moreover, it is this celebration of diversity which prevents unity in Christ from being interpreted as uniformity in Christ.

The African theologian John Mbiti describes the gospel as coming "to each culture as a stranger, a stranger who settles down. The gospel does not throw out culture—instead it settles in the culture and makes its impact on the lives of the people within that culture."[6] Perhaps there is a sense in which Asian and other ethnic Christians can use this understanding of the incarnate gospel as a model for their own lives. The gospel does not reject culture, but transforms it and takes it forward. Similarly, the encounter between Asian and western cultures can be a transforming experience, rather than rebounding into separateness and alienation. Moreover, the gospel is not lessened or extinguished by the culture where it settles, but rather it speaks as a prophetic voice out of it; culture is judged by it and challenged by it. Young people from minority ethnic groups can be a prophetic voice in their society rather than becoming conformed to it beyond recognition.

For the Christian faith to be part of a process of positive social change for young people, making sense of their relationship with God must not be separated from making sense of their cultural identity. It is when they can begin to make personal and theological sense of what is truly meant by the term "multicultural" that they can become partakers and creators of a society which uses the term with integrity—a society which embraces the richness and values of a future Kingdom. The task for youth ministry is to make it so.

Endnotes

1. A note about terminology: In Britain it is common practice to use the term "ethnic minority" to define those people or groups who are not the dominant majority in terms of their ethnicity. I have reservations about the use of this label, and prefer to use the term "black." I use the terms "black" and "ethnic minority"—or more preferably "minority ethnic"—interchangeably. However, the term "black" has several meanings and applications, and I use it in different ways in the course of this essay. In general, I use "black" as a general label for all people who would not define themselves as "white" in terms of their ethnic identity. An exception to this is where I make the distinction between Asian and African or African-Caribbean, where "black" may be used in reference to the latter. In Britain the term "Asian" generally, and inaccurately, refers to those from the Indian subcontinent; I have rather shamefully adopted such usage for the sake of brevity in this paper. The term "African-Caribbean" is used to refer specifically to those people from the West Indies whose ancestry originated in Africa.

2. K. Ghandi and D. Oakley, *The Asian and African Caribbean Youth Project: The Way Forward* (Oxford: Oxfordshire County Council, 1966), 1.

3. OFSTED, *Recent Research on the Achievements of Ethnic Minority Pupils* (London: HMSO Publications, 1966), 80.

4. Maya Angelou, *Conversations with Maya Angelou* (Reading: Cox and Wyman Ltd., 1989).

5. B. McGinn, *Ephrem the Syrian: Hymns* (Mahwah, N. J.: Paulist Press, 1989), no. 17, v. 11-12.

6. T. Lane, *The Lion Concise Book of Christian Thought* (Tring, England: Lion Publishing, 1986), 227.

The Evangelization of Hispanic Young People

Ramón I. Aymerich

Go therefore and make disciples of all nations, baptizing them in the name of the Father and of the Son and of the Holy Spirit, and teaching them to obey everything that I have commanded you. And remember, I am with you always, to the end of the age. (Matthew 28:19-20)

By and large, Anglicans tend to look at the catholicity and universality of the church a bit differently than many other mainline denominations. Our point of view is that "making disciples of all nations" involves maintaining the tension between being faithful to the commandments of the Lord and the practices of the church *and* respecting individuals and cultures and their ways of expression. Catholicity for us, then, means the many and varied expressions of the church as it becomes incarnate throughout the world. The "Anglican Communion" is not the "English" way of doing things, but rather the many ways in which our rich legacy, history, and beliefs are manifested and celebrated throughout the world. Although Episcopalians tend to forget they are part of something larger, as people (many of them Anglicans) from all nations continue to come to and settle permanently in the United States, the Episcopal Church will continue to be challenged and will, in my opinion, become more and more "Anglican" and less and less "Episcopal." After all, we are incarnational people, which means that just as God took on human flesh and human nature, so the church needs to take on human flesh in its varied and many forms.

⌁ Links with the Gospels

Keeping that in mind as a very important foundational principle for what I want to say, let me share with you some links I see among the gospels, the church, and Hispanic young persons. More specifically, I want to ask, "How do the lives of Hispanic young people parallel the life of Jesus as a child and as an adolescent?" We who profess to be Christians are called to imitate Christ in our life, to be Christ-like. That, as all of us know, is not easy. If I were a young Latino-Hispanic person, I would appreciate knowing that as I am invited to imitate Christ, there are many things that the Jesus of the gospels and I have in common. The following are some examples.

Born in a foreign city

At least as far as Luke's gospel is concerned, Jesus was not born in Nazareth, the city where his parents were living. Luke tells us that Joseph and Mary, who was with child, traveled up to Judea to the town of Bethlehem. Caesar Augustus had ordered a census of the entire world, and Joseph, a descendant of David, had to register in Bethlehem, the town of David. Traditionally, the birth of Jesus has been depicted as having taken place in very humble surroundings. Regardless of the actual details of the birth, if it happened away from home and the familiar surroundings, it must have been difficult to say the least.

These difficulties are also experienced by first-generation Hispanic parents who have not been in the United States long and who have children here. Because of their immigration status, they are often not given the services that most people with medical insurance or eligibility for Medicaid are provided. And in most cases, when the delivery and accompanying charges are paid by Medicaid, the parents are asked to repay the government, as if Medicaid was a loan rather than assistance in time of need. I have accompanied church members to immigration hearings where the judge has asked the Nicaraguan mother or father of a United States-born child how they plan to *repay* the government for the assistance they received during the birth of the child. In one instance, the judge went on to humiliate a woman by telling her that the birth of her child had been paid with taxes that he and her attorney and other legal United States citizens had paid to the government for work they had done. After the hearing was over, I pointed out to the judge that this woman and her husband were both working and paying their share of taxes, but because of the miserable wages they were being paid, they qualified for Medicaid—which is government assistance and not a loan.

A family in exile

According to the gospel writer Matthew, Joseph, Mary, and Jesus had to flee to Egypt for political reasons:

> The angel of the Lord appeared to Joseph in a dream and said, "Get up, take the child and his mother, and flee to Egypt, and remain there until I tell you; for Herod is about to search for the child, to destroy him." (Matthew 2:13)

Mary and Joseph were somewhat lucky. They were able to leave for Egypt with the child. I know so many parents—including my own—who had to send their children alone ahead of them or who had to flee their country of origin and leave their children behind. The gospel according to Matthew is silent about the time that the holy family spent in Egypt. However, knowing the type of relationship that Egypt and Israel had, I am sure that their sojourn there was not a bed of roses.

The same thing has happened to so many families who have come to the United States, escaping political persecution. I have had many people in my office crying and telling me that if they knew how life was going to be for them in this country, they would never have left their country of origin! And yet there was nothing they could do about it. They were caught between a rock and a hard place.

Multilingual and multicultural

Again, the gospels do not say anything about the number of languages that Jesus spoke. But if in fact he lived for a time in Egypt and often traveled to Jerusalem, it is not farfetched to presume that he spoke several languages. Additionally, Jesus was very welcoming and receptive to people who were outside mainstream Judaism. He was very much what we would call a feminist and affirmed and encouraged women, whom society considered second-class citizens. In the parables Jesus is very clear about how we are to consider the marginal and the downtrodden. The parable of the good Samaritan is the best of many examples of what Jesus thought about those whom society and religion rejected.

In this area the church has a tremendous responsibility and a challenge. We need to let our Hispanic and Latino young persons know that the fact that they speak several languages is something enviable and not shameful. They need to know what a valuable gift this will be for them someday. The church also needs to encourage them to be faithful to their past even in the face of pressures to give up their rich heritage and to adopt a new way of life.

The family as a most important unit

The gospel according to Luke tells us that when Mary and Joseph

> had finished everything required by the law of the Lord, they returned to Galilee, to their own town of Nazareth. The child grew and became strong, filled with wisdom; and the favor of God was upon him.... His mother treasured all these things in her heart. And Jesus increased in wisdom and in years, and in divine and human favor. (Luke 2:39-40, 51-52)

It is not unusual for three or four generations of several families to be present at a Sunday eucharist at the congregation in Miami where I am rector. It is not unusual for me to walk or drive around the neighborhood and to see young men or young women walking hand in hand with someone who is five or six times their age, but with whom they obviously have some kind of a family or love bond. When my parents were finally given permission to leave Cuba in 1966, my father refused to leave unless my mother's mother came along. They missed one opportunity to leave and risked missing another when at the airport in Cuba they were told that a seat was not available for my maternal grandmother. My father's decision was final. Either she went with us or we all stayed. He knew how difficult it had been for all of us when we were first separated due to my earlier departure, and he did not want to go through that pain again.

Family is extremely important for Latinos and Hispanics. Often the extended family unit is preserved in spite of the difficulties that keeping the unit together may bring about. It is much easier to put great-grandma in a nursing home, but it is much more important to take care of her at home, regardless of how difficult that may be. I often encourage young persons to look up to their parents for guidance and example. They know the immense sacrifices their parents have made and continue to make to ensure a proper future for their children, and their children's children.

Just recently I stopped unannounced at the home of a parish family. As I made my way through the house to their backyard, I realized that one of the sons of this large family was engaged in refinishing a chair, a trade he was learning from his father. Thinking I should say something, I told him to continue to improve those skills that someday may be very beneficial to him in a country like ours, where such artistry has been taken over by computerized machines. I could not help but think of Jesus, the son of Joseph the carpenter, who must have learned his father's trade. In fact, there is a religious folk song in Nicaragua that speaks of Mary wanting her son to be a carpenter just like his father.

↩ The Church and the Celebration of the Sacraments

While the majority of Hispanics and Latinos I know call themselves "Catholics," and in fact were baptized in the Roman Catholic Church in their respective countries of origin, there is no doubt that a large number of them never practiced their religion back home. In fact, the Roman Catholic Church in the United States has realized that unless they do more aggressive evangelism, nontraditional religious groups will continue to "take from the church" immigrants who have not had an opportunity to become members of a particular congregation.

I have to be honest with you and tell you that when it comes to the celebration of the sacraments, I have done a one-hundred-eighty-degree turn. I know that the church wants the celebration of the sacraments to be for its members. I fully understand that the sacraments are the celebration of a people that belong to a particular Christian community who have committed themselves to worship, study, prayer, and stewardship. In my twenty-one years of ministry I have even declined to baptize or marry people who had no desire to be incorporated into the body of Christ and into a particular congregation.

I now think that if I had been more patient and more understanding, those people (or a good percentage of them) would have eventually chosen to belong to the congregation and to participate fully in the life of the church. Several years ago a young couple came to me asking me to marry them. The rector of a neighboring congregation had consented to do the service, but in the meantime decided to retire and the interim would not go along with his decision. They were in a bind, and so was I. What was I to do? I chose to celebrate their wedding. To this day, I have no regrets about it. They became members of this congregation, something which was not part of any condition that I placed on them, and have continued over the last two years to come to church. They have invited me to their home on several occasions, where their friends have asked me many questions about the church. This year, on Thanksgiving, they bought provisions to make sandwiches for the poor and homeless of the area, which they themselves distributed with the assistance of members of our youth group.

Was my decision to celebrate the wedding of this young Hispanic couple the right decision? As far as I am concerned, it was. Would I do it all over again? Definitely. Will it always net that result? Absolutely not. In fact, I know that many people come to our congregation seeking baptism, marriage, or another one of the sacraments because we may be a little easier to deal with than our neighbors. But as far as I am concerned, the church should not be another place where immigrants or new arrivals to this country experience further problems and are confronted with what they perceive to be unreasonable demands.

People do have needs, physical as well as emotional and spiritual. People who come to this country from traditionally religious countries, as most are in the Caribbean Basin and Latin America, also come with their own religious traditions. Should the church be in the business of asking them to throw those traditions away, or should it rather be about honoring those customs, which are and continue to be important to these people who have left just about everything else behind?

For example, Holy Communion in the Episcopal Church is open to all baptized persons. That means that every baptized person, from an infant to someone dying of old age, is welcome to receive the Body and Blood of Christ. I would never deny Holy Communion to a baptized infant who is brought by his or her parents to the communion rail. However, I also realize that in many Latin countries the tradition is that a child will make his or her first communion around the age of seven, a practice which the Roman Catholic Church has upheld since the time of Pius X.

At Holy Comforter in Miami, where we have a large number of members who are first-generation Latino-Hispanics, we honor that custom while making sure that everyone knows that any baptized person—regardless of age—can receive communion. As the children are prepared for their "First Communion" through our Sunday school program, we meet with the parents regularly and emphasize to them the importance of continuing the religious formation of the children once the celebration of their first Holy Communion has taken place. At the same time, we make our Sunday school program attractive and interesting enough that the children will want to come back once they have made their communion. Word has gotten around the neighborhood about the quality and attractiveness of our program. Consequently, we now have the celebration of First Communion twice a year—in May and in December—with an average of thirty children each time.

I am not naive, nor do I pretend that everyone who is prepared for their first Holy Communion, or for confirmation or marriage, will remain in the church. However, the number of people who are integrated into the active life of the church is enough, in my opinion, to warrant taking this departure from the traditional way of doing things.

I think the same thing can be said for non-sacramental celebrations. For example, on December 8, Nicaraguans celebrate the Feast of the Immaculate Conception, in honor of the Patroness of Nicaragua. This is exclusively a Roman Catholic feast day, and in fact, a day of obligation for Roman Catholics. With a church filled with Nicaraguans, I would be a fool to ignore such an important feast. Do I make it a holy day of obligation in our congregation? Obviously not. Do I observe it by bringing to that tradition what is best from our tradition? Of course. And so, when I am invited to join in the celebration of *la purisima* in someone's home, I always tell the host family that I will be happy to be with them as long as I can celebrate the eucharist and speak about the importance of Mary as a role model in the life of every Christian. This is evangelism at its best: a home filled with neighbors and friends, where young and old alike for the first time experience the celebration of the eucharist outside a church building and are given a substantive and encouraging message to take with them. Often the response is: "Gee, that priest is not a bad guy. He has a good sense of humor. He seems to relate well with us adolescents. I think I am going to go to his church."

Another non-sacramental church celebration which is very popular here in Miami is the *quinces,* a Latin version of "sweet sixteen." Often, no expense is spared in this celebration of a girl's (and sometimes a boy's) rite of passage. Needless to say, on those occasions the church is packed with people, most of them teenagers who are either part of the "court" attending the honoree or friends who have come to celebrate. Most want a *Te Deum,* which I embellish with readings from scripture. Two of my favorites passages are Ecclesiastes 12:1-8, where the young person is exhorted to remember the Creator, and Luke 2:41-52, the story of

Jesus who at the age of twelve is brought to the temple in Jerusalem by his parents for the feast of Passover. During the homily, I speak directly to the teenagers assembled at church and tell them how important it is to rely on the power and the grace of God during this period of great growth and change. I also invite them, if they are not already members of a church, to come and worship with us on Sunday and explore the opportunities we offer to young people at Holy Comforter.

Another rite of passage that is very important for adolescents is obtaining and wearing a high school graduation ring. Considering the expense of rings these days, they represent not only a lot of blood, sweat, and tears, but also a financial challenge for many first-generation Latino-Hispanic young persons who do not have a legal status in this country, and whose parents often have to work two jobs to make ends meet. For these reasons, on an appointed Sunday once a year, I ask those young persons in the congregation who are wearing a recently purchased high school ring to come to the altar at the time of the offertory so that they and their rings can receive a blessing. This simple gesture can go a long way in helping high school seniors realize what they have accomplished and what lies ahead of them as God, through the actions of the church, promises to continue to bless them.

✥ The Church as an Institution

The church is not only the people of God gathered to celebrate the sacraments. It is also an institution respected by other institutions in our society, as well as most Latino-Hispanics who have had a relationship with the church in their own respective countries. Consequently, the church can become the place to which young persons come with non-religious issues and requests. It is up to the church's leadership—both clergy and lay—to insure that as we serve these young persons with their concerns and issues we also make them aware of the message of Jesus and the spiritual and sacramental dimensions of his church. The following are some examples.

The church and "community service hours"

At least once a week, a young person will come to the offices of Holy Comforter Episcopal Church asking to see me, the rector. In one hand he or she holds a yellow piece of paper, which I immediately recognize as a referral for community service hours, usually as a result of a petty crime or some other infraction of the law. It is my responsibility to make sure that this young person completes the hours and returns to court or its agency with the paper signed by me. But I and others who are members of the Holy Comforter Ministry Team see this young person as another opportunity to proclaim the great love of the Lord, particularly in light of the infraction committed and how the young person may feel about it. I immediately make the young person feel at ease in my office, asking him or her to sit down and let me know what happened. I do this not because I am nosy but as an opportunity to start some dialogue.

If it is possible, I try to place this young person in one of our outreach ministries. Every Wednesday at Holy Comforter Church, approximately two hundred bags of food are distributed during a religious service. A young person who has to perform community service hours and who can accomplish the hours doing something for others in the name of Christ walks away feeling good and knowing that he or she has been able to help others in need.

The church as a place to "hang out"

The church in most Latin American countries plays a very prominent role and is often located in a strategic place, usually near the town square. As young persons in Cuba, my sister and I would often visit the parish house during the week, and on occasion would stay overnight either at the rectory or at the convent adjacent to the church. Back in those days there were no personal computers, but I am sure if the sisters or the parish priest had had one, they would have let us use it to do our homework.

Several years ago, with financial assistance from the social concerns commission of the diocese of Southeast Florida, the Church of the Holy Comforter set aside a series of rooms to be used exclusively by the young people of the church and the neighborhood. The rooms, which include a kitchen and a bathroom, have several computers, a pool table, and state-of-the-art audiovisual equipment. Here young people can, with the supervision of adults, gather and do homework, play pool, eat pizza, listen to music, watch a movie, or just plain hang out. One of the church's acolytes, who at one point drifted away from the church and became a member of a gang, once in a while invites local gang members to come with him and play pool and listen to music. In this day and age, when curfews for youth are becoming the norm, it is important for the church to provide places and opportunities for personal interaction and development while at the same time letting young people know that they are valued as human beings.

The church as a promoter of cultural diversity

At the very beginning of this essay I mentioned that the catholicity and universality of the Anglican Communion presupposes a variety of cultures and nations. Several years ago the national church gave us a grant of three thousand dollars for the sole purpose of purchasing attire and music and providing training for an emerging group of folk dancers. While the church does not have any native North American members of the congregation, a large number of its members come from countries where there is a substantial indigenous population. The group is off and running. Early in 1996, our dancers performed for the Presiding Bishop and Executive Council during their meeting in Miami. In October, at the diocesan Hispanic Heritage Festival, they impressed everyone with their vitality and professionalism. Later that year, at a convention center in downtown Miami, they were introduced as the "Young Folk Dancers of Holy Comforter Episcopal Church" to an audience of five thousand Roman Catholic charismatics who were gathering for their annual prayer and praise meeting. As their rector, I was so choked up that when I arrived backstage to congratulate them, the words could not come out. All I did was cry, which embarrassed the kids but at the same time let them know how proud their rector was of them. In a world where homogeneity is so often stressed the church needs to tell its youth, who come from countries where strong traditional values and customs are upheld and celebrated, that diversity is wholesome. They need to be proud of and celebrate who they are.

I hope the examples I have shared with you will offer you starting places from which to proclaim the good news of our Lord and Savior Jesus Christ. Latino-Hispanic young persons are ready and willing to hear the good news, particularly when they are taken seriously and shown that they are not the future of the church, but its present.

Youth Culture and Evangelism

Dean Borgman

As those committed to youth ministry, we may paraphrase the promise of our Lord in this way: "You are receiving power from the Holy Spirit to be witnesses of me in all the youth cultures of the world" (Acts 1:8). The key question of this essay is, *"Why and how should we make more critical use of information about adolescence and the youth culture in our ministry these days?"* Information about the many cultural influences that affect the lives of young people is crucial to effective evangelization with them. The information to which I am referring has to do with changing configurations of adolescence, youth, and popular cultures, and of youth ministry itself. Five assumptions underlie the approach of this essay.

First, adolescence is a social structure as well as a stage of growth. It is the transitional age between childhood and adulthood, and it is greatly affected by expectations and influences from parents, schools, and society. From biblical cultures to societies today, no one is exempt from this passage from childhood to adulthood. The primary socializing systems in which most children and teenagers live today are family, school, the media, and their peers. Seven-year-olds are probably influenced by those four systems in that order; by the time they are teenagers in secondary school, the order may change to peers, media, family, school.

Second, the prolongation, isolation, confusion, and restriction of youth are significant factors in the creation of their culture. To the extent that the dominant culture undervalues, neglects, or oppresses particular groups of teenagers, youth may form unique and sometimes oppositional subcultures.

My third assumption is that significant changes in the world and in the dominant culture create corresponding changes not only in the youth culture, but in adolescence itself. Most who work in the youth culture or study it are impressed with the rate at which it changes. To the extent that the influences on children and youth change, we may expect a change in young people and their culture—and youth ministry must also change to remain contextualized and relevant.

Fourth, a common thread among those involved with the evangelization of young people is to see relevant youth ministry as incarnational and relational. This emphasis reflects an understanding of youth culture as subcultures. Relevant youth ministry does not simply invite youth into the adult church; it is driven by missiological urgency to enter the various subcultures of young people today. It does so as Christ entered human culture, and with the desire to become involved with young people on their own turf.

Finally, there are youth workers who, without any prior training, love young people and want to serve them. Although we respect such concern for young people, we are also committed to training youth workers with the best information and principles available. While we recognize that youth ministry is the Lord's, who took fishermen without ministerial training to found the church and can still work through the untrained to do exploits, we think striving for excellence in youth ministry calls for some degree of sophistication.

∿ Professionalism in Youth Ministry

Much fine youth work has, in fact, been in reaction to the condescending and irrelevant efforts of some social workers and religious leaders. Many of us became youth workers saying, "We refuse to be nine-to-five desk-sitters who remember clients by numbers and diagnoses." Of course, we still resist bureaucratic and programmatic institutionalism that loses the relational touch. But, should we not also strive to move youth ministry and concern for the evangelization of young people more into the mainstream of the church?

As a young youth worker many years ago, I was driven more by numbers than a deep and theological sense of our calling. When our group reached a hundred members, we were successful. When it topped two hundred we were really going places, and by the time it reached three hundred we were the greatest! We did not need training or the wisdom of experience: we used the cult of personality and the key-kid concept to build up a Saturday night movement in our church basement. Along with many secondary teachers and students, we had no idea there was life after high school or university. We were so committed to kids in the here-and-now that we thought little of what their lives and faith would look like fifteen years down the road.

This ministry contains many characteristics of immature youth work. Still, whenever we see young and fervent youth workers in such a ministry, we should guard against making quick judgments and writing it all off. For God has and still does bring significant results from such efforts. Professionalism certainly does not guarantee kingdom results, but we are striving to combine youthful spontaneity, the creativity of the Spirit, and sound professional wisdom.

By "professional" I mean youth ministry that is well thought out as well as prayed through, that is holistic rather than superficial, that considers long-term as well as immediate results, that empowers young people rather than making celebrities of its leaders. Admittedly, it is not easy to determine what is or is not a profession in today's cultures. Traditionally, professions have played a special role in a society. They have a special responsibility for society's treasured resources—be it the life of a baby, the education of children, or the reputation and freedom of a citizen. This is what doctors, teachers, and lawyers do. Clergy have traditionally been considered professionals because they deal with people's souls. What makes a group of workers professional is specialized knowledge, practical training, acceptance of a set of standards, and oversight and discipline. We are called "professionals" because we have a responsibility for the souls of young people. With that responsibility comes the challenge to be well-informed.

↵ Youth Culture

Some very sophisticated denominational youth leaders in the United States and elsewhere still act as if youth ministry is primarily a family affair in a pleasant church setting. Certainly, all of us are deeply committed to family and church. But most young people are growing up in a different world—a world of friends, pop culture, sensationalized news, and spicy commercials, a world symbolized in videos of house, jungle, rap, heavy metal, and alternative music. Not all young people are getting high or having sex on the weekends, but studies show that the percentage of those from "nice" churches who do is higher than their leaders and parents would like to admit.

Human beings must have a culture as a context in which to survive, reproduce, and socialize their young—as well as to live with dignity and fulfillment. It is only within human culture that personal identity and status are achieved. In the culture of today it is difficult for young people to work out their identities and to achieve a sense of their status. Years of further education, experience, and the paying of dues are usually expected before they are ready for adult responsibility and rewards in business or even family. Teenage sports stars are the exceptions that prove this rule—they are still playing as "big kids" and relying on sometimes unscrupulous agents. We may like to think that young people are adults now, but that is not their reality.

American culture has greatly segregated and prolonged adolescence. Influenced by media and advertising which cater to and prey upon them, adolescents establish a culture with their own language, humor, fashions, and music. This youth culture is not monolithic; it is divided into many subcultures. When the folk language (or slang), folk fashion, or folk music of a particular group becomes popular enough, it is quickly exploited by the media in way that makes it mainstream—mass or pop culture rather than folk culture. Young people with a need for unique expressions of their identities may feel compelled toward alternative, punk, or neo-punk cultures. There is, then, a constant reshaping of youth culture and special subcultures within the larger culture, and these are the contexts of our ministries.

↩ Two Disciplines of Youth Ministry

There are really two disciplines of youth ministry that are as different from each other as the disciplines of teaching and social work. The first discipline might be described as *youth ministers* who work from *within* the church, hoping its young people will bring in outsiders. The second could be called *street workers* who work from *without,* hoping to lead young people into the church at some point. Within these groups there are those whose style and framework is "inside-out" and others whose style is "outside-in."

Both styles or disciplines need a keen knowledge of the youth culture, though perhaps for different reasons and with different emphases. The youth pastor has the greatest temptation to assume that church culture, be it ever so "youthful," is the culture within which group members are really growing up, making their life commitments, and being discipled. Actually the church youth group may well be a kind of subculture that is itself only one compartment of the busy, fragmented lives of the group's members. The values they learn from youth ministers are their church values, and these may have little to do with their school values or peer values. This does not reflect superficiality in the church's teaching, but the fact that hurried children are growing up to be "patchwork selves" as teenagers.[1] If a youth minister is with a young person two hours a week, that is a minute fraction of that teenager's life. The youth minister needs an understanding of the other compartments of a teenager's life, and must also be familiar with the whole context within which the church's young people are being discipled. Church youth leaders ought to see beyond what is sometimes a Christian or denominational subculture to various other shades of secular subcultures influencing the members of their youth group.

By contrast, the outreach worker, or street worker, is really a missionary who needs an anthropological understanding of the culture in which he or she is involved. Missiology is a delicate and sensitive discipline. We must see the beauty and positive aspects of all cultures before we can earn the right to be heard. We enter other cultures as learners before we can become teachers. We do not take God to other cultures; we wait to discover God there and be surprised as we find new revelations of Jesus Christ. This is not meant to diminish the singular and unique revelation of Christ as a Jew two thousand years ago, nor the revelation of the word of God in Holy Scripture. Discovery of God in other cultures has to do with the continuous and unique manifestations of grace in all cultures.

No culture has a corner on God's truth—though we have to admit that westerners have tended to act as if they do. The spiritualities of other peoples and the instances of common grace in particular cultures can bless and instruct us in many ways if we are open to them. On the other hand, the evils of cultures are best judged and corrected by cultural insiders; missionaries are there to share the good news of such hope. Until recently the underestimation of culture in many religious circles, and in most youth ministry writings, has been a crucial vacuum needing to be filled. Without a deep understanding of culture as an idea and of cultures in particular, dynamic theologizing is limited and youth ministry is less effective.

✓ Research and Youth Ministry

I see research as the second of nine stages in youth ministry, after the first task of developing a strong pastoral support base and varied leadership. Here I mean research in the broadest sense, as the informational base needed for relevant and holistic youth ministry. *Webster's* defines research as "searching, diligently examining with continued care," while the *American Heritage Dictionary* calls it "scholarly or scientific investigation." To the occasional students who object to my wide and more popular definition, I suggest we distinguish two types of research: primary or scientific research, and secondary research. Secondary research includes all careful observation, inquiry, questionnaires, surveys, and collections of news and magazine articles, as well as scholarly studies in journals. We are talking here primarily of this secondary and broader use of the term. Few of us are called to scientific research on a focused and unusually narrow aspect of adolescent behavior or the youth culture, although we applaud those who are. But all of us are called collectively, I believe, to organize our observations and inquiries about where young people are at these days and how they may be most effectively encouraged in their growth and spiritual quest.

It seems helpful to further distinguish two types of secondary research in youth ministry: community research and topical research. The first inquiry of the youth worker should be a survey of the context of a particular ministry, identifying the interests, assets, and needs of young people, along with the needs and resources of the community. Such investigations promote critical networks that encourage holistic ministry with young people. Out of this community research comes further need for information on various issues among young people, which we call *topical* research. Files of clippings from local newspapers, along with national and international information, can become a resource center for a local network of youth workers.

Examples of broad observations and inquiries

You can tell a lot about a culture by looking at what it is giving its children. The giant toy stores of the early 1980s were filled with sexy Barbie dolls and toy machine guns. Children's cartoons tell us the new, product-driven stories. Not content with directing commercials at children every ten minutes, toy manufacturers have created whole television programs promoting violent toys. We also began to notice three strong messages that dominated movies, television programs, and commercials by the mid-1980s: "You should be wealthy and therefore successful. You should be sexy and therefore popular. You can be strong, dominant, and violent, and therefore sexy." To what extent do you think these three statements express the culture in which American children were growing up in the 1980s? By the time these children became teenagers at the end of the decade, America was experiencing a wave of date rape and even fraternity gang rape. Are there any causal relationships here? Does this information suggest any implications for youth ministry?

Let's take a look at another postindustrial nation, Germany. By the late 1970s there were signs of spiritual revival among German young people. An understandable caution about large group rallies, along with the German tendency toward bureaucratic and socially-oriented youth programs, might have discouraged evangelical happenings. Instead, renewal movements and large rallies came not only to be tolerated but even supported by the German church. Especially notable is *Kirchentag,* a conference attracting more than one hundred thousand youth each year. It is run one year by the Protestants and the next by Roman Catholics. Themes of peace and care for the environment are prominent, but there are also programs aimed at personal commitment and piety using sophisticated technology and music.

By the 1980s we were learning of a rise in neo-Nazi propaganda in Germany—including computer games that "sent Jews to concentration camps." The removal of authoritarian restraints in East Germany unleashed the incipient antisemitism and xenophobia that had never completely gone away; problems of unemployment and immigration were also serious factors. Published reports informed the world of a growing number of skinheads and hate crimes. (Predictably, the American media seized on such news even though the phenomenon was probably more widespread in this country.) In response, the German legislature created remarkably strong legislation against discriminatory words and actions.

Spiritual revival continues, especially among the young in Germany. Roland Werner is a young musician and evangelist who has taken over a four-day rally called *Komme forge Jesus* (Come Follow Jesus). Skeptics wondered how many would come to the East German town of Dresden in 1996 and how organizers would cover the cost of over four million dollars. But Werner's dream of bringing together twenty thousand young people was exceeded, as thirty-two thousand gathered for a series of creative activities climaxed by a rally that filled the Dresden football field. The planning group was well aware of the various groups that would be attending—Jesus freaks, straightedge skinheads, environmentalists, those heavy into techno music, and others. This knowledge helped them plan a program with appeal and relevance for all.

In the United Kingdom, the Maranatha Community has recognized the importance of gathering and disseminating crucial facts about children and young people. In December 1993 they read a forty-five-page document in Parliament called *What On Earth Are We Doing to Our Children? An Appeal to the Nation's Conscience by the Maranatha Community*. This launched "A Call to the Churches" sent to three thousand Christian leaders throughout the land at the feast of Pentecost in 1994. Here are some of the statistics from this document, facts with which we all have to live:

- According to the United Nations, more than 17 million children in the world die each year of starvation and malnutrition.
- According to Children of War—Save the Children, more than 1.5 million have been killed in wars worldwide in the past decade. Over 4 million more have been disabled, maimed, blinded, and brain damaged, and more than 12 million children have lost their homes in this period.
- According to a 1984 U. S. Justice Department Study, seventy percent of all adult criminals in American jails suffered childhood sexual abuse.
- According to a 1994 article in *The Independent,* more than 250 million copies of child pornography videos are circulating worldwide.

The implications of these statistics demand careful consideration. What are the results of sexual and physical abuse on children? What havoc does the trauma of violence play in young lives, and how may we respond? The answers to these questions and others related to the conditions of young people within our culture have a direct relationship with those concerned with the evangelization of young people. Effective evangelization depends on our ability to access important research regarding young people, and then to relate that data to our ministries with young people.

Some children and young people are more resilient than others, but all respond to loving care and secure structure. Researchers now believe loving relationships also can help older children "reset" their automatic response to stress when it has been derailed by abuse. This is not always easy: even a loving touch can sometimes set off a tantrum. Fortunately, researchers are also discovering drugs that can check the fight-or-flight response. If we fail these children and teenagers, researchers remind us, they are less likely to live up to their economic potential, and more likely to wind up in prison, on drugs, or in psychiatric units—at an enormous cost to society.

My main argument is that we need readily available information in our ministries of healing, liberation, and empowerment. The research and information contained in this chapter is not esoteric: it is available to anyone who works with badly bruised young people or discusses such issues with young people who are more fortunate. It should shape our preaching and teaching. The task of gathering such information should be done collaboratively, with input from local resource centers and international organizations, such as our various denominations and the Center for Youth Studies. My suggestion is that we decide what is most important for youth workers "in the trenches" to know, how we can get at that information, and how it can most readily be made available. There is already established the beginning of a global network, with methods for gathering information, a writing guide for abstracting information, and a CD-ROM with the *Youth Workers' Encyclopedia* and other program and biblical resources.[2]

Theology is best articulated by those who have a Bible in one hand and today's newspaper in the other. For the same reason, we need research to help frame the theologies behind effective youth ministry wherever we labor. May all our endeavors keep young people and the youth culture clearly in focus, and may they begin and end in the Spirit of God and our Lord Jesus Christ.

Endnotes

1. See David Elkind, *The Hurried Child: Growing Up Too Fast Too Soon* (Reading: Addison Wesley, 1988) and *All Grown Up and No Place to Go: Teenagers in Crisis* (Reading: Addison Wesley, 1996).

2. For information on these resources, contact the Center for Youth Studies, 130 Essex Street, South Hamilton, Massachusetts 01982. Phone: (978) 468-7111, ext. 573; e-mail: cys@gcts.edu.

part three

Evangelism and Liturgy

Preach It and They Will Come

Clayton L. Morris

It once was common to expect that young people would abandon their church connection somewhere during high school or college, that they would return briefly to have their marriage blessed, and that they would finally begin an adult relationship with the Christian community of their childhood when their first child was in need of baptism. In these closing years of the twentieth century, however, those assumptions are all in question. Many people between the ages of fifteen and thirty have never been in church. Young people do not see marriage as an unavoidable option, as did many in earlier generations. Church is no longer an integral part of people's lives. Everything has changed! And so has the question of how and why young people might or should see Christianity as an organizing structure for their lives.

This essay will examine the attitudes of young people today toward the church, not in the hope of discovering deficiencies in their perspectives, but by wondering what it is about the church that makes it irrelevant or distasteful to many thoughtful young people. While the purpose of this essay is to provide suggestions about how to help people between the ages of fifteen and thirty find their way into a vital relationship with the church, its subject is the connection we have—or do not have—to the church's worship life and how those connections can be nurtured and (perhaps) redirected. This will not be a description of the creative *hooks* one might use to seduce youth into an existing ecclesial institution. Rather, we will explore the possibility that the church fails to attract people because its institutional assumptions and patterns of behavior have failed to maintain and proclaim an animated vision of the gospel and its demands on those of us who would call ourselves followers of Christ.

✌ Developing Church Connections

Why do people develop a connection to church? We like to think that we go to church for *spiritual* reasons, making a genuine, personal response to a call God has issued. But to get some sense of how people are drawn into the worshiping community, it may be better to set aside the altruistic issues for a moment. It is reasonable to assume that we attend church because being there meets a need for us. The need is not necessarily personal or selfish, but something gets us out of bed on Sunday morning.

We are drawn to worship for a variety of reasons. Some of us maintain a relationship with a Christian community and a regular attendance at worship out of a sense of holy obligation. We learned, probably at a parent's knee, that being *Christian* is a necessary part of life, and part of being *Christian* is showing up on Sunday morning. The church connection, in this context, is just something we feel compelled to maintain.

Others of us find in a congregation of Christians the opportunity for social engagement. Maybe it is the young singles club, the altar guild, the youth group, or the Saturday gardening crew. When we are asked about our association with the church, we say something about our preference for socializing in a *Christian* context.

Still others of us are interested in improving ourselves—becoming better people, better life partners, better parents, better citizens—and we look to the Christian community to provide educational opportunities and motivational, inspirational experiences. For us, the church is a continuing education opportunity with a strong moral-ethical focus.

There are dozens of reasons, like these, which draw us into Christian community. But curiously, these religious and sociological considerations that identify a rationale for maintaining a church connection do not relate significantly to the teachings of Jesus, which serve, presumably, as the primary rationale for the continued existence of the church. Sometimes when listening to people talk about the reasons they like their congregation it is impossible to find any specifically *Christian* content in the rationale.

Any institution which expects to gather people in community will be a complicated, multifaceted organization. We should not expect everyone who is drawn into the life of a Christian community immediately to articulate a cogent description of the ministry of Jesus or even an accurate recital of the baptismal covenant. But neither should we assume that the claims of the teachings of Jesus on members of Christ's Body can be taken for granted. We should not expect that the founding principles for the establishment and maintenance of Christian community are simply given, unexamined and hidden beneath the interesting and varied textures of congregational life.

Over the course of this century people have increasingly sought to meet their social and religious yearnings apart from specifically ecclesial associations. Local newspapers and magazines offer a seemingly endless variety of support groups, meditation strategies, personal growth opportunities, and informally organized para-religious communities. What gives rise to this epidemic of new expressions of human spirituality? Does the growing popularity of these institutions and organizations say something about the nature of Christian community and our attraction to it?

During the past several decades the church has slowly recognized that fewer and fewer people are attracted to traditional, mainstream churches. Institutional responses to this threatening trend have fallen, roughly, into three categories. Some communities have retreated into the security of apparent past glory and have attempted to reconstruct a kinder, gentler, safer world of an earlier time. The fact that these late-twentieth-century recreations of life in the 1950s are reconstructions of a world that never existed is apparently of less concern than the comfort offered by a world-view whose image projects an illusion of safety. As much as we try, pretending will not bring back a world we invented in the 1950s to take our mind off the issues of conscience and justice we did not want to face then.

Some have attempted to attract us by offering responses to our natural curiosity about religion. These communities take seriously the pain and anxiety we feel in our attempts to survive in an apparently hostile world, and offer resources from the disciplines of psychology and spirituality to assuage the negative feelings we have about our lives, our neighbors, our communities, the nation, and the world. It is certainly a good thing to be at peace with ourselves, our lives, and our environment, but the fact that I feel better about *my* life does not solve the crushing problems that exist in the world just outside my door.

Some congregations have rediscovered the imperatives of the gospel of Jesus Christ (as they are expressed in the prayer book's baptismal covenant and catechism) and have allowed the teachings of Jesus about ministry in and to the world to form a primary rationale for belonging to an ecclesial community. These congregations are part of an important trend to restore the teachings of Jesus to a central place in the life of the church by putting the eucharist at the center of the congregation's worship, emphasizing the initiation of unbaptized adults in light of that eucharistic focus, and surrounding the whole with the baptismal covenant's call to the restoration of universal human community and wholeness.

It is this third strategy which may offer hope for the future. In the Episcopal Church it has been our habit to *meet people where they are*. We are not a confessional church, expecting adherents to subscribe to rigorous doctrinal positions or strenuous devotional habit. We have tried instead to proclaim the gospel of Jesus Christ in word and sacrament and to encourage people to make a faithful response to what they hear and experience. At an earlier time, when we expected the problems of human existence to be gradually but surely worked out in the arenas of science and technology, this relaxed approach may have been sufficient or even appropriate. But as we come to grips with the fact that the modern world has not managed to eradicate suffering and evil from our lives, we begin to recognize the need for a new approach in response to a new understanding of how the world works.

✙ The Baptismal Covenant
What do the baptismal covenant and catechism say about the church and its ministry? The baptismal rite in the *Book of Common Prayer* begins by proclaiming that

> There is one Body and one Spirit;
> There is one hope in God's call to us;
> One Lord, one Faith, one Baptism;
> One God and Father of all. (BCP 299)

Then, in the renunciations that follow the service of the word, the candidate for baptism is asked to renounce "the evil powers of this world" (BCP 302) in order to embrace Christ. This profound shift of focus and allegiance is spelled out later in the liturgy, especially in the last three questions of the baptismal covenant, which ask the candidate to proclaim the gospel, to serve Christ in all persons, and to strive for justice and peace among all people, loving all people—*all* people—as neighbor (BCP 304-305). The catechism is even more explicit, identifying the mission of the church as the restoration of "all people to unity with God and each other in Christ" (BCP 855).

If these references seem extreme, it is because of a common element of our ecclesial behavior we would just as soon forget. In communal life we fall into habitual patterns. We tend to gather with people like ourselves. We come to know the people with whom we pray and socialize, and so we come to distinguish between those who are in the community and those who are not. Unless we exercise extreme care, our level of comfort with those we understand to be our sisters and brothers in the community makes it easy to see those we do not know but who, according to God, are also sister and brother, as the enemy. Thus, our gathering in search of unity can become divisive.

If we can set aside for a moment the lenses with which we view the church as we have come to know it, and look with a fresh eye at the *Book of Common Prayer* and the story of Jesus as it is recorded in the gospels, we find a call which compels us to live as if there is a place at the table for all people, and enough sustenance for everyone to feast into eternity. This gospel of hope is compelling to an increasing number of us who find ourselves living in a world that divides us into camps and that fails daily to care for others or even for the planet upon which we all depend for sustenance.

The starting point for any exercise hoping to draw people into the community of faith who are, for whatever reason, alienated from it is a recovery of gospel passion for the world the church seeks to serve. When we try to create a lovely but naive world-the-way-we-think-it-should-have-been, or when we seek to build psychological and spiritual defenses from the feelings of guilt and despair we suffer when we catch a chance glimpse of the world as it is, we are simply not involved in the Christian project to restore the unity of creation.

∿ The Catechumenal Process

It comes as a shock to many Christians to discover that our world, which we were taught to think of as a *Christian* world, is full of unbaptized adults. It is not merely that these people have been neglectful of their Christian duty; they have no experience or knowledge of what Christian duty is. They have never been exposed to the church or its view of the world. When we thought of ourselves as a *Christian* nation, we assumed that everyone was initiated into the church as a matter of course. Perhaps we did not notice as families abandoned that tradition along the way, but it finally became apparent to us that there are significant numbers of well-educated, intelligent, highly motivated people living lives of purpose and responsibility who do not have a clue about the church.

In the 1960s, the Roman Catholic Church began to react seriously to this emerging situation. They saw in society's abandonment of traditional religion an opportunity to articulate the gospel in a new way. By recovering the catechumenate, a highly structured journey of initiation for adults developed in the first few centuries of Christian experience, the church provided a forum in which the inquiring adult might live through a carefully considered encounter with the Christian faith and community, moving through four stages, beginning with inquiry and ending with reflection on the experience of baptism.

The word *catechumenate* does not fall easily from the lips. Those of us who have enthusiastically found our way into the world of catechumenal process probably need to admit that it is a system whose structure and vocabulary often seem complex and intimidating. Some critics have wondered why the church would attempt to resurrect a sixteen-hundred-year-old process for use today. These concerns notwithstanding, catechumenal process works, and it works because it is simple, direct, and effective.

The catechumenate unfolds in four stages. It depends, first of all, on a congregation's assumption that God calls people to ministry. It assumes that the primary role of the church is to restore the unity of creation. The congregation that has taken the baptismal covenant seriously will recognize that the core of Christian experience is its ministry, and the community will be on the lookout both for ministers and opportunities to minister. Thus, when a potential adult baptismal candidate arrives in the community asking whether or not baptism will lead to opportunities for ministry, the community will welcome this newcomer into an exploration of the faith.

Stage one of the catechumenate is a period of connecting and getting started. The inquirer is invited into dialogue with the community so that connections between personal aspirations and congregational life can be made. If the inquirer discerns that the road toward baptism is the right path and the community sees in this newcomer the seeds of Christian consciousness, a rite of Admission to the Catechumenate introduces and welcomes the newcomer and reminds the community that there are people among them preparing for baptism and life as Christians.

Stage two of the process is the lengthy period during which the catechumens, in the company of sponsors and catechists (Christians prepared to teach and converse with the candidate about the church, scripture, ministry, and community) spend time, week by week, hearing God's word and reflecting on it, praying, and exploring the possibilities for ministry open to the candidate and the community. This is a time during which the Christian community, represented by catechists and sponsors, listens with the catechumens for God's call to ministry, and during which catechumens begin to discern what form that ministry will take. Stage two comes to an end when the catechumen decides to begin the journey toward baptism, which is announced to the community in a liturgical rite of Enrollment of Candidates for Baptism, and stage three begins.

Stage three usually occupies the time between Ash Wednesday and Easter, and is a time of intense preparation for baptism in which the candidate is accompanied by sponsors and catechists and attended by the constant prayers of the entire community. This is a time of conversion, a time for the candidate and the community to die and rise with Christ in newness of life. Stage three ends at the moment of baptism, usually at Easter.

Finally, stage four is a time during which the newly baptized reflect on the experience of journey into baptism with sponsors, catechists, and the rest of the community. It is during this time that they begin their particular ministries in the world.

In each of these catechumenal stages, four aspects of the life of the church characterize growth in the faith. Throughout the process, the study of scripture encourages the community to hear God's voice as it sheds light on every aspect of daily life. Through common prayer and life in community, the communal nature of

God's call to ministry is brought forth. In the context of weekly eucharistic worship, the community celebrates its common identity in Christ and offers itself to be sent out in mission. And thus the life of the community at prayer transforms the daily lives of each member of the congregation, so that the unity of God's creation can be restored.

The importance of the catechumenate is that it holds up the primary reason for the church's existence. The Christian community is asked to consider the circumstance of a person with no church experience who feels an intuitive call to deal with the social and ethical issues facing the human community. They hear in that call a stranger's response to the hard but hopeful demands of the gospel. The process of inquiry, inclusion, and initiation creates a new and wonderfully dynamic vision of the interaction between church and world. In the process of initiating a stranger into the community, the entire congregation gets a new glimpse of its own journey of faith and a new reminder of what it means to be set apart as the body of Christ.

✧ Young People and Worship

It has been clear for a long time that during the early teenage years it can become increasingly difficult for many young people to maintain a connection to church and worship. Perhaps we should rejoice in that disconnection. If nothing else, it means that these folks are stepping aside to evaluate the structures to which they devote time and energy. They must take a step or two away in order to see to what they are giving their energy. But will they come back?

The American church of the late twentieth century has lost its children. They are lost not because they are bad, insufficiently spiritual, inattentive, or lazy. They have wandered away from a church that is attempting to form them for a world that no longer exists. They have gone, not because they were not paying attention, but because they were. So to wonder about getting young people back into the Christian community is to commit ourselves to a serious evaluation of the way the church is and to exploring how the church should be.

What kind of strategies will work? It is not difficult to gather a crowd, but that is not the point. We can *hook* people into participation in the life of the Christian community, but if a new member program is not rooted in Christ's ministry it is finally counterproductive. It is not difficult to find new ways to attract newcomers, but if we are interested in attracting young people to ministry, we have to make clear to them what the church's ministry is.

The baptismal covenant provides the rationale for being the church. Addressing the problems, prejudices, and deficiencies that prevent people from eating, sleeping, and enjoying useful work, and finding ways to increase understanding, common respect, and genuine compassion among people—these are the liturgical actions that identify our belonging to the body of Christ. And these are the actions that will attract the attention of many young people as they struggle to find their place in the world.

We live in a hostile world. The gap between the few who live well and the many who struggle is growing. Life seems increasingly dangerous. But as is always the case when the human community faces danger, there are ever-increasing examples of loving and heroic responses to human need and misery. It seems that while life appears to be increasingly painful and difficult, people are likewise increasingly attentive to the implications of the gospel message for human life. If God wants everyone feasting at the same table, then perhaps we should get on with inviting them to the feast.

We are concerned, as a church, that the emerging and next generations of adults in our population are not going to be involved in our common life. How do we respond? How do we draw them into the circle of worship? How do we help them find their connection to the body of Christ? And what stands in the way?

Nothing is more likely to silence us than the sense that our opinions are not worthy or wanted. Yet we do that to young people all the time, and not just to young people, but to every newcomer. We invite them into *our* world—whatever world we occupy. We make it clear that they are welcome to stay and participate as long as they see the world through our eyes. What we fail to grasp is the fact that their perspective, especially because it comes from outside the enclave, is exactly right. It is not the insiders who should be catechizing the strangers, but the strangers who should be teaching the established community.

✌ What Strategies Work?

First, we must learn to rearticulate the gospel. Examine the baptismal covenant. Wonder what it means to live among equals, in a community in which everyone is whole, well-fed, and content. Preach the promises of Jesus.

Then we must learn how to recognize the unique gift every generation brings to the table. We are a community which consists of infants, children, youth, young adults, adults of middle age, and elders. Each age group brings to the table its particular offering: perhaps it is blissful innocence or precocious playfulness, certainly challenge, often impossible optimism, eventually a sense of being settled that often gives way to a sense of crisis with the realization of advancing age, and finally, the graceful maturity that is the attractive mark of old age. Each is a delicious flavor of life which deserves to be savored and enjoyed.

The almost-adult young people among us frighten us. They bring to the table levels of hope, honesty, encounter, fearlessness, and sometimes folly, which seem to threaten the whole. But with all those threatening gifts they bring the essence of life and renewal. We reject their presence at our peril, for if we want to evangelize our youth, we need to find in their open, questioning, forward-looking attitudes about life the key to understanding our own commitment to the gospel. As we invite them (or re-invite them) into the community of faith, we need to be alert to listen to what God has been telling them along the way.

Finally, we must think about the liturgical life of the community. How might we worship in a way that articulates, in the context of our common prayer, the notion that God yearns to draw all creation into one circle? How might the younger generations among us help us to forge that new articulation? What *hooks* might we place in the liturgical round to attract missionaries of the gospel? Do the possibilities offered by the catechumenate provide the hooks we need?

Two things seem clear. The gospel of Jesus is alive and well. The church is moving toward a prophetic and hopeful articulation of the teachings of Jesus that will gather a community of God's creatures in a feast of abundance. But the habit of the church is not yet prepared to articulate, celebrate, and live that good news. Do we want to attract another generation of people to inhabit the church? Of course we do. How will we do it? Preach it, and they will come!

Evangelism and the Catechumenal Process

Ann E. P. McElligott

The ministry of evangelism includes both proclamation of the good news of Jesus Christ and formation in Christian community. Indeed, when Christians proclaim the Word, they are inviting persons to be formed, or transformed, in Christ. St. Paul invites the faithful to be formed in the mind of Christ: "Let the same mind be in you that was in Christ Jesus" (Philippians 2:5). In this formation, the faithful become a new creation: "So if anyone is in Christ, there is a new creation: everything old has passed away; see, everything has become new!" (2 Corinthians 5:17).

The church has tended to think of the work of formation, or Christian education, as being distinct from that of evangelism. In so doing it has followed the traditional understanding that the ministry of proclaiming and inviting are distinct from that of nurturing people in the faith. Part of this distinction results from the false assumption that Christian education or nurture is directed primarily to children, especially those of school age, while proclamation is directed to adults, especially those who are "unchurched." In the late twentieth century, however, a number of factors have led the church to question many of the assumptions undergirding such sharp differentiations among ministry categories.

First, as the baby boomer generation matured it challenged the assumption that Christian education was directed only, or primarily, to children. The notion of ongoing, or lifelong, learning became more prevalent. Second, the "schooling model" of Christian education was challenged by a new understanding that Christian formation takes place in the very process of engaging in worship, caring for one another, and ministering to those in need. Third, Christians became increasingly aware that the mission field commenced at the doors of their own churches rather than beyond the boundaries of their society or culture. The so-called Christendom model of the Christian community no longer pertained, and the work of evangelism became an urgent concern for congregations. All of these factors supported the recovery of an ancient model for preparing and forming adults for baptism and membership in the body of Christ.

Following Vatican II, the Roman Catholic Church developed a set of rites for adult initiation and established the adult catechumenate as a normative pattern for adult preparation for baptism. Following their lead, the Episcopal Church has also adopted the catechumenal model as a process of faith formation appropriate for preparing adults for Christian baptism and for ministry as members of the body of Christ. Here evangelism and nurture are reintegrated into a single process, along with engagement in worship, pastoral care, and service. As congregations began to implement the catechumenate for unbaptized adults, they found many baptized adults who were also seeking to learn and grow in the Christian faith. This work with adults raised questions about the quality of formation being offered to parents and godparents of infants and young children. Accordingly, new liturgical rites were also developed for preparing baptized adults to reaffirm their baptismal vows and for preparing sponsors of infants and young children for their roles. The catechumenal process now consists of four distinct stages, each set off by its own public liturgical rite through which catechumens and the whole congregation share and celebrate the transforming and converting work of the word of God in the gathered community.

In its essence, catechumenal formation is a process of conversion through the agency of the word of God. The word "catechumen" comes from the Greek word meaning "to sound in the ear"; a catechumen is a "hearer of the Word." The word of God, reaching its fullest expression in and through the person of Jesus Christ, is the active agent in conversion. Conversion is not an abnormal or extraordinary process. It is the lively process of growing into a fresh new way of being or into a renewed way of acting or into a new place of belonging. The person making such changes follows a natural evolution. This transformative process, leading to commitment and membership, can be described as having four distinct stages. All adults seeking to enter or renew their faith commitment will tend to follow such a pattern.

⌇ Inquiry

In the first stage, a person initiates the process by inquiring about entering into a new or a deeper relationship with the body of Christ embodied in a local community. The inquiry may be occasioned by a life crisis, by the evangelization activity of congregation members, by the approach of a significant life passage such as a marriage or the birth of a child, by simple curiosity, or by the restlessness of the soul for God. However the individual and the Christian community initiate the engagement, the inquiry process immediately becomes a communal activity. Individuals approaching the local congregation are inquiring about whether they want to enter into relationship with and establish an identity within that community, while the community is inquiring both about the individual and about themselves. The members of the community must discern whether or how they can expand to include the inquirer within their number. The primary function of the inquiry stage is to provide an open environment where inquirers can question the community freely to determine whether they can, with integrity, enter into a time of deeper formation preparing for membership. Such discernment is always mutual, as the members of the community come to know the inquirers and discern how they can incorporate and support them in the community.

This period of inquiry may be accomplished quickly, or it may require time for the inquirer to deal with significant life issues. Inquiry is focused first on those questions participants have about Christian faith and commitment, and then on the stories they share about their own journeys to God. The inquiry stage of the catechumenal process provides a structure where representative members of the community can meet on a regular basis to respond to the questions of the inquirers, to share their own faith stories, and to be formed through the word. During this time the inquirers begin to reflect on their lives and their stories in light of the dynamic word of God in the gospel. Regular reflection on the cycle of liturgical readings in the gospels provides a ground through which inquirers explore their questions.

Participants are ready to move to the next stage when they have sufficient answers to their questions to commit to a period of deeper formation to God and membership in the community. Participants who make the public commitment to move into the second stage are joined by sponsors who accompany each individual through all the succeeding stages of formation.

✧ Formation

The second stage is basic formation for Christian living. During this stage catechumens are not simply being instructed about Christianity, but being formed as Christians in the daily places of their lives. The primary agent of the formation continues to be the word of God in the community of the faithful. During this time participants and their sponsors continue to study the Sunday lectionary, allowing this cycle of scripture texts—especially the gospel—to aid them in confronting issues of ministry in their daily activities. This formation involves four aspects of Christian living: they become people of prayer by entering into the regular practice of praying; they become people who worship God by joining the community in its regular worship; they become part of the Christian community of faith by reading and reflecting on the story of salvation history as recorded in the scripture and tradition of the church; they begin to follow Jesus Christ by serving others—the poor, the outcast, and the needy.

Critical to this stage of formation is engagement in ministry, both in the daily places in one's life and with those who are most in need of Christian care. Christian formation engages the whole of one's life. While regular church attendance and study of scripture are part of normal Christian practice, disciples of Christ carry their faith beyond the gathered community into the whole of life, into their daily places of work, home, family, community, leisure, and civic life. Catechumenal formation is more than engaging in the activities of the church; rather, it is joining with the Christian family in discovering how to carry the proclamation of Jesus Christ out to serve the whole of God's creation.

As in the inquiry stage, the members of the church are as involved in formation as the participants. The congregation is being formed anew by the presence of new members and is finding its ministry to be both expanded and revitalized. The length of time that participants stay in this stage will vary according to individual needs. Participants have completed this stage when they are prepared to make a firm commitment to be baptized or to reaffirm their baptismal vows. The completion of this stage will most often coincide with the beginning of the season of Lent.

ᴧ Preparation for the Rites

During the third stage, participants are focused intently on the approaching rites of passage, generally during the solemnities of Holy Week and Easter. This is true whether participants are preparing for their baptisms or for a public reaffirmation of the solemn vows of their baptisms. This time is characterized by the intensity of final preparations, with all the profound focus and discipline that such consummation entails. During Lent, the whole congregation joins in a season of preparation and is reminded of the ongoing need of all Christians to renew their repentance and faith. Participants and their sponsors, along with all members of the congregation, are disciplining themselves to join with Christ in the holy baptism of dying to the old and rising to the new. It is in and through the paschal mystery of dying and rising that we become a new creation in Christ. During this stage, participants question their own readiness and discover that their worthiness is wrought totally through the grace and generous self-giving of God.

ᴧ Reflection

The catechumenal process does not, and must not, conclude with the observance of the rites of passage, whether baptism or reaffirmation. A fourth stage of reflection is crucial to the fullness of the process. The participants, accompanied by their sponsors and witnessed by the assembled community, have moved through a transforming process culminating in a rite of dying and rising. Their pilgrimage resumes with a period of time when they can reflect on their risen lives in Christ and explore how they have been reshaped and revitalized. During this fourth stage, participants look back on their recent journey and, through that lens, on the whole story of their growing relationship with God. In doing so, they consider how the ground of their existence has been renewed and what consequences that will have on all aspects of their daily lives.

Traditionally, this fourth stage has focused on a study of the sacramental life, the living mystery of Christ dying and rising in the sacraments of baptism and eucharist. It has been called *mystagogia*, or study of the mysteries. Beyond studying the mystery of the holy sacraments themselves, participants discover how their own lives are sacraments, outward signs of the love of God in the world.

◡ The Catechumenal Process as Evangelism

The mission of the catechumenal process might be described simply: to make disciples. Disciples are those who go into the world to proclaim the gospel of the risen Lord and invite others to hear the good news of God in Christ. When Jesus commissioned his followers he commanded them to "go therefore and make disciples of all nations, baptizing them in the name of the Father and of the Son and of the Holy Spirit, and teaching them to obey everything that I have commanded you" (Matthew 28:19-20a). He described an integrated process of proclamation, baptism, and formation. The catechumenal process involves the whole congregation in this central mission of being a baptizing community.

The catechumenal process always commences with proclaiming the good news. A congregation taking its catechumenal ministry seriously must engage in intentional activities to proclaim the healing gospel to those who have not yet heard, to open their doors to all inquirers, and to minister to the particular needs of people in the community of which they are a part. Proclamation begins with hospitality. Beyond a hospitable welcome to those who have courage to knock, the congregation must extend an open invitation to those who do not know how to reach out for a deeper relationship with God. It is part of "presenting Christ to men and women who do not know him," noted Bishop Datak Yong Ping Chung, Bishop of Sabah, in a recent talk on evangelism. "These men and women could be people in our churches, sitting in our pews, baptized and confirmed, but with no real-life transforming faith in Jesus."

A catechumenal congregation is one that welcomes those who question. Its members are willing to engage all questions, not because they possesses all the answers, but because all questions lead them to encounter and know the living Christ more deeply. The catechumenal congregation is always seeking the inquirers, always ready to be upset by their questions, and constantly poised to be renewed in its recognition of God's activity in its midst.

◡∶ The Catechumenal Process with Young Adults

Catechumenal formation invites young people into a process of discipling, acknowledging that they come to the process with gifts, skills, and a story worth telling. Here they find a community that celebrates their presence and encourages their growth in faith. Many young adults, although baptized as infants and raised in the church, have ceased to have a regular relationship with a community of faith. Some have lost interest in church, some felt rejected by the church or never found themselves at home in the Christian community, some fell out of the habit of regular church attendance, and still others found no adequate means of making the transition to adult membership in the community.

In my counseling with young adults, often in preparation for marriage, I regularly listen to them explain how they were raised in the church and then fell out of the church habit during their teen years. They usually describe themselves as believing in God, and they expect to join a church when they have children. Yet they seek no active involvement in the Christian community for themselves. One young man described his discomfort in approaching the Sunday worshiping community when he said uneasily, "You know, I don't know how to go to church." He had lost the comfort, or at least familiarity, of attending church as a child within a family. He did not know how to cross the threshold and take his place among the worshipers as an adult.

Increasingly, many young adults in our society are either unbaptized or were baptized as infants but given no experience of participating in the church beyond that long-forgotten ceremony. It is a sad commentary on our age that the golden arches of McDonalds are recognized more readily by young people than the symbol of the cross. And yet these young adults are no less likely to feel the stirring of God in their hearts than those who have a long history of church membership and attendance.

The church has a significant responsibility to seek out these young adults and welcome them into the community of the faithful. But this welcome must do more than usher them to an empty pew. They are seeking a community of faithful friends who will accept them without judgment and who will welcome them and respond openly to their questions. Young people often turn to the church at the time of a significant rite of passage—their marriage or the birth of a child. They feel safe in approaching the church as consumers requesting its known commodity: sacramental services. At these threshold moments, the church must offer more than a building and an officiant for their liturgy. This is a time when the community can invite them to renew their relationship with God and to enter the faith community. The seekers need to be welcomed into the faith community, not simply into the rector's study. When the congregation is engaged in the catechumenal process, a welcoming community is always available to receive the young adults. Here, too, they can be linked with sponsors who can help them to find their way through the daunting traditions of worship and into the other activities of the congregation.

Many young adults are isolated from nurturing communities, whether by circumstance or choice. They need a new and diverse community where they can talk freely about spirituality and where their stories will be honored. In a world where people tend to be segregated increasingly by age, the catechumenate will, ideally, offer a diverse group representing all generations of a congregation. In this setting, the young adults can find how much they have in common with different people of all ages and discover that they need not feel marginal in the church. Likewise, older adults can discover the common ground they share with the young adults.

The catechumenal model of evangelism and formation is ideal for ministry with and to young adults for a number of reasons. First, catechumenal formation differs radically from the traditional schooling model. They are not being returned to "church school," with the implication that they somehow have failed to complete their necessary study for full membership. Furthermore, inquirers of whatever age are treated as adults and invited into full participation in the community. The only distinction made is that those seeking baptism will not be admitted to communion until after their affirmation of faith and baptism. All others would be nurtured in the congregation, fed at the eucharistic table, and included in the full ministry of the congregation.

Formation with youth and children is traditionally done apart from the congregation, but one of the hallmarks of catechumenal formation is that it takes place in the midst of the life of the parish. While those seeking to belong are being formed, the whole congregation joins with them. The young adults are not sent to the basement of the church until they have achieved the necessary knowledge to be accorded full membership. Rather, they join the congregation in its ongoing pilgrimage of growth into the fullness of Christ, and they are invited to share the stories of their faith journeys and their experience with God. No stories are more important than others—they are simply longer!

Finally, the catechumenal process connects the concerns of daily living with Christian faith. Participants are encouraged to discover how to be Christian in the daily places of their lives. They explore how to bring their faith into their homes and relationships and working environments. The journey of faith is not one which removes them from their daily concerns, but one which provides help and strength in the other aspects of their lives. Further, the catechumenal group provides an environment where they can talk about the tensions of trying to be a person of faith at work and home and leisure.

↜ The Courage to Begin

The process of catechumenal evangelism and formation is demanding. Indeed, the most common objection is that it is unrealistic to ask people in this frenetic world to enter a time-consuming formation process. Many feel it is unrealistic to suggest that people devote as much as nine months to regular meetings in preparation for baptism, confirmation, or baptismal reaffirmation. Others feel such a demand will simply lead people to "shop elsewhere" for their sacramental services. Considered from the "mass-market" perspective, the catechumenal process may not appear to have a competitive edge, especially with young adults already overburdened with too many commitments. Yet in my experience with both young adults and old, I have found that those who have listened and responded to the restless stirrings of God in their hearts are not looking for an easy path. They recognize that such questions about the ultimate things of God and eternity deserve time and attention.

Catechumenal formation takes time because it deserves the devotion and patience that anything worthwhile requires. Effective pastoral care and formation depend not on how carefully we construct a short, brilliant program for people to attend, but on whether we have enough time together being the body of Christ. Thus, we who are the gathered community need to move beyond our own reticence and dare to invite young people to join us in a birthing process that takes time. Rather than promising that "it really won't be much bother or work," we need to find the courage to speak the truth that Christian living is worth the effort. Yes, the journey may be arduous. But as pilgrims of faith we are always supported in the companionship of Jesus Christ, who taught us that the yoke is easy and the burden is light.

Note:

Additional information on the catechumenal process may be obtained from the North American Association for the Catechumenate, 651 North Berwick Avenue, Indianapolis, Indiana 46222.

Journey to Adulthood

David E. Crean

"What ceremony else?" Laertes demands at the funeral of his sister, Ophelia, in Shakespeare's *Hamlet*. It is a question many teenagers might legitimately ask. What ceremonies are there in today's church that mark the teenager's passages through life?

Puberty is a time of enormous change, arguably the time of greatest change outside the womb. Young people at puberty develop in all sorts of ways—physically, physiologically, mentally, and spiritually. Physically, young people undergo enormous growth spurts: young men develop facial hair, their testicles descend, and their voices grow deeper; young women develop breasts, their hips widen, and they begin menstruation. Physiologically, young people's bodies are virtually awash in a "sea of raging hormones" that bring about these changes. Mentally, young people are able to conceptualize, to create, to integrate their thoughts in ways impossible for children. Spiritually, too, they are changing, as they begin to form their own faith structure instead of taking what they have been taught for granted.

Psychologically, teenagers are also declaring their independence, cutting the apron strings, if you will. This move toward independence is shown with some exactitude in Luke's story of Jesus in the temple, in which Jesus separates himself from his parents, who then have to go searching for him—an all-too-familiar scenario for parents of teenage children: "Assuming that he was in the group of travelers, they went a day's journey. Then they started to look for him among their relatives and friends" (2:44). When they find him, Mary, as one would reasonably expect, explodes: "Child, why have you treated us like this? Look, your father and I have been searching for you in great anxiety" (2:48). Like a typical teenager, Jesus gives her some back talk: "Why were you searching for me? Did you not know that I must be in my Father's house?" (2:49). This response may even have resulted in a grounding: "Then he went down with them and came to Nazareth, and was obedient to them" (2:51).

In today's world, young people are seeking meaningful ways in which the community can affirm the changes they are experiencing, as well as their growing independence. But as far as I have been able to discover, the church has no ceremony that marks the passage from childhood to adulthood, which simultaneously celebrates the birth of the adult as it mourns the death of the child. No ceremony exists to reassure the parents of the adolescent that they are not alone, that this passage has happened in the past to other parents of teenagers, and that eventually the young person will return to them as an adult and a friend, but not as the child he or she once was. We need these ceremonies, and if we do not develop them young people will initiate themselves, as has been shown quite clearly, frequently with disastrous results.

In the Jewish *bar/bat mitzvah,* at the age of thirteen the adolescent stands before the congregation to be recognized as an adult member of that community. At the close of the service the young Jew proclaims, "I am no longer a child." The young Jew is now, literally, "a son [or daughter] of the commandment." This rite can be traced back to the second century, the time of the second diaspora of the Jews following the destruction of the temple in Jerusalem in A.D. 70. Thus, it seems likely that the *bar mitzvah* arose as a means of establishing and affirming a separate Jewish identity when the people were scattered abroad in a sea of paganism. There were, of course, Jewish congregations spread throughout the Roman Empire even before the diaspora, as we read in the Acts of the Apostles, but these groups had a central focus at that time—the temple in Jerusalem—for their religion. The Jews of the diaspora did not.

Today, we face an analogous situation. We appear to be drifting into a situation not unlike the one faced by the Jews of the diaspora, but instead of paganism we face a rampant secularism that is, at best, indifferent, and, at worst, hostile to Christian values and beliefs, if not to Christianity itself. The situation is well summarized by theologian Ellen Charry:

> Raising children in our culture has…persuaded me that *the intentional formation of young Christians is the most important ministry contemporary churches can undertake.* Modern liberal education, stemming from Rousseau, assumes that children flourish when given the freedom to select among many options in developing their own unique gifts and talents. This approach can succeed with Christian children, but probably only in a culture that is sympathetic to Christian practices and beliefs. That is no longer our situation. Becoming a Christian today is, as it was in the earliest centuries, an intentional choice made in the face of other options. While children do need freedom, they also need to be deliberately shaped by Christian practices so

that they may have a genuine chance to understand and respond to the gospel.[1]

Charry states the dilemma exactly: on the one hand is the secular world with its seductive and glamorous images, on the other, the world of the community of faith. This community witnesses to a reality that transcends the world. Moreover, this community celebrates its unique heritage and world-view with liturgy, which is simply another word for ceremony. Precisely because the world is unsettling and confusing, we need ceremonies, public ceremonies, that affirm the intrinsic worth of young people.

Of course the secular world also has its ceremonies. One has only to look at the pomp and circumstance that surrounds college football games and reaches its apotheosis in the Super Bowl to realize that the secular world has developed ceremonies which almost completely eclipse those of the church. The president of the International Olympic Committee, Juan Antonio de Samaranch, has equated the Olympic movement with a new, and even more popular, religious experience!

What the church brings to its ceremonies is something very different, and very important. We are the people of a story and this story, which we tell and retell every Sunday, marks us. Our liturgies tie into this story, the story of a community that comes together, as it has done throughout the centuries, to be blessed, broken, and shared. Our task, then, becomes to make the young people in the church rooted and grounded in this story so that it becomes for them *their* story, which they can claim for their own and in relation to which they can see their own individual stories.

The importance of rooting and grounding the young people in our congregations in the story of Jesus Christ cannot be stressed too highly. When young people are secure in their story, seeing it in relationship to the story of Jesus Christ, and when that story is reinforced by meaningful liturgy and ceremonies, they will be better able to resist the glamorous powers of the world. It is our task as the church to make sure that our young people are secure in themselves and, to put it in theological terms, are clad in "the whole armor of God" (Ephesians 6:11).

⌁ The Role of Confirmation

Ah, yes, one may claim, but in the Episcopal Church, as in many other denominations, we have confirmation. Once one is confirmed, is not one inoculated with Christianity against the world? Emphatically not. Confirmation as inoculation simply does not work, nor was it ever intended for that purpose. It may also have been a puberty rite at one time, somewhat akin to the *bar mitzvah,* but it certainly is not today. Confirmation at age twelve used to be normative in the Episcopal Church, and reception of communion by the unconfirmed was forbidden. (In the Church of England the practice continues to this day.) Confirmation thus took the place of a rite of passage, an initiation into full participation in the life of the church.

This view of confirmation has changed. Holy Baptism today is "full initiation by water and the Holy Spirit into Christ's Body the Church" (BCP 298). (Cynics note that while baptism is the entrance ritual to the church, confirmation has become the exit ritual.) Given this new understanding of baptism, which includes partaking of Holy Communion, the role of confirmation needs to be rethought. The notes in the *Book of Common Prayer* concerning the rite of confirmation assert that "in the course of their Christian development, those baptized at an early age are expected, when they are ready and have been duly prepared, to make a mature public affirmation of their faith and commitment to the responsibilities of their Baptism and to receive the laying on of hands by the bishop" (BCP 412). Thus confirmation, as liturgical scholar Leonel Mitchell notes, "is the renewal of the baptismal covenant, not its completion.... It is not a 'puberty rite' for adolescents, but the appropriate liturgical and sacramental act by which a baptized person personally accepts the faith into which he or she has been baptized and renews the promise to live the baptismal life."[2]

Can confirmation be made more "relevant," more of a puberty rite for teenagers? Unless we are prepared to jettison confirmation as a "mature public affirmation of their faith and commitment to the responsibilities of their Baptism," probably not. Margaret Mead, while serving on the Drafting Committee on Christian Initiation, said that our culture could probably not produce a uniform puberty rite "unless you can get the state to let the bishop dispense first driver's licenses from the cathedral steps on Pentecost."[3] However, confirmation can be a meaningful ritual for a young person in a certain narrow sense. Being freed from the ambiguity of confirmation as both a rite of passage (something it was never intended to be anyway) and an affirmation of mature faith, we can concentrate on the latter. As we will show later, confirmation, in its proper perspective and at a proper time in the development of the young person, can become a meaningful experience in the life of that young person, a means of grace and a full validation of his or her faith experiences.

⌁ Rites of Passage

The term "rite of passage" has been generally misunderstood. A rite of passage is frequently confused with an initiation ceremony, but the two are not synonymous. While a rite of passage may, and usually does, contain an initiation ceremony, the initiation ceremony does not comprise the whole rite. A rite of passage is a process which takes place in several stages over a period of time, while an initiation ceremony occupies one point in time. Many anthropologists, working in widely disparate cultures and geographical areas, have identified three stages: a physical separation from the community, an extended period of initiation (which may include instruction in the customs and history of the community as well as a physical ordeal), and reincorporation of the initiate into the community with a new adult status and often with a new name. This rite of passage involves the community as a whole, which is also an important theme in Christian initiation.

In the catechumenal process of the early church, moreover, this process of separation, initiation (including instruction), and reincorporation was carried out rigorously. The catechumens were physically separated from the congregation for the whole of Lent. During this time they received rigorous instruction in the faith, notably in the areas of prayer, scripture study, and Christian living.[4] There were also ordeals to be undergone, in remembrance of Jesus' period of temptation in the wilderness. At the Great Vigil of Easter they were brought back into the church to be baptized, usually by full immersion, and immediately after that confirmed by the bishop when they became fully fledged members of the Christian community and were able to receive communion. Sadly, this process has been allowed to lapse; indeed, some have suggested that perhaps in the present century it would be impossible to recreate.

The church in the postmodern era has neglected the needs of young people for meaningful, appropriate rites of passage. The closest we come today to a rite of passage is high school, when young people begin to separate from their parents. They go apart into an area to which the parents have little or no access, to be instructed by elders of the community. If they are lucky, they will encounter a wise shaman who can make a difference in their lives—if they are lucky. There are ordeals to be undergone. There may even be some sort of initiation ceremony, but never is there an encounter with the divine, at least not in this nation in which church and state are rigidly divided. After high school, they are (sometimes) recognized as adults. Sometimes they even manage to change their names.

"Without a ritual to contain and inform the wounds of life," says Mircea Eliade, "pain and suffering increase, yet meaningful change doesn't occur."[5] The question thus becomes: Can we provide such meaningful experiences, or sets of experiences, for young people in the church?

✎ Journey to Adulthood

In the spiritual formation program for young people known as *The Journey to Adulthood*, the provision of such ceremonies is a key element. The ceremonies that have been developed for this program all contain elements of the general rite of passage described above: separation, initiation, and reincorporation.

The journey begins when the young person is between eleven and thirteen years old, and it unfolds in three sections, each lasting two years. The first is known as Rite-13. This section derives its name from the ceremony called "A Celebration of Manhood and Womanhood," which is kept on or soon after the young person's thirteenth birthday and is very loosely derived from the *bar mitzvah*. It is conducted in the church, before the congregation. The service comprises six main sections:

~ The young people are issued a charge by the celebrant on the responsibilities that they are undertaking as they begin the journey toward adulthood:

> As men and women, it is given to you to share God's power of creation. Human beings, because they are made in God's image, are the only creatures on earth who can choose how to use their creative power—not only to create new life, but also to shape the world according to God's purpose. God calls us to use this gift to build and not to destroy. Are you aware of God's gift to you and the responsibility to use it wisely?

~ They lead the congregation in saying a portion of Psalm 139.

~ This is followed by a prayer for the parents. Petition is made to "strengthen them that they may support their sons and daughters as they begin the journey toward adulthood." The prayer concludes with a further petition:

> Carry them all safely through this journey, so that one day they may stand together as adults and friends, a joy and a comfort to each other all the days of their lives.

~ Next comes a charge to the peers of these young people:

> Will you stand by them, knowing that there may be times when your support means more than any other?

~ There follows a charge to the congregation to support the young people in their journey. This asks two things:

> Will you, as a community of God which spans the generations, share your knowledge and experience with these young people as they become young women and men? Will you guide, guard and sustain them as they grow into the full stature of Christ?

~ The service concludes with a blessing.

This brief ceremony has all the conditions identified above as being important. It is relevant to the present time and it is appropriate to the particular stage of life of the young people. First, it recognizes that these young people are indeed men and women, in the sense that they are biologically capable of reproduction. Second, it recognizes that the young people, like all teenagers (and like Jesus in the temple), are beginning to draw away from the parents. They are creating their own identity. This is affirmed not only in the prayer for the parents, but in an important feature of the ceremony. At the beginning, the young people undergoing the initiation sit with their parents (and siblings, grandparents, other relatives, and godparents) while the rest of their peers sit in a group. Following the ceremony (which concludes with the exchange of the peace), they cross the aisle to sit with their peer group. In terms of a rite of passage, this ritual addresses the separation and the initiation ceremony. Nothing is asked of the young people. They are not committing themselves to any course of action, unless it is to be aware of their responsibilities and to be faithful to them. All that is being acknowledged is that they are now young men and women beginning their journey toward becoming adults.

The experience of St. Philip's Episcopal Church, in Durham, North Carolina, after some ten years of conducting this ritual, is that while the young people taking part are understandably nervous, they recognize its importance. Newcomers to the program are told: "You've got to do it. You'll hate it at the time, but you've got to do it." The celebratory nature is emphasized by a party afterward and the awarding of a handsome certificate.

The second part, "The Journey to Adulthood" (J2A), follows the two years of Rite-13. At the beginning of this two-year period, the young people in this age group are separated from other teenagers and from their parents and siblings and are taken into the church for another ceremony. This consists of the Holy Eucharist and includes a Litany of Separation and Dedication in which the young people pledge to support each other on their journey together.

At the end of the two years of J2A (or sometime during the second year, depending on the bishop's schedule), the young people decide on their confirmation. It is a decision that they make for themselves; it is not made for them by their parents or even by the peer group. By this time, the decision on whether or not to be confirmed is truly the "mature public affirmation of their faith and commitment to the responsibilities of their Baptism" called for in the prayer book. By placing the sacramental rite of confirmation in this context and at this time, it serves to place a seal on their spiritual experiences. In a real sense, it is an essential step in their spiritual formation.

The young people also go on a pilgrimage, which is, in the words of the *Oxford Dictionary of the Christian Church,* a journey "to a holy place or sacred shrine to obtain special blessings from God or as an act of devotion, penance, or thanksgiving." They, quite literally, go on a pilgrimage to encounter the Christ. They discover that "although God is present always and everywhere, we still need to go to a special place where, once we have discovered God there, we discover that he is everywhere."[6] When they return, they are reintroduced to the congregation in yet another ceremony, as young adults in the church. In this ceremony, we use the rubrics in 1 and 2 Timothy to instruct and exhort the young people in their new roles as young adults. This segment of the program, known by its acronym of YAC, gives the young people the opportunity to function in the church in a variety of adult roles—lay readers, chalice bearers, and members of committees.

✢ The Role of Education

This program would not enjoy the success that it has without education to back up the liturgical experiences. Throughout Rite-13 and J2A, the teaching is aimed at enabling the spiritual formation of the young people, by which we mean providing "an environment in which new Christians can experience the living of the Christian life and can learn to live it themselves."[7] The teaching falls into four broad categories: self, sexuality, spirituality, and society. These take their validation from the development of Jesus: "And Jesus increased in wisdom and in years, and in divine and human favor" (Luke 2:52). As Jesus increased in wisdom, he became aware of himself as a person. As he grew in years, he underwent a physical development, which also included sexual development. His growth in divine favor reflected his deepening spirituality. And his growth in human favor reflected his involvement with society.

These four categories, which we see as essential components of the human condition, are important. They all need to be kept in balance. The problem with a discussion of sexuality without seeing its connection to spirituality, for example, is that it leads to a rampant sexualism in which promiscuity and sexual misconduct become almost normative. The secular world is prepared to talk about self and society, and about sexuality *ad nauseam,* but any mention of spirituality either evokes New Age religion or a desire to rush for cover. By contrast, the church addresses the issues of self and society to some degree, and spirituality to a greater degree, but is so threatened by any discussion of sexuality that meaningful dialogue becomes well nigh impossible.

This having been said, the teaching in the Rite-13 and the J2A components of the program differ from one another. Rite-13, which celebrates the gift of manhood and womanhood, and its concomitant gift of creative power, is lighthearted and celebratory. The latter is based on two premises: manhood and womanhood are gifts from God, and adulthood must be learned. Because adulthood is skills-based, the second component concentrates on the acquisition of certain skills. These premises are in contrast to the surrounding society which states, implicitly if not explicitly, that one has to prove that one is a "real" man or woman (whatever that means); the program thus takes away from the young people the awful burden of having to prove their masculinity or femininity. All the teaching, though, is carried out in the fourfold context of self, sexuality, spirituality, and society.

ᕀ The Role of the Teacher

Any discussion of the role of education raises the question of the role of the teacher in *The Journey to Adulthood*. What kind of person or persons are we seeking to guide young people through this critical stage in their lives?

First and foremost, the teachers—the preferred term is leaders—are not there to impart information to the young people, although some imparting of information is necessary. This is a program of spiritual *formation* rather than *information*. The leaders are mentors rather than teachers. They are not authority figures, but rather spiritual guides. They are invited, as one reviewer of the curriculum astutely noted, to participate at the same level as the young people and to grow spiritually along with them.

We seek two adult leaders for each class, one male and one female. There are good reasons for this. Often teenage boys are more comfortable talking with men and girls with women. We also expect the leaders to model healthy relationships between the sexes. Maturity is also an important factor. Too often the church gives responsibility for the youth group to young adults who are barely out of their own teen years themselves. I do not subscribe to this concept. In the classical rite of passage, instruction is given by the elders of the tribe, those with the most wisdom and experience. We would do well to bear this in mind in selecting youth leaders.

In an articulate and compelling essay, "Adolescence and the Stewardship of Pain," Frederick Buechner calls for adolescence as the time when young people start to keep score and become stewards of their pains:

> Adolescents are Adam and Eve in the process of tasting the forbidden fruit and discovering that in addition to good, there is also evil, that in addition to the joy of being alive, there is also the sadness and hurt of being alive and being themselves. Adolescents are Gautama the Buddha as he recognizes the first of the Four Noble Truths, which is that life is suffering, that at any given moment life can be lots of happy things too, but that suffering is universal and inevitable and to face that reality and to come to terms with that reality is the beginning of wisdom and at the heart of what human growing is all about.[8]

It follows that the best teachers are those who are familiar with suffering and have learned to grow through their own personal suffering. It is only the truly exceptional young adult who has reached this stage of spiritual development. While many elderly are probably not completely suitable as youth ministers except as occasional advisers (ministry with young people does require a certain degree of athleticism and energy), I would make a strong plea that, in any spiritual formation program for young people, we consider not just those who are young, vigorous, and athletic to lead the program, but those who are older and wiser and who are good stewards of their pain.

The church today is facing a crisis in attracting and retaining young people. This crisis has been largely caused by taking their presence for granted and by failing to evangelize them. My experience in *The Journey to Adulthood* program[9] has convinced me that this trend can be halted through the creation of meaningful ceremonies and liturgies which recognize, affirm, and celebrate the often traumatic passages that young people undergo on their journey toward becoming adults. These liturgies need to be backed up with strong education programs directed toward spiritual formation.

Endnotes

1. Ellen T. Charry, "Raising Christian Children in a Pagan Culture," *The Christian Century* (February 16, 1994). Italics mine.

2. Leonel L. Mitchell, *Praying Shapes Believing: A Theological Commentary on the Book of Common Prayer* (Wilton, Conn.: Morehouse Publishing, 1985), 119, 122.

3. I am grateful to Leonel L. Mitchell for supplying this anecdote.

4. Mitchell, *Praying Shapes Believing*, 94. He goes on to note that "the early Church felt that three years [in the catechumenate] was a good standard for converts from paganism."

5. Mircea Eliade, *Rites and Symbols of Initiation: The Mysteries of Birth and Rebirth* (Dallas: Spring Publications, 1994), xx.

6. David Adam, in Margaret Pawley, ed., *Prayers for Pilgrims* (London: Triangle, 1991), ix. He adds: "Sometimes we need to return to that special place so that we may strengthen our vision which is becoming dim, and reaffirm our faith that is weakening."

7. Mitchell, *Praying Shapes Believing*, 91.

8. Frederick Buechner, "Adolescence and the Stewardship of Pain," in *The Clown in the Belfry: Writings on Faith and Fiction* (San Francisco: HarperSanFrancisco, 1992), 5.

9. Details on *The Journey to Adulthood* and its offshoot, *The Adult Journey,* may be obtained by contacting the publisher and distributor: LeaderResources, 38 Mulberry Street, Box 302, Leeds, Massachusetts 01053-0302; phone: (800) 941-2218, (413) 582-1860; e-mail: info@LeaderResources.com.

The "Youth Church" Question

Pete Ward

Recent discussions in Britain have suggested that the unique needs of young people require an expanded sense of what we mean by "the church" if we are to take the evangelization of youth seriously. The word "church" typically carries a number of different meanings. For many people the church is simply a building, for others it is a reference to the people who meet there. The word can refer to a national organization or a denomination, but it also can be used to speak of the ecumenical unity of all Christians everywhere—the universal church. Church also has a spiritual connotation, as in "the body of Christ"; in this use of the term all believers are part of the church whether they attend worship services or not. Indeed some who attend these services may not be part of this mystical body. For a number of Christians "church" is a fairly clear term, denoting authenticity and characterized by the authorized and proper ministry of both word and sacrament: church is where we enjoy the fellowship of people with whom we share a set of beliefs. The various meanings which are associated with the word "church" can be confusing, but they indicate the importance of the term for Christians, as well as the possibility of a variety of interpretations as to what kinds of groups and activities should properly be called "the church."

While I see a real need for whatever we consider to be "church" to be well-defined, I would argue that if we are to take young people seriously, our current thinking needs to expand. Indeed, there is some evidence that in popular expression "church" is wider than the definitions I have already mentioned. For example, "house church" is commonly used for relatively informal gatherings. Christians attending worship in a recognized church on a Sunday might express this kind of feeling by saying, "I go to church but my home group is my real church." There is something which we regard as being "church" about community groups. The same could be said of the many missionary activities which Christian people undertake. Outreach to homeless youth and similar projects are often regarded as an expression of the missionary concern of the church. Thus we speak of these missionary projects as "the church reaching out to people," or in our case, reaching out to young people. I would therefore suggest that it is possible to regard the church as existing in three forms: missionary project, community group, and institution.[1]

From the time of the New Testament, the church has existed both sequentially and simultaneously in these three forms. In many cases churches can trace their origins through the gathering together of an informal group of believers to the establishment of a more formal organization. Some churches still have memories of the first missionary initiative which brought the original community group into existence. In the New Testament we see a similar progression, where the missionary activity of someone like Paul results in the formation of a community of believers. As time goes on these communities begin to organize themselves by developing specific ministries and rules of conduct for the whole group. Paul's letters to the church in Corinth are a good example of the way this kind of ordering of the church evolved. Thus even in the New Testament we can see community groups that have arisen out of missionary projects starting to institutionalize.

The sequential progression from missionary project to community group and then to institution is well accepted. The temptation is to see these as a linear progression, with one stage superseding the other and rendering it obsolete. This is a mistake, since it is also possible for these three aspects of church to coexist. Indeed, I would argue that it is important that church be expressed as institution, community group, and missionary project in every town and locality.

❖ The Church as Institution
In recent times many Christians have sought to downplay or even avoid the institutional nature of the church. Local churches, often under the influence of charismatic renewal, have sought to express their life in communal rather than institutional forms, valuing fellowship and intimacy above organization and structure. Some Christians have self-consciously turned away from existing denominations and formed their own fellowships and house churches. While these developments bring much that is good, there is a sense in which by seeking community they have failed to appreciate the importance of the institutional characteristics of the church.

In order to discern how the church can become more responsive to young people today, it is important to ground the discussion in an understanding of the components of the institution itself. The institutional nature of the church has six basic elements which make it essential to the pattern of the life of the people of God: tradition, longevity, organization, universality, legitimacy, and fellowship.

Tradition

It is the institutional nature of the church that keeps the historical legacy of the church alive. Those of us seeking new ways of being church with young people are increasingly turning to the tradition of the church for inspiration. Thus, many alternative worship services are using forms of worship that many would associate with the Roman Catholic or Orthodox traditions. Without the church as institution these traditions would be largely inaccessible. The tradition of the church links us with Christians of previous generations and as such it is an important corrective to the tendency to be too closely linked to our particular cultural expression of the faith.

Longevity

Related to tradition, institutionalization is essential for social movements to ensure their survival. The informality of community groups means that they tend to burn themselves out. They avoid this by finding ways to routinize their leadership and community life. Ironically, what many have sought to renew in recent years—the regular, habitual worship of the church—has also been its strength. There is merit in the way that the church has developed sustainable forms of worship and organization that are able to exist through the centuries. The church exists for us now because these regular patterns of life have withstood spiritual apathy and have found ways slowly to adapt and change in the light of spiritual enthusiasm. Our impatience with the church as institution must to some extent be tempered by an admiration for its ability to endure.

Organization

Institutionalization is an inevitable result of success. Community groups need to regularize their life as time goes on, and patterns of leadership, worship, finance, and administration tend to become more organized. The same is true of relationships with other Christian groups and the wider society. These relationships, which quickly follow the establishment of a group, are essential not only to ministry, but also to a sense of identity and acceptance. Relationships outside the community group demand a more formal means of communication and leadership. A practical example of this would be the fact that most churches wish to acquire charitable, nonprofit status and thus must fulfill governmental requirements for exemption from taxes. This kind of advantageous development inevitably demands an organized and legal structure.

Universality

The institutional nature of the church reflects the gospel imperative of all Christians—of whatever racial or social group—to be united in Christ. The institution of the church is the means by which we keep alive the need for all Christians to be in association with each other.

Legitimacy

It is the institution of the church, through its leaders, which alone is able to give legitimacy to both community groups and missionary projects. The institution is the means by which innovation is recognized and valued. An example of this in England would be the youth church Soul Survivor Watford, which has been accepted into informal relationship with the Anglican Church by the Bishop of St. Albans. Another example is the way that Cardinal Basil Hume has made a place within the Roman Catholic Church for the Upper Room, a charismatic community of young people.

Fellowship

The church as institution should not be seen as a purely bureaucratic organization because it also functions through relationships, even though these relationships are distinct from those which exist within the community group. Relationships within the institution have been regularized and ordered, and they are relatively undemanding: weekly attendance at a service and/or meeting can be regarded as sufficient commitment. The community group, by contrast, emerges from "below," as charismatic leaders come to the fore with authority derived from the members of the group rather than by the selection and training of the institution. The community group will often demand a much higher level of active involvement from members, such as a communal lifestyle or a common purse.

✌ The Church as Community Group

Most churches can point to aspects of their life which are more akin to community groups, such as home groups or base communities. These community groups enrich the life of the institution, giving it a focus and a cohesion that might otherwise be missing. Community groups are often the places where people feel a sense of belonging and identity, but they can also be a forum for innovation and change. Community groups may reflect some of the age, racial, or social divisions within a society. Thus, a student Christian Union would in some respects be a community group, as would be a women's group meeting to develop new liturgies.

At times the relationship between community groups and the institutional church may be stormy. Community groups may challenge the comfort zones of the institution. For its part, the institution may feel threatened and try to close them down or, if that fails, use more subtle means to undermine their legitimacy. A healthy and dynamic church, however, needs both. These two aspects of the church need each other. The institution looks to community groups for energy and periodic refreshment; community groups need the institution to provide a tradition to react against and to renew.[2]

When a community group severs itself from the institution and sets out to become a church in and of itself, it soon finds itself institutionalized. At the same time, community groups may find themselves taken over by the institution of the church. One example of this would be the way that music and styles of worship originating within groups such as the Iona Community in Scotland and the Taizé Community in France—both with large youth followings—have slowly begun to find their way into mainstream church life. This is the role of community groups. At first they are radical and innovative, but over a period of time their way of doing things becomes accepted by the wider church. The institution thus responds by slowly incorporating the life and energy of community groups into its own life, and in this way community groups renew the church. If a community group does not continue to innovate and grow, its independence from the institution will become less important as the life and worship of the mainstream church life reflects its values. Eventually the community group will cease to have a reason to exist and will wither away.

✓ The Church as Missionary Project

The missionary aspect of the church involves a small number of individuals who make a deliberate physical or cultural journey to reach out to a particular community or to focus on a defined need in society. Christian work among the homeless would be a good example of this, or a Youth for Christ Center. The missionary group are a committed and trained "band" who set themselves apart from the main body of believers to prepare themselves for their chosen aspect of missionary service. In many cases, their missionary journey will involve leaving their jobs behind or seeking paid support from the rest of the church so that they can devote themselves to the task.

The missionary project is essential because without it many aspects of the call of God upon the church would go unheeded. The church as institution and the church as community group need the church as missionary project. Not all church members are called to the same kinds of evangelistic or social service. The missionary project is the means by which the church makes room for experimental work reaching beyond the formal structures of the institution. It is also distinctive because it generally involves an incarnational engagement beyond the social, racial, or generational boundaries that characterize community groups. The missionary project is a prophetic witness to the rest of the church that those in need and those who currently are outside the institution of the church and outside the community group are close to the heart of God.

Youth ministry must take the church much more seriously. The problem for many youth ministers in Britain is that the institutional church has attempted to locate all three aspects of the church's life in its own structures. Local churches have wanted to play down their institutionalized structures and emphasize fellowship and belonging. The net result has been that community groups linked to churches have been very closely controlled. Most of these groups are set up to serve institutional ends rather than develop new forms of worship or social engagement. The spread of institution-sponsored groups has meant that genuine community groups find it hard to gain acceptance by the institution; dissent and innovation are quashed and the groups themselves are marginalized. This has been the experience not only of some of those involved in alternative worship, but also of some women's groups. In this way the institutional church has generally failed to maintain the dynamic relationship it should have with community groups that might provoke and challenge them. It is extremely difficult to be "owned" as part of a local, regional, or national church without totally fitting into the structures. This does not mean that there are no examples of positive relationships—the Upper Room in the Catholic Church and Soul Survivor Watford in the Anglican Church are proof of this—but these examples are comparatively few and far between. More often the existence of such groups has been discouraged, as the local church has sought to be both institution and community group at the same time.

Similarly, the local church in recent times has tended to see itself as the focus of missionary work in an area. The idea of freestanding missionary projects has been discouraged as churches have increased their staff numbers by appointing their own workers. The policy, particularly in youth ministry, has been for churches to try to cover both the needs of the children of Christian parents and some strategy for outreach in one staff appointment. Thus incarnational patterns of ministry are often neglected. Churches feel they are doing their part by employing a youth minister and therefore have a tendency to see no need to donate money to community groups and other religious groups concerned with the evangelization of young people. The result of this has been a decline in some of these ministries and an increasing sense of isolation among youth workers.

If we accept that the church can be seen as existing in three modes—institution, community group, and missionary project—it follows that some of the contemporary aspects of youth ministry can be more readily accepted. Each of the three elements is itself the church; at the same time, each element needs the others to be fully itself. Thus, a youth church could be recognized as truly church without autonomy in its leadership or even its finances. To be fully church it needs a relationship with the institution, since it is only the institution which can bestow legitimacy. The consequence of my argument is that missionary projects are able to remain independent from the institution of the church, but they must also build relationship. These relationships are what guarantee their integrity as church in missionary mode. Of course, the other side of the argument is that an institution without relationships with community groups or missionary projects is not fulfilling itself as church. It is the role of the institution to seek both unity and diversity.

This threefold understanding of church would allow for generational groups (such as youth) to speak of themselves as church. It would allow for the independent reality of such a community group based on young people and would accept that certain church activities, like the administration of the sacraments and appointing of leaders, are a legitimate part of their life in relationship with the church as institution. This independence may create problems for churches such as the Anglican Church, which has traditionally linked unity and its sense of identity to the priesthood and sacraments and located these in designated parishes, schools, and hospitals. The organization and self-understanding of the Anglican Church effectively denies true authenticity to community groups, and such a position will need to be revised if the threefold understanding of the church is adopted. It is the role of the institution to find ways to adapt to grassroots community initiatives. The spirit of being church arises from the community life of the new group, but status and recognition come from the institution.

As far as the community group is concerned, there is a need to work at relationships with the institution. The latter will at times favor caution over innovation; even if resisted, this tendency must be treated with understanding. At the same time, the community will need help and guidance; this must be sought and accepted. The relationship between the institution and community will at times be stressful and extremely fragile, and the community will be tempted to go it alone. That would be a mistake. The success of any congregation with young people will require the ability to walk the fine line between cautious inactivity and maverick creativity, between following the Spirit and sticking to the rules.

✎ Creativity: A Sacramental Approach

Worship is both a divine encounter and a cultural activity. The two are intimately connected; you cannot have one without the other. We experience God "incarnated" within culture, and worship is similarly incarnational. The starting point for the development of worship that connects with the subcultures of young people is the realization that worship is both a divine encounter and a social construction.

One way of thinking about the way human creativity and divine inspiration combine in worship is to use the language of sacrament. Theologically, a sacrament is a sign or symbol of a deeper spiritual reality. For most Christians there is one defining sacrament seen in the bread and the wine of the communion service. The "elements" of the bread and the wine point beyond themselves to the fact that in some way during the worship service Christ comes and meets the believer. Definitions of how this comes about will vary among Catholic and Protestant Christians, but this kind of sacramental understanding is common to both. The eucharist and baptism are recognized as sacraments because in the scriptures God promises to meet us at these moments. The precise form of the ritual which makes up the sacrament varies according to culture and theological tradition. This means that Christians celebrate these two sacraments very differently, but we do so in the faith that however we frame the sacrament God's Spirit will come and honor us within our worship. Some churches have traditionally added to the number of sacraments by including confirmation, confession, marriage, ordination, and the anointing of the sick. In more recent times, sacramental thinking offers an understanding of how we encounter God in the normal circumstances of life. For Leonardo Boff, a sacrament is an ordinary reality, something from this world that evokes a different reality.[3] Everyday items thus can become signs and symbols.

A sacramental understanding of worship is vital for a contextual approach to work among young people. At the heart of this understanding is the genuine spiritual energy and encounter with God that many Christians experience in church worship. If worship is sacramental, then it is possible to see that there might be a number of cultural forms for worship within which God might encounter different groups of people. Problems arise when God's presence is linked to a particular style of music or liturgy, for it is a perennial temptation for the church to become identified with only one subculture or culture. Real encounter with God leads to the baptism of a style of worship which is itself culture-specific, although increased emphasis on sacramental understanding should caution youth workers and clergy against this kind of problem.

The aim of youth ministry should be to set free young people's creativity in worship. They have their own expressions of celebration, lamentation, and community life that can become the building blocks for a new expression of worship and church life. A sacramental understanding of encounter between God and humanity offers a framework for understanding how the culture of young people and the work of the Holy Spirit may coincide. Young people who are creating worship for themselves will need to establish rituals of worship that are appropriate within their own setting. Of course, youth culture itself comes with numerous ritualistic behaviors: dance, dress, greeting, performance, and language all hold power. Christian worship set within popular culture will transform these existing ritualistic forms of behavior with a sacramental theology. Some aspects of the existing rituals will need to be abandoned in the light of the gospel story, but others will be seen as helpful for Christian worship—the use popular forms of dance or music, for example.

❧ Imagination, Risk, and Play

Creativity is a mystery. When we hear a good piece of music, look at a painting, or read a novel, a part of us is in awe. Most of us have asked the question, "How could we ever create something as clever or beautiful as this?" We consume the creative products of other people, but in so doing we can become alienated from our own ability to create because we lose the power of our imagination in adult life. The creativity of professional artists can leave us feeling wanting in our own skills or abilities. And it is a good deal easier to play a worship song written by someone else than it is to write our own.

Much of the worship in the church today is largely unhelpful for young people because it has been shaped by the cultural sensitivities of the generation that currently attends church. For young people and youth workers seeking to develop worship for a particular context, creativity is essential in finding ways to worship in words, songs, and rituals that ring true. Creativity itself is a process of developing the imagination, merging new ways of looking at things with other older ways of expression, largely through a process of trial and error. The artist creates something and then takes a step back to assess how it looks. With what has been learned, hopefully, the next time something better can be achieved. The sacramental view of life asserts that this creative process is charged with the presence of God. The Christian artist is one who is seeking God by the exercise of a Spirit-filled imagination. When an artistic creation is to be used in worship, the artist's desire is that God will become present to the whole community through it. Creativity in worship is linked to the need for worship to be meaningful and "meaning-making" for the Christian community.

Imagination is a basic element in this approach to creativity in worship, and one way of understanding imagination is to look at the way that children use play as a way to understand the world. In discussing the education of young children, Jerome Berryman points out the importance of "godly play" as a means of creating meaning:

Godly play is the playing of a game that can awaken us to new ways of seeing ourselves as human beings. It is the way to discover our deep identity as godly creatures, created in the image of God. The possibility of godly play puts the games played for glory, fame, and wealth, even for salvation into a new and astounding frame. This larger frame, staked out at the limits of our being and knowing, reveals how limited the other games are and how they turn play into work so that the player winds down into self-destruction.[4]

For Berryman, this form of play involves working with spiritual issues in the light of sacred symbols and stories. When young people begin to construct worship for themselves symbols are used to make sense of this experience.

Young people in the church today are experimenting with new worship services that use a number of different media. Music, the visual arts, and rituals are being explored in new ways. Contextualized worship comes about when young people make their own sacred space by drawing on elements from within their own subculture, as well as from the more traditional aspects of Christian worship. Godly play describes the way popular culture and Christian tradition work together to create something that is located within the life of a particular community. The key point is that play is a serious activity with an experimental element.

Play is a metaphor for the way that creativity can be developed in worship. New forms of worship arise out of youth culture when we combine one symbol from popular culture with another from the Bible: a picture of a Coke bottle with the story of Jesus turning over the tables of the money changers in the temple, or a picture of a terrorist juxtaposed with the celebration of communion. Play involves trying something out to see how it feels or looks. This process inevitably involves some risk. There will be times when we get it wrong. The use of the term "play," however, gives a lightness of touch to the process in which we are engaged. Play sees worship as an arena for taking risks and occasionally getting things wrong. The appropriate response when things fall apart is to laugh, learn from the mistake, and do it better next time, just as young children will occasionally bump themselves or fall over trying to learn a new dance step or play football. Godly play is serious, but it is also good fun. Our primary task as youth workers should be to enable young people to encounter the sovereign God in worship. In doing this they bring their own culture and identity and find it transformed by God's presence and perspective.

Endnotes

1. These distinctions are based on the typologies of Ernst Troeltsch in *The Social Teaching of the Christian Churches* (London: George Allen, 1931) and Ralph Winter, "The Two Structures of God's Redemptive Mission," *Missiology* (January 1974). For a longer treatment of Winter, see Pete Ward, "Distance and Closeness" in *The Church and Youth Ministry,* ed. Pete Ward (Oxford: Lynx Communications, 1995).

2. These insights are based on Leonardo Boff, *Ecclesiogenesis* (London: Collins, 1986) and Rosemary Radford Ruether, *Women-Church: Theology and Practice* (New York: Harper and Row, 1985).

3. Leonardo Boff, *Sacraments of Life, Life of the Sacraments* (New York: The Pastoral Press, 1987).

4. Jerome W. Berryman, *Godly Play* (New York: HarperCollins, 1991), 7.

part four

Church and Academy

Our Church's Ministry in Higher Education

Edmond Lee Browning

I wonder what we might discover if we were to do a survey of clergy in our church today and ask, "What were the critical times in your faith journey?" From my own experience, I believe we would find that a large percentage see their college days as a particularly significant time, when they were mentored by the chaplains on their college campuses who recognized and encouraged their vocations to ordained ministry. The same is true of many of our lay leaders, for whom the college years were formative in so many ways, including in the life of faith.

It was said years ago that the college and university community is the greatest domestic mission field of the church, and these words continue to ring true today. I would add that it is also our oldest domestic mission beyond the congregation. Anglicans have always valued learning as a means of informing the life of faith. We have insisted on an educated clergy and devote significant congregational resources to Christian formation and education for all ages. Many distinguished educational institutions have their roots in our tradition, including the College of William and Mary (1693), Trinity College, Hartford (1823), and St. Augustine's College, Raleigh (1867). Over the years we have also established and funded ministries in higher education at both private colleges and state universities—Yale University, for instance, and the University of Oklahoma.

Although we can look back to a distinguished past, we cannot rest on what has been. Today's ministry in higher education is not an afterthought that we do "if we can afford it," but a necessity for the health and vital witness of our church. Campus ministers proclaim the gospel of Christ in places that are central in shaping both the next generation of leaders and the future direction and values of our nation itself. They are evangelists in a fertile mission field.

Ministry in higher education proceeds from the gospel mandate. It is named in our baptismal covenant and anchored in the presence of the living Christ. In all these things, campus ministers resemble those who minister in other settings, but there are also important differences: campus ministry occurs at a critical time, in a critical place, and from a critical theological base.

✢ A Critical Time

It is essential that the church reach out to young adults during a critical time in their lives of intense spiritual questioning, vulnerability, and enormous possibility. Such connections can have a lasting effect on their lives, especially on their commitments to faith. Many of these interactions are with young people from another faith or no faith at all, some of whom become Episcopalians and assume an active role in the church's leadership. Additionally, campus ministers can be an important presence at times of stress or crisis, when students are far from family, friends, or other support.

This time is also critical for higher education. As the cost of college escalates, pressure increases on students and families to justify what can be an extraordinary expense. As a result, both individuals and institutions are becoming increasingly driven by a kind of bottom line, "return on our investment" mentality; the most important value in education becomes success, often defined as financial success. Institutions of higher education themselves are struggling with the temptation of brokering education as a commodity rather than providing a place for inquiry and exploration for the development of individuals and society. So it is essential that gospel-based values and visions of reality be clearly articulated and embodied.

✢ A Critical Place

While campus ministers find roots in faith communities within the institution they serve, they also have a ministry and witness to the entire educational institution, believers and non-believers alike. In this they resemble the apostle Paul preaching to the Athenians in the Areopagus and, as Paul found in his time, many will say, "May we know what this new teaching is that you are presenting? It sounds rather strange to us, so we would like to know what it means" (Acts 17:19-20). Our campuses are at the forefront of important conversations in our culture around gender, race, equity, and the use of science and technology. While the church's views are not always solicited, we are compelled by our mission to proclaim the good news of God in Christ by word and deed.

Unfortunately, as our presence on campuses diminishes, there are many who are eager and anxious to take our place. Not only do we minister in a context of knowledge disengaged from faith, we also compete for the attention of young adults alongside cults and parachurch groups offering the security of community without the challenge of discernment. Our Anglican tradition embodies an openness and willingness to tolerate divergent views and opinions, which gives our church its special affinity for modern universities and colleges where open discussion and the exchange of ideas are valued.

✣ A Critical Base

Some campus ministers are marginal in the places they minister, far from the center of attention or power and rarely holding the academic credentials that command status. They live out Paul's observation that "God chose what is foolish in the world to shame the wise; God chose what is weak in the world to shame the strong" (1 Corinthians 1:27). What can be learned about ministry from this base can be critical to informing the church's witness to the wider world, where the church can often be similarly viewed as marginal or as irrelevant, foolish, and weak. In preaching the gospel, campus ministers are not only ambassadors of our community of faith, but also eyes and ears for the church.

✣ What Can We Do?

Knowing that the number of institutions of higher education greatly outstrips the number of our congregations, we see that the mission task is as enormous as it is compelling. Yet in the work of mission discernment how can we be sure that college and university campuses are not overlooked? Can we understand that our congregational resources can do much in this local mission field? Let us think of congregations hospitably offering an open hand and a compassionate heart to students and young adults as well as to others in the community.

Congregations need to offer hospitality to students on neighboring campuses as part of the difficult work of making disciples. This hospitality implies carving out staff time, space, and opportunities to gather for worship and learning that are appropriate in timing and content for students. We can also place young adults into significant leadership and decision-making roles that make a difference.

Although on campus we see the regular gathering of an intergenerational community, these gatherings are almost exclusively centered on academic matters. Congregations, however, offer an intergenerational community that can involve young people in a different way: as peers or friends seeking the same common good. By being part of a congregation, students can reach out to others beyond the campus, in doing service and making witness. In many ways, the specialized work of ministry in higher education would be done if congregations met the challenge of fully becoming themselves, that is, being communities of faithful people responding to the needs of the world around them with the joy of the good news.

We know that the university plays an important role in contemporary culture, just as we know that the church has been shaped by the college experiences of its members. If we take seriously the priority of campus ministry, then we have much to share with the young women and men at institutions of higher education. We have gifts of our faith to offer, and they yearn to receive these gifts, even though they might not necessarily express it in that way. We also have much to receive from these young people. The gifts of openness, energy, vulnerability, and a sense that much good is yet to be are there for us to receive as a church. Let us open our hearts and our churches so we may give and receive one another's gifts. In so doing we will be making incarnate the community that God wills for us.

Campus Ministry and a Hungry Heart

Cathleen Chittenden-Bascom

You shall love the Lord your God with all your heart, with all your soul, and with all your mind... [and] you shall love your neighbor as yourself. (Matthew 22:37-39)

Before I went to college, my world was compartmentalized. In the suburban Denver of the sixties and seventies my life seemed to be a series of boxes connected mainly by vehicles—be they Saabs or VWs—much like the squares on the board of a Monopoly game. There were places of recreation (especially the Rocky Mountains) and places of culture, places of education and places of entertainment.

More to the point, there was a box called religion. For seventeen of my first eighteen years of life, I felt only tenuously connected to our local parish church. I know now that my mother's Christianity and private prayer life influenced how I view things. Yet on the whole, the church was a place visited. Sometimes as a young child when I read or heard words from *The Book of Common Prayer* a sense of power and awe would come over me and the beauty and wonder of God would touch me. But as soon as we left the shade of the sanctuary, the Broncos and one's golf game quickly became the topic of conversation and seemed, in the sunlight, more solid realities. Once a year our congregation did send a beautiful woven bookmark on my birthday in a weighty envelope—a sort of annual whisper that God could enter my world, even if through the mail. On the whole, I was an apt example of what Mircea Eliade terms "modern Western consciousness," for in my expectation the sacred and the secular were separate and distinct.

But then, at seventeen, I had a conversion experience. And at eighteen I went to college. A lasting vision of my faith development in college is that the walls came tumbling down. The dikes and dams which had attempted to keep God safely contained gloriously collapsed! Jesus said, "You shall love the Lord your God with all your heart, with all your soul, and with all your mind... [and] you shall love your neighbor as yourself." The call became clear. No more boxes. No more Sunday Christian. No more compartmentalized human being.

The Canterbury House at the University of Kansas can be found atop the renowned—and mythical—Mount Oread (there are, of course, no real mountains in Kansas). In 1980, that one block in which the Canterbury House stood in dignified simplicity, a good-sized forest green clapboard house with a red door, was the one block connecting most spheres of my being. It was the block between my dorm to the north and the campus proper to the south—my social life and my academic pursuits. Down the hill to the east was the "real world" of the boutiques, the coffee houses, and the bars, and to the west the art museum and football stadium of the university. The "church" stood unapologetically in the middle. There on the crossroads of my young adult journeys, like the very question of the existence of God itself, the Episcopal campus ministry sat where I could neither ignore nor get around it.

Peter Casparian, the chaplain, was also hard for me to get around. The first time I saw Peter, he rode up to the Canterbury House in his collar on a motorcycle. The moment he took off his helmet and it dawned on me that this was the priest, that wall between the sacred and profane felt an important tremor. For my main image of an Episcopal priest came from my childhood: Father Barnes was an ancient wisp of a man who dressed in black, with the dust of books hanging about him and a beatific kindness in his blue eyes. And yet, in my experience Father Barnes was one with the church building and grounds, almost one of its shadows. To me it was as if he were kept there in some magnetic field of the church bell, a holy man living in a holy place.

So I was taken aback by this priest who so freely rode his motorcycle back and forth between the secular and sacred worlds. The face that emerged was not sunken with age, but almost childlike in its roundness, with ruddy color. His sandy hair was long, and only the hint of a receding hairline suggested he surpassed most students in age. He wore tortoise-rim glasses, Top-Siders but no socks, and was built like a fireplug. Peter was no shadow, but solidly human.

ᴠ᷅ Love the Lord your God with all your heart

Our valentines and medical sketches of the human heart are featherweight next to the full-bodied understanding of the biblical "heart." The heart is the innermost center of our natural condition. Eating and drinking strengthen the heart. The heart is the seat of love and of hatred, of all feelings and affections. It is the center of the moral life. Bruce Springsteen was very popular when I was in high school and college, and although I think the lyrics of his other songs are more profound, "Hungry Heart" remains a refrain for my youth. Springsteen's music, with Clarence Clemons on the saxophone, wailed out the pain of our disillusioned but survivalist era. It expressed the existential anger of those of us who have the assassination of Martin Luther King, Jr., as an early memory, who waited most of our childhoods for the Vietnam War to end, and who cut our junior high political teeth on the Watergate proceedings and the resignation of a maligned president.

As a generation, many of us hungered, longed for something we were too despondent to believe existed. Thus, in my opinion, came the preppie and the yuppie movements: if there are no real values or hope, why not make as much money and be as powerful as you can? And if you cannot take the emptiness of such ruthless materialism, find some stylish drink or drug to numb yourself. This may be too cynical. The children of the sixties and seventies do possess much creativity and drive, but to me, much of it seemed obsessive and empty.

Of course, that was also the condition of my own "heart." There was much that was beautiful about my childhood. Even though I was the youngest of four daughters, seven years younger than the last and undoubtedly a "mistake," I never doubted that I was wanted; I felt delighted in. Also, born to middle-aged parents from the middle class, I wanted for very little. In a family so laden with women, I felt much freedom and encouragement to be and do anything my imagination could grasp. I loved school. I had friends. I loved sports. I wrote plays and acted them out. Both in the Rocky Mountains to the west and the wheat fields of Kansas to the east, I romped and explored with ferocious energy.

But as an adolescent, life became less beautiful. A deep sense of abandonment came over me as my older sisters left home, my mother returned to her career, and one by one my beloved grandparents became ill and died. Sadly, the loss I felt, combined with body image pressures, translated into eating disorders. *A hungry heart.* By the time I entered college, pendulum swings between food and exercise were a rhythm of my life. Blessed with enthusiasm and a zest for learning and life, nonetheless my self-image rested largely on whether or not I had eaten a beckoning piece of pie, and my sense of a good day depended, sleet or heat, on whether I had made it out of bed to run a few miles.

It makes me vulnerable to write and remember, except that through ministry I have come to learn that I am far from alone in such struggles. So many of us have given the strangest things power in our lives. We all need to know ourselves as "the beloved," but deep down run with the fear that we are not. Pascal called it the God-shaped hole. It is true: *everybody has a hungry heart.* But what Jesus said is also true, "Blessed are you who hunger now, for you will be satisfied."

My struggles with overeating and obsessive exercise have been calmed and healed over the years. But it was in college that the foundations of that healing, and of deeper things, were laid. How? In some mysterious way the answer is simple: *communion* and *community.*

As I understand it, the Hebrew heart is the belly of the person, and when I think of those years I think of the belly of the Canterbury House: the common dining room. In the early 1980s this space—with its green shag carpet, suspended stained-glass in the windows, and the small oak table which we used as an altar—served as the site of both our eucharistic feast and the meals that followed. When I first came to college, although I had a conversion experience on a Campus Life ski trip late in high school (a first moment of prayer followed by an overwhelming sense of a "person-on-the-other-side"!), my beliefs about Jesus were fluid and forming. When I entered college, I believed Jesus was only a human being. I saw him as the greatest human, an amazing source of wisdom, an elevated teacher. But then I had a dream.

During a nap upstairs at the Canterbury House, I dreamt in vivid color and light. There was a gentle waterfall and a river. I felt myself peacefully going down through the surface and depths of the warm water. My shoulder blades softly touched the sand and pebbles at the bottom. Though I saw no one else in the dream, I knew I was being baptized. As I began to float back to the surface I had a sense of well-being and my eyes were mesmerized by a dance of sunlight on the transparent green water. Back and forth the light would move. Then a shadow appeared on the surface. "Of course," I thought, "it is my own reflection." But as I floated up and met the surface of the water, I saw a face. But it was not the face I expected, even in my dream: the face was not my own. It was a collage made of bars of shadow and bars of light, a beautiful, penetrating, Jewish-looking face. The face of Christ.

I immediately woke. But from that day to this, and most powerfully soon after the dream, that face is present to me whenever I am with others gathered for the eucharist. It was a dream which took me beyond where my intellect easily wanted to go, to the belief that Jesus is divine. There, as a young woman standing on that green shag rug in the Canterbury House, with my hands folded and lifted, I would receive the broken bread and see that face, and experience myself as loved and known as I had never been loved or known before. The piece of bread was small, the wine but a sip. But as Jesus promises in the Beatitudes, my hunger was being satisfied. *Communion.*

Then the table would be reverently cleaned and pushed to the side. We would end the worship with the exchange of the peace and then the peer ministers would carry out something like baked potatoes and cheese. Waves of laughter would soon replace waves of chant and song, and then Jesus would come to me again, in his more human form, in that group of believing people.

There are so many faces to remember. As I was empowered to love and was seeking to learn to serve, others so often served me. Ted studied ten hours straight with me at a coffee shop so that I would pass a geology exam. David jump-started my much-loved '64 Plymouth Fury again and again on subzero days. Lissa told me she thought I had an eating disorder. Amy carried boxes to the third floor when it was one hundred ten degrees with eighty-five percent humidity. We all listened to Tib as she remembered sexual abuse in her family. We tried to minister to Jim in his depressions. It was part and parcel of living, but somehow because of that bread we broke together, and the One we remembered, we did it more closely, with a stamina beyond our own, and less touched by despair. In a fast-paced world we made the time for one another and learned from our own experience that what you give is given back sevenfold.

It was not an accident of architecture that our sanctuary and dining room were one: it was perhaps the deepest symbol of Peter's sacramental theology, which was also evident in many small details of his ministry. He did evangelism by handing out popsicles to passersby in the heat of August, with sweat rings around his collar. Perhaps he had Benedictine leanings: he worked at endless fix-up projects around the Canterbury House, and for those of us who became peer ministers he expected physical labor to be a part of our spiritual discipline.

In my junior year I made the rather drastic change of leaving my sorority house, with its full sets of silverware and its virtual servants, to live at the Canterbury House, where as peer ministers we were to be servants as Jesus was. We cooked a meal for the worship community (sometimes up to one hundred twenty-five people) and prepared meals for one another four nights a week. We would clean the chapel, dust, vacuum, and clean toilets. I remember Peter teaching Ben, a postdoctoral biology student, to use a shovel. I was in no better shape! But I found, to my own surprise, that physical work was therapeutic, healing to my heart.

And servanthood was to extend beyond the church and university. In those days folks would come by the Canterbury House for help and we did not turn them away. We were not to give money, but always gave food and drink and, hardest of all, our time. "For whatever you do to the least of these…" was taken literally by us, and we tried to act it out. Because we were a community living there, we felt safe and supported and enabled to invite others in. Troubled students, as well as those who were not students at all, sat in that common dining room for a sandwich or for an audience. It could be inconvenient, sometimes disturbing, or even a little frightening. Such service is not easy, but it brings joy; it helps to create heart. *Community*.

↳ Love the Lord your God with all your soul

The epitome of Peter Casparian's incarnational activity was the building of St. Anselm's Chapel. When a church burned down in the small Kansas town of Tongonoxie, Peter claimed it as an opportunity for resurrection. With the help of architecture professor Kent Spreckelmeyer, he had the beautiful wood of the remaining parish hall moved piece by piece to Lawrence and rebuilt into a small, graceful sanctuary adjoining the Canterbury House. When I think of my spiritual development in college, this chapel is where my memory dwells. With its pebbled rock floor and a wall of windows, combined with that old wood, it carried something of the outdoors about it. At the same time it had the scent of an ancient holy place: maybe the pews retained the incense of years gone by. I experienced moving liturgies there—Easter Vigils and ministry celebrations and the Stations of the Cross—and once a week and every day in Lent we gathered there in the early hours for morning prayer. But for me it was above all a place of contemplation and solitude. A place where one could bask in prayer, in the presence of God.

One Holy Week I practically lived there. On Maundy Thursday, Marguerite Casparian and her mother prepared the chapel for the night watch. Her mother came from the South and I imagined she drove all those wondrous flowers up from a warmer clime. They nearly filled the chapel with budding boughs—forsythia, honeysuckle, and lilacs. Bucketfalls were arranged as only a textile artist might, as if weaving the Garden of Gethsemane again from God's own threads right there in our small chapel.

That year the peer ministers had determined to watch all night. A thunder and lightning storm stirred itself up outside. I sat and prayed, and tried to pray, and slept, and woke and tried to pray, and prayed, and the rain was slamming down on the roof, and the whole chapel would light up with lightning blasts. The pebbles wore themselves into my knees. The present and eternity merged (the power of liturgical remembering), and I was there with them, one of the Marys perhaps, trying to watch. That night I felt what the disciples felt and what is so crucial for us all to feel—Jesus' forgiveness was palpable in that room. His presence remains steady even when ours fades in and out.

My final peace about my sense of vocation would come a few years later, across the Atlantic in England. But that chapel received my first questions: I spent some hours there, saying to God, "Me—a priest? Ridiculous!" Although at first I ran from the idea, Peter was constantly putting articles about women clergy in my mailbox. The chapel was where I preached my first sermon and felt the joy of it. That priest and that community of people could not have been more encouraging, prayerful, and honest in my discernment process. Only later in England and in seminary would I observe and experience the climates of patriarchy that tragically block women from offering their gifts to God's people.

There is no way we can love someone we do not know, and it is hard to love if we do not know who we are. Campus ministry gave my soul a place and time to pray, to come to know God, and to come to better know myself.

◌ Love the Lord your God with all your mind

Before I moved into the Canterbury House I would pad through the thick snow on winter nights to study in Peter's office. I would grip the road with my toes through my boots in order not to slip on the ice, driven and intoxicated by the idea of some quiet studying, since the sorority house was no haven for academic pursuits. There was a brightly painted study hall with lights on all night, but it mainly harbored chatting women and pizza. One friend and I would occasionally wear our Walkmans there while we studied, which proved a good social buffer. But a nicer option for me was a trek to the Canterbury House and Peter's office.

There was a time when religion had seemed to me the antithesis of the intellectual life. In fact, at the time of my conversion, one of my strongest fears in pursuing the Christian life was its threat to reason. But this book-filled office was symbolic of a truth that to me was new: the rich intellectual reality of the Christian faith. The space was interesting in itself, too, with its roll-top desk, photographs of children from around the world, pipe, pieces of small pottery and sculpture, stacks of paper.

But most interesting of all were the books. When I pulled the little stool around and gazed at the titles and the authors on the shelves, a new world and community opened up before me. Thomas Merton, Fyodor Dostoyevski, Mother Teresa, and Carl Jung. Julian of Norwich and Dorothy Day. John Donne, George Herbert, Madeleine L'Engle, Dorothy Sayers, and C. S. Lewis. I would take down volume after volume and read beautiful prose and poetry that took God seriously. I would learn of thinkers who thought about reality in terms of a Creator, and social activists who held as their example the radical person of Jesus Christ.

And at the Canterbury House I began to realize that this tradition was not merely in books, but was part of living as well. On Wednesdays at noon we had a small service at the Danforth Chapel on campus, and with some amazement and trepidation I would find myself kneeling next to one of my professors. On Friday afternoons I started a gathering at the Canterbury House where we invited professors to speak with us in more depth about something that related to their discipline and their faith. We heard about a Manx poet, about nuclear weapons policies, about the environmental crisis—all in relationship to Christian faith. I found some of these speakers, far from being ignorant, were among the smartest people I had ever met. I saw that religion was not marginal but a living force in any number of arenas in our society. And I began to realize that knowledge was most beautiful when it too was a servant.

In the center of Peter's office, on the coffee table, a dog-eared Bible usually sat, obviously the most gazed-into book in the room. It was in that study I first tried praying before reading scripture. I prayed to have *eyes to see and ears to hear,* and

Jesus' words came alive on the page! The books on the shelves attested to the living, experiential nature of our faith, and to the fact that the Spirit speaks through people of all generations. Far from cutting me off from vibrant thought, the church offered companions and tools for doing the work each of us is called to do with our minds.

Heart. Soul. Mind. Of course the edges blur; they overlap, they defy boundaries, and they all involve our bodies. But Jesus' point was clear: he meant our whole selves, and he underlined that fact with his own life and his own death. As I watch the young adults I minister with now, I see the same unfolding development. Day by day the love of God heals and strengthens every facet of their being. The same staples seem to feed them: communion and community; solitude and prayer, scripture and Christian thought. They become more satisfied, and more solid, for these things work on us to make us more like Christ. Jesus' love of God was no separate compartment off to one side, and my experience of campus ministry is that it beckons us and invites us to follow Christ with our whole being.

On Engineers and Evangelism

Jane S. Gould

Every Wednesday afternoon I celebrate the eucharist in a windowless chapel surrounded by a moat. Designed by architect Eero Sarinen in the 1950s, the building plays brilliantly with themes of light and water. Where most chapels have plaques that affirm the building's creation to the "Glory of God," this one's plaque reads, "This building gives embodiment to the responsibilities of the Massachusetts Institute of Technology (MIT) to maintain an atmosphere of religious freedom wherein students may deepen their understanding of their own spiritual heritage, freely pursue their own religious interests, and worship God in their own way."

The MIT Chapel completes a critical triangle on the west side of campus with Kresge Auditorium and the Stratton Student Center. Even so, religious life has never been central to MIT. Whether the tall brick walls and moat are to protect the rest of campus from spiritual influences or to create an island of peace in the midst of the stress and strain, the chaplains have no illusions: God and the life of faith are not central to discourse on our campus.

My predecessor, Scott I. Paradise, often described the religion of MIT as "scientism." In an essay titled "A Ministry to Scientists and Engineers," he wrote:

> MIT is a thoroughly secular place. If it has an established religion, it is the religion of science, that is, the belief that the pursuit of scientific knowledge and the harnessing of nature for human ends is the great human enterprise. The scientific method is the only reliable path toward truth....Chaplains are easily ambushed by the feeling of being the priest of one religion in the temple of another.

Among the books he left for me when I assumed my position as Episcopal chaplain at MIT was Andrew D. White's two-volume opus, published in 1896, dedicated to Ezra Cornell, and titled *A History of the Warfare of Science With Theology in Christendom*. Although I admit to having only browsed a few chapters of White during my two years at MIT, the title staring down at me in stereo reminds me of the critical tension within which I work.

I came to MIT from a position as associate rector of an Episcopal congregation in Lawrence, Massachusetts, the youngest and poorest city in the Commonwealth of Massachusetts. My job at Grace Church involved me in creating and sustaining programs for children, youth, and families in the congregation and in the largely Hispanic neighborhood around the church. When I accepted the invitation to become Episcopal chaplain at MIT, people uniformly expressed surprise at the huge shift I was preparing to make. It is undeniable that the MIT community possesses vastly greater access to self-determination, education, wealth, and power than the people of Lawrence. Still, the critical issue for both places seems the same to me. What, if anything, does the church have to say to young people in a secular, post-Christian culture?

Clearly, there is no possibility for evangelism unless we believe that the church has something to say to young people and they have something to say to us. We offer very little when we invite them into congregations obsessed with institutional survival, worried about building repair, dominated by the fifty-something crowd, cemented to ancient liturgies and hymnody, divided over social issues, besieged by scandal, and fearful of change. In any case, young people find precious little welcome in most of our congregations. Episcopalians have come to accept that teenagers leave the church after confirmation and, if all goes well, return when they have children. Some bemoan this tendency but most treat it as the norm and view young people who violate the norm as either saints or weirdos.

When students go to church they feel keenly the culture gap between their own eighteen-to-thirty crowd and the rest of the congregation. Usually no one speaks to them. If they do, a white-haired greeter says, "So nice that you're here," implying with every word and movement that they are out of place. The student-visitors feel as if they are being observed as exotic creatures — "twenty-somethings" who go to church. MIT students find the gap broadened by their vocations as scientists and engineers. All too often they tell stories of going to church and finding themselves standing in a corner at coffee hour, the regulars terrified at the prospect of having to speak to a young scientist.

Congregations further alienate students by classifying them as "non-adults." One graduate student complains that her younger brother gets treated as an adult because he is married and has a job while she is relegated to the inferior status of student. Her problems and joys are not regarded as those of real life. Some parishes even maintain separate lists of members and student members. They see college and graduate students as useful youth group leaders and church school teachers, but they rarely integrate them fully into the life and governance of the parish. Many congregations talk about young adult ministry but either do nothing about it or plan activities without involving young adults in the organization and execution of the events. Needless to say, both of these strategies fail to yield a vital ministry, and the young people are blamed for not being responsive.

In a recent retreat with MIT students, I asked them to draw pictures of whatever came to mind when they heard the words evangelism and "Christian witness." As they created images of blaring trumpets, brightly burning candles, witness boxes, flowers being distributed at airports, conversations over coffee, soap-box speeches, door-to-door canvassing, lamps burning on hill tops, crosses, people under spotlights, and hands joining, the students displayed a wide variety of interpretations. Quickly, it became clear that neither evangelism nor Christian witness carries with it a clear definition or a pure legacy. Even so, all the students had stories of "being evangelized." Whether targeted by the Boston Church of Christ, Inter-Varsity Christian Fellowship, Jehovah's Witnesses, Mormons, Assemblies of God, Maranatha, or the Campus Crusade for Christ, they all remembered times when people pushed their religious convictions on them. They all resist evangelism that communicates the message of "one way, my way."

Although the students with whom I work at MIT want to invite friends and colleagues to worship with them, although they want to take more risks in witnessing to their faith, although they want to affirm their faith more boldly, they fear how others will hear and receive them. They do not want to be lumped together with the "evangelical Christians" who are active and effective at MIT. They are not drawn to the seemingly easy answers proffered by these groups, even as they see that the clarity and orderliness of evangelical Christianity can have great appeal for the mind of the engineer.

In any case, evangelical groups thrive on campus and seem to provide the public definition of what it means to be Christian. Many non- and lapsed Christians assume that there is a monolithic Christian identity that holds to certain theological positions, political affiliations, and social attitudes. One graduate student described a meeting in which one of her colleagues suggested that she might feel uncomfortable inviting a particular astrophysicist to speak to their research group on the origins of the universe because she was a Christian. She stammered something about being sure he would be a fine speaker and tried to figure out how her colleague even knew she was a Christian. With our small group, she wondered aloud, "Since when are being a Christian and being a creationist synonymous?"

✧ A faith tradition that holds in tension reason and mystery

The Episcopal community at MIT will never be very large, but what we can offer is a thoughtful articulation of Christian faith that recognizes our global context and values the richness diversity brings. Our students seek fuller knowledge of their own and other religious traditions. They have no desire to proselytize; however, they do want to be able to answer questions and affirm their faith with both passion and precision.

It is important for students to be able to affirm that people of faith do not need to check their intelligence and rational capabilities at the door when they go to church. They cherish the fact that our tradition values intellectual pursuit and understands that God reveals Godself through it. One graduate student recently reflected that in both her academic work and her life of faith "there is a need for intellectual nourishment and stimulation. What I realized when I started reading the Bible again this year is how much my faith had died because I wasn't feeding it anything to help it grow. In the same way, my academic research was in danger of falling apart because I wasn't getting any input from outside sources—I was finished with my classes and didn't have an advisor."

Anglican theology affirms the centrality of scripture, reason, and tradition to God's ongoing revelation. Study of scripture, theological discourse, conversations about faith and science, and discussions of their own experiences of God all appeal to the probing intellects and hungry souls of the students. The tolerance of ambiguity and diversity within Anglican interpretation and expression of doctrine gives them space to question, inquire, and explore their own understanding of faith. In classic Anglican style, their contexts shape how they interpret and articulate their encounter with God. As I spend time with them, I can never forget that these young people are scientists and engineers. During one Sunday evening Bible study I could not help but smile as a graduate student explained in enthusiastic and great detail how the Incarnation was like quantum physics. I marveled at the analogy as he opened God's word to us in new and meaningful ways.

Yet, even as the students with whom I work emphasize the importance of bringing all of themselves—including their fine, critical minds—to their life of faith, they are quick to reject notions that God can somehow be scientifically proven. They cringe when nonscientists use and misuse scientific language to demonstrate God's existence. Similarly, they become uncomfortable when scientists who are Christians attempt to use science to prove God's existence. A group of students recently had a good laugh as they thought of poorly conceived and executed research projects motivated by religion. One student wondered, what becomes of the faith of those who came to believe in Jesus because of the Shroud of

Turin? Carbon dating clearly proved that it was not the shroud in which Jesus was wrapped. Are those people to stop believing because the shroud was not authentic?

Even as one undergraduate affirmed that it is possible to have "semi-religious experiences solving linear algebra," the students agree that the precision and even magnificence of the problems and their solutions do not constitute proof of God. One electrical engineering graduate student wrote, "Do I believe that I can see God in my own research? Absolutely. Some days the patterns I see in the data or the way that the pieces of a puzzle fit together are so amazing that I feel grateful for the opportunity to study these things. Other days, the acoustic wave equation seems downright evil. If my faith in God relied upon my feelings about certain aspects of science, I'd be in real trouble. To believe in God because fractals are cool, chaos theory is fascinating, and butterflies are masterpieces of aerospace engineering is fraught with peril. Believing because of science diminishes faith and often seems to be bad science (i.e. it doesn't usually involve a logical line of reasoning). If there is absolute proof of God's existence, where is the room for mystery? For mercy? For God's incredible grace?"

As scientists and engineers, they know how to make "engineering approximations," they know that lines are not really straight and that astronomers are surprised at every turn. Theirs is not the world of absolutes that nonscientists sometimes assume. Furthermore, these bright young scientists insist that the life of the spirit must not be viewed as totally imprecise and fuzzy. After all, even as we acknowledge our inability to know God fully and affirm our need to enter into the mystery, we know that God is quite clear that we are to have no other gods and that we are to love our neighbor as ourselves.

ᴗ: A faith tradition that cherishes them as children of God

One of my ancillary responsibilities at MIT is as an admissions reader. Every regular admission applicant's folder is read by two faculty or staff readers in addition to the admissions staff. Never have I seen so many SAT and Achievement 800s, straight A's, glowing recommendations, and lists of prizes. Yet I know that when these bright and ambitious young students come to MIT, fifty percent of them will be in the bottom half of their class. They have never known anything less than excellence, but most will suffer failure or at least significant setbacks during their MIT career. MIT is an intense and highly competitive place; it can undermine a student's self-confidence, values, and sense of joy.

For students working in this competitive and highly technical world, their faith provides them with freedom and perspective. A materials science graduate student noted that, in his research, every problem has a solution somewhere. When he comes to worship, on the other hand, he does not come looking for solutions. He opens himself fully to God's presence, freed by the awareness that there is not an answer he needs to find. He gains perspective on life and work as he steps back and stops seeking certainty. Similarly, an undergraduate computer scientist commented that he knows that all the problems given to him—no matter how mysterious they seem to him—have right and wrong answers. He finds freedom in recognizing that "God is far more complicated than I can figure out. I just have to trust God and let things play out."

"Trusting God and letting things play out" does not mean abdicating personal responsibility, but it does mean letting go of the notion that we are in control. MIT students know that they, their parents, their professors, their advisors, and God all expect them to use their talents to the best of their ability. Yet they also know that they are more than MIT students. They are more than the last test result or the next problem set or the dreaded dissertation. Members of the Lutheran-Episcopal Ministry at MIT see themselves as possessing, or at least trying to hold onto, a sense of perspective that is often missing elsewhere in the Institute.

One undergraduate told me of a conversation in her dormitory shortly after a tragic murder-suicide in a Harvard dormitory in June, 1995. As a group of students watched the news one asked, "Aren't their exams before ours?" Another asked, "Aren't they already done?" A third commented, "Maybe grades just came out." The conversation proceeded along these lines for several minutes before my friend asked, "Did it ever occur to any of you that she might have had problems that weren't academically related?" Their faith helps students remember that there is more to life than grades. They know themselves to be Christians who happen to be students and techies at this point in time. The center of their existence is God, not circuits or organic chemistry.

Conversations at MIT tend to begin with how are your classes or how is your research, rather than how are you. Last year one graduate student experimented by asking people to tell her something good that was going on in their lives. She reported that most people did not know how to answer the question. Indeed, some felt threatened by the way in which she had violated the social code. They could talk about their research, their advisor, and their future employment prospects but they had put the rest of life in a box—out of view and consideration. The intensity and focus required for doctoral candidates easily obscures any life beyond the lab. When it came time last winter for this graduate student to choose her future employer, she turned down the University of Michigan, where she would have been one of several tenure track mechanical engineers competing for a single tenured position. Instead, she chose to affiliate herself with the University of Toronto, where she experienced a sense of community and collegiality that she knew she needed to sustain her work and herself.

An undergraduate once told me that he got very caught up in the competitive spirit of MIT and found himself checking how others were doing on every problem set and test. As he compared his performance to that of others he become more and more discouraged. He was working hard and God was letting him down. He was not getting the grades that he deserved. Even as he knew that God did not give grades—good ones or bad—he felt that his hard work should be rewarded. Now, as a junior, he has realized that the more he focused on tests, grades, and competition, the further he drifted from God and God's purpose for him. Now he tries not to ask people about classes, tests, problem sets, and grades. He asks instead, "How's life?" or "What's up?" He still studies hard and tries to do well. Now, however, it is his own vocation as a Christian and an engineer that he is trying to work out, not his position compared to all the other engineers on campus.

⌇ A faith tradition that gathers people in community

In a place as competitive as MIT, many view community and companionship as luxuries. Although lab groups and study groups work together, only certain aspects of life provide the content for these relationships. At home, students may attend church because their family does, because their friends do, or because it is the right thing to do. Once they reach MIT, however, there are no institutional supports for maintaining a life of faith. On the contrary, the pace of life, negative stereotypes about Christians, and assumptions that only goodie-goodies go to church clearly make church attendance a bold and countercultural move.

Episcopal and Lutheran students gather for the eucharist every Wednesday evening at 5:10. We have other eucharists, Bible studies, retreats, outreach projects, and social activities, but the heart of our ministry is our Wednesday evening eucharist. When I first arrived at MIT I wondered whether we should shift to a Sunday service, but as I have lived with our Wednesday worship I have come to appreciate the tremendous symbolic power of celebrating the eucharist in the belly of the secular beast. Students come to worship straight from classes and labs and they leave to return to classes, labs, libraries, and problem sets. We truly worship in the midst of MIT, and as we gather for the eucharist we challenge its value system. As MIT drives its students to strive independently to achieve more than they ever dreamed possible, we acknowledge gratefully our dependence on God; we give thanks that the world is neither ours to make nor ours to save.

One student comments, "I go to church because I desperately need God and people. As I've learned over the past year, my faith, and ultimately my life, can only be sustained if I have a place to hear and be nourished by God's word within the context of a community." Another explains, "I really believe in my education, but sometimes the jolts and stresses of MIT get in the way of my real education; going to a worship service helps me see through what's going on." A third says, "Here I can worship God and discuss my faith with other members of the MIT community who value science and engineering and who believe in the good news that God has given us through his son, Jesus Christ."

In the final years of the twentieth century, it is important to note that our community is not built and strengthened only when we gather face-to-face. Our MIT faith community does not consist simply of those who come to worship and other events planned by the ministry. Through our web site we provide information to and converse with Christians around the world. On campus, students looking for a sympathetic person with whom to explore questions of the meaning and purpose of life or seeking help for a depressed friend can find the chaplains and student religious groups on the web. Through our e-mail list, members of the ministry post announcements, ask for prayers and thanksgivings, launch discussions, and organize weekly worship. Many people on the list never post notices, nor do they come to worship. Yet, with some regularity, they or a friend of theirs appear at my door or call my phone number asking for help. Although e-mail can never take the place of face-to-face communication or even words on paper, we miss a tremendous opportunity if we do not use electronic communication as a method of building and strengthening our communities of faith. I cannot imagine any strategy for evangelism among young people that does not use online communication. Young people today know how to navigate in cyberspace and the church needs to sail there in order to reach them.

✧ A faith tradition that expects us to stand with the poor

MIT students know that they are richly blessed, but they have little discretionary time or money. Last summer one just-graduated senior joined our team of volunteers at a church-based supper program and signed up to teach summer Sunday school at a local parish. Before she headed off to graduate school on the west coast, she wrote to me about the people she met serving supper and eating with the homeless in Harvard Square; she told of teaching scripture to children and encountering God as they learned together. She wished that she had connected with these programs sooner so that her world would have embraced more than MIT and so that she could have been more attentive to God's presence in her life. Yet she concluded somewhat wistfully, "I'm not sure that I would have thought I had the time earlier, though. I don't know how you push people to do more without making them feel guilty. But try."

As a twenty-something seminarian, I joined with other divinity school students and organized a shelter for the homeless based at University Lutheran Church in Harvard Square. My classmates and I had visions of shelter-based advocacy and training programs; we planned to engage the seminary community in responding concretely to the systemic causes of homelessness; we knew we could make a profound difference. The shelter still runs at Uni-Lu from November to April and it provides respite from cold hours spent on the streets. However, we failed to usher in the reign of God as we had imagined. What we managed to do was open our own eyes, ears, and hearts to Joe, Peter, Billy, and dozens of others whom we had always avoided or acknowledged with a few coins as we passed by. What we succeeded in doing was creating a network of college-age volunteers whose lives, like our own, would never be quite the same for having spent time in conversation with one of the outcast.

Whether we design and build houses for Habitat for Humanity, spend the night in a shelter, go on a mission project to the Mississippi Delta or El Salvador, volunteer in a tutoring program, prepare food for a supper program, help out in a summer youth camp, teach job skills to city kids, or run a computer camp, we all are called to serve. Certainly, we do some good for others as we give our time and talent, but that is not the real reason young people need to be involved in service. We serve so that we might remember how richly we are blessed; we serve so that we might honor God's preference for the least, the last, and the lost; we serve so that we might realize that there is more to life than problem sets, exams, and dissertations; we serve so that we might be drawn out of our ivory-tower insularity and encounter people whose lives are vastly different from our own; we serve so that we might be converted.

✌ A faith tradition that reminds us to contemplate ethical implications

How do these students integrate their vocations as Christians and scientists or engineers? How does their faith influence their science and their science their faith? How should their faith influence their professional choices? For first-year students to find out that their calculus professor is an articulate and faithful Episcopalian is a stunning discovery. For student researchers to realize that a mechanical engineering professor changed his area of research from munitions to prosthetic devices because his Christian faith would not allow him to support the war industry alerts them to ethical questions that reside in the research they do.

At MIT students struggle with questions about the ethics of research. Some assert that there are fields of research that they personally would not do—genetic engineering, biotechnology, nuclear engineering, for example—but they believe that all are "good" research that someone should do. Others contend that some research should not be done because the potential for its misuse is too great. However, most agree with mainline MIT thinking that maintains that increased scientific knowledge and technological advances are necessarily good because they "enlarge freedom." MIT orthodoxy insists that discovery itself is morally neutral, although it can potentially be used for good or ill. According to the MIT ethic, researchers have a responsibility to expand the horizons of knowledge, not to make moral decisions about what might be useful knowledge and what might be destructive.

As students contemplate how they live their faith as informed Christians in a complex world, it is important for them to confront the MIT ethic and recognize that no activity is morally neutral. Even doing research that is benign or possessing social value does not free the individual from reflecting on such questions as how funding happens, what gets funded and what does not, how research is conducted, how research teams function, and who has access to publication in the leading journals.

Nearly thirty years ago, still under the shadow of the mushroom-shaped fruit of the Manhattan Project (with which MIT had numerous connections), Episcopal chaplain Myron Bloy recognized the need for faculty and students to have the opportunity to discuss the ethical implications of technological advances. He gathered members of the MIT community for seminars on critical issues related to science and technology, with programs focused on the arms race and the U. S. military establishment. During the last couple of years, most of our programs have focused on the Internet, the global economy, and the environment. Our students live on the *infobahn* and it is critical that they consider such issues as democratic access, feeway or freeway, identity development, the future of higher education, privacy, censorship, and ownership of information. As MIT students prepare to assume leadership in business and industry, it is imperative that they reflect thoughtfully on questions raised by the global economy and the impact of technology on employment. Environmental concerns frequently inspire programs on issues such as sustainable development, government regulation and the environment, and the future of nuclear power.

Most days I do not wear a clerical collar to work. The only events for which I invariably wear a collar are Technology and Culture Forum programs. Between seventy and seven hundred people attend these programs and most of them have no explicit religious affiliation. I wear my collar to make clear that the issues of the forum are the issues that concern the church in the late twentieth century. The church needs to be present, raising questions and fostering dialogue on the moral and ethical implications of science and technology. Students need to know that the church is a place where their questions and concerns are given voice and thoughtful consideration. The work of the church needs to be in the midst of their secular world and not simply within the bounds of the moated chapel.

There is much within our faith tradition that appeals to young people. They seek respect for themselves and others, acceptance, thoughtful dialogue, opportunities to serve, critical ethical discourse, and community. The challenge for the over-thirty crowd is to let go, to listen, and to learn. The substance of our faith is sufficient to draw young people to the church if we can resist making idols of who we are and how we worship. Now is the time for the young to interpret and reinterpret the tradition we know. If we have the courage to open ourselves to conversion, all will be made new. And, in the process, their friends and colleagues will join them in church.

In a sermon preached at the installation of Constance Parvey as Lutheran chaplain at MIT, Krister Stendahl warned her not to think of the students who gather for worship as her congregation. Rather, he said, "Think of them as your support system for the work of the kingdom of God in this place." Whether at MIT or Grace Church in Lawrence, our faith communities constitute support systems for all ministers as we seek to be God's people in the world. The task of evangelism must not be simply to draw people to worship on Sunday mornings. If the church is to have a place in our secular, post-Christian culture, we must be bold and rejoice in being "the priests of one religion in the temple of another." Being acceptable and mainline, being the "religion of the Empire," tames us and separates us from the great mission to which God calls us. We, indeed, are called to baptize, teach, and make disciples of the nations. We must understand these responsibilities in new ways if we are to hear the voices, engage the minds, soothe the hearts, and enkindle the spirits of the young.

Eating the Seed Corn

The Abandonment of Campus Ministry   *Timothy J. Hallett*

The idea of a decade devoted to evangelism in the Episcopal Church looked promising at first, beginning with a high-profile consultation on ministry in higher education and an opening eucharist at the National Cathedral in Washington, D. C. There was substantial, nationwide representation at the consultation, including faculty members, administrators and other university staff persons, lay and ordained chaplains, rectors of churches adjacent to campuses, diocesan representatives, and a bishop or two. A few campus ministries even brought students, though this seemed to fluster the organizers, who had not envisioned a significant student presence at such a prestigious event. There were some addresses and some overly structured group sessions, and then everybody went home, and that was that. The consultation had consulted. No follow-up occurred.

The consultation was not without an enduring moment, however. It occurred during a sermon by John Worrell, chaplain at Rice University, when he observed that in our demographically aging church, cutting campus ministry is like "eating the seed corn." He did not intend to be prophetic, but prophetic he was. The church has been chomping away ever since.

This same decade has witnessed the elimination or drastic curtailment of long-standing campus ministries at a range of institutions. Their names compose a litany: Kenyon College, Columbia University, the University of Maryland at Baltimore, Grambling University, the University of Memphis, the University of Illinois at Chicago, Northern Illinois University, Mankato State University, Western Michigan University, Michigan State University, Wayne State University, the University of Southern California, the University of California at Los Angeles, the University of California at Irvine, the University of California at San Diego, the University of Washington. This is only a partial list, augmenting the wholesale abandonments of the 1970s and 1980s. It does not include a number of ministries in more primary stages of dissolution, nor does it enumerate the ongoing reductions of support for our remaining ministries.

Disregard, even disdain, for campus ministries has spilled over in both directions. Youth ministries are a shadow of their former selves. Too many congregations have forgotten that there used to be lots of young people in the pews and hardly anyone remembers that we once attracted young adults. There was a long stretch of time, from the beginning of this century until the early 1960s, when campus ministry was a priority. In a phrase since repeated *ad nauseam* by college chaplains, the church used to call it "our greatest domestic mission field." Chaplains and chapels and Canterbury Houses proliferated over university landscapes, linked by a national network of Canterbury Associations and a staff of full-time provincial coordinators for college work. Bright young clergy were sent to the campuses, some to move on to other things, others to make a career of it. And it paid off. Wherever one goes in the Episcopal Church, whenever people talk about their involvement with the church, one finds person after person, lay and ordained, who came into the church, or came back to the church, or stayed in the church because of some campus ministry. Others came later, but also because of some seed planted then, and countless priests first discerned their vocation in college days.

That was then. Priorities have changed. Now, formerly generous agencies specifically exclude funding for campus ministries, and in most dioceses the budget for ministry in higher education is easy pickings when crunch time comes. After all, we have to support those perpetually dying missions in dead-end towns. Something happened in between, something not much examined, not much noticed at the time, but clear in retrospect and in implication: the church gradually, deliberately turned its back on young people.

It began in the mid-1960s, with the escalation of the war in Vietnam and the proliferation of the peace and civil rights movements at home. It was exacerbated by the countercultural and sexual revolutions, and even liturgical renewal. The growth of feminism and the movement toward the ordination of women soon played a part. The campuses were hotbeds of these movements, and chaplains were in touch with them, touched by them, and more often than not, in sympathy with most of them. In large segments of the broader church, this support did not play well. Chaplains found themselves trying to interpret these movements to a church that did not want to hear, while trying to interpret the church to a constituency that was increasingly hostile toward organized religion. These chaplains soon learned that it hurts to be on the cutting edge of change. What got cut was their budgets and their jobs.

Let us admit that not all chaplains handled themselves well in those heady days of the sixties and seventies. Some became so wrapped up in social and political issues that they lost touch with the church; some forgot that the people who pay your salary may have legitimate expectations; some became alienated and alienating. But too often what was essentially a personnel problem was solved by eliminating the position, not merely by removing the incumbent. Chaplains had become suspect and their positions expendable. Retreat from campus ministry gained force.

Lest this jeremiad seem too harsh, let it be said that these patterns do not necessarily apply in some of our southeastern and south central dioceses. There are places where ministry in higher education is a priority. In the same places, strong diocesan youth programs are in place and there is emphasis on outreach to young adults. Not surprisingly, the church is actually growing in those areas, while most of the rest of the church has forgotten what that is like.

That the church's suspicion of students and universities can be traced to the upheavals of the 1960s and early 1970s is perhaps understandable, though not to be excused. What is baffling and disturbing is the church's unwillingness to get over it: to face its hostility toward the young and repent of it. Suspicion of chaplains has extended to a major part of their constituency, the students. For decades, college and university chaplaincies had been a primary source of aspirants to holy orders. It requires some effort to recall that the usual path to the priesthood in those days was from college to seminary to ordination, with no or little space between. Most clergy began their careers in their mid- to late-twenties. But in the midst of the Vietnam War, that progression was disrupted. Since postulancy also conferred deferment from military service, the church began to suspect male aspirants of draft-dodging. Instead of taking a hard look at vocational discernment, most dioceses took the easy way out: "Go work for a couple of years, get some real life experience, then come back and see us." Which, being interpreted, meant, "We don't believe you. Go expose yourself to the draft. Maybe we'll listen to you later. You're not wanted now."

As for young women, it was easy to tell them that their ordination was problematical. Surely they would not want to take the time and make the effort and endure all the hostility just now, would they? Better to go to work for a few years, get some real life experience, then come back and see us. Which, being interpreted, meant, "We don't want to match your commitment with ours. You're not wanted now, if ever."

Not surprisingly, young people got the message that the young need not apply. Most went off and worked for a couple of years as they had been told, and never came back. The church was spared the embarrassment of young clergy who were "too close to the concerns of their own generation," who might hold advanced views on any number of topics, and who might have had some real life experiences that were frowned upon. The church was also spared their energy, vivacity, and commitment.

At the same time, the church had begun to indulge a fascination with "late vocations." It was thought wonderful that someone might overthrow a secular career, with all its pomps and perquisites, to take holy orders. Unlike callow youth, these people brought a wealth of real life experience, a maturity, a perspective of the real world, a knowledge of the people in the pews. And indeed, some of them did. Some of them abandoned successful careers. Some of them made fine priests. And some of them, in the midst of a mid-life career or identity crisis, abandoned unsuccessful careers and unsuccessful relationships. Many of them were recent converts or proselytes with little experience or understanding of the Episcopal Church. Many were too well- or ill-formed in their religious understandings to benefit from theological education. Many had real life experience that was of little, no, or negative value to an aspirant to ordination. Many of them did not make very good priests. But at least they were not infected with the ferments and conflicts and turmoil of the rising generation. And it was easy to overlook the fact that mistakes, arrogance, and overconfidence are not limited to the young.

No one thought to ask why the late vocations of converts are more precious than the early vocations of the sons and daughters of the church, or why twenty-one years of experience in the church counts for nothing. No one bothered to ask why other professions are confident of their ability to discern and develop youthful potential, while the church alone flounders. The seasoned physician, attorney, teacher, businessperson, artisan, laborer—one who has spent a lifetime in the field—is sought out in most professions. But in the case of the clergy, the church decided less is more. Soon you hardly ever saw a priest under thirty, then under thirty-five. Soon the median age in our seminaries was thirty-nine. Soon middle-aged people at entry-level stipends were struggling to pay off huge educational debts, while the church insurance system was faced with clergy demographics skewed toward higher age and risk factors.

Suspicion of the young had even further consequences. Youth camps and conferences, for years another seedbed of leadership for the church, were staffed primarily by college students on summer jobs. But who could trust them? Who could trust the high school kids who were their campers? Faced with the specter of drugs and sex, the church simply panicked. High school camps and conferences were abruptly shut down in many places. Not a few dioceses even sold off their camps, terminating work with younger children as well. The church decided that it was safer not to be part of young people's experience.

In just a few years, a carefully constructed, highly effective structure for eliciting commitment from youth had been dismantled, and a "Not Wanted" sign hung in its place. The remaining campus ministries could not in good conscience encourage young people to consider ordained ministry, knowing that they faced summary rejection. In the absence of young clergy who had worked so naturally and effectively with young people, youth and young adults began to vanish from the pews. And with no young clergy as role models, it stopped occurring to young people that they might consider the priesthood as a vocation.

So the church lost contact with one generation, then another. Now, the census tells us, some sixty-nine percent of Americans are forty-five or younger, but at the same time some sixty-nine percent of Episcopalians are forty-five or older. The church, to the degree that it is aware at all, finds itself out of touch with the aspirations and illusions of the rising generation, oblivious to the burning issues and problems, values and blind spots, of Generation X.

The graying of the church will not be reversed by lip-service to youth and young adult ministries, or by adding titles while reducing positions, or by pretending that congregations are afire to reach out to adjacent campuses, or by exploiting lay professionals for full-time work at half-pay, or by placing unreliable or troubled clergy in campus ministries where the only harm they can do is to prove so unsuitable and ineffective that next time round we can eliminate the position entirely. Those are the current strategies, but they will not work.

From time to time one sees an article in the church press noticing the absence of the young—and of young clergy. But while these phenomena are noticed, the direct correlation between them is not, and there is distressingly little evidence of concrete actions being taken throughout the church to fill either void. Commissions on ministry continue to place hurdles in the way of young aspirants to holy orders, while removing obstacles for those of riper years. Although in recent decades the average age of seminarians hovered in the late thirties, several years ago it moved up to forty—precisely the wrong direction for a demographically challenged church. For some reason we consistently deny a full-blown Anglican theological education to people in their twenties because they are too young, while we routinely consent to piecemeal, patchwork theological education for people over forty because for some reason a full-blown Anglican theological education is too demanding for them. This aberration has become so much the norm that we do not marvel at it.

What might work is to take seriously the few remaining young adults we have by giving them access to leadership and influence in the church, hearing the hard things they have to say, and putting them to work with all their vigor, confidence, arrogance, and vision. It has been so long since we have had that kind of energy in the church at large that we have forgotten what it is like.

About midway through the "decade of evangelism" there was another consultation of sorts. The office of young adult and higher education ministries organized a young adult forum, which brought together a diverse group of eighteen- to thirty-five-year-olds for conversation about their experience of life in the church. Most of them had grown up in the Episcopal Church and many had been active in youth or campus ministries. Some were trying hard to be included in congregations that seemed oblivious to their needs and presence, others were clinging to their commitment in circumstances of rampant indifference, and more than a few had given up. But the church they had known and loved had called them together and seemed to want to listen, so they spoke with energy, candor, passion, frustration, and almost wistful affection. Their conversations were videotaped for future use. During an off-camera break one of them asked, "Now just who is this video for?" One of the organizers responded: "It's for the church—you know, parishes, dioceses...." There was a little pause. Then someone said, "Oh, for the *church,* not for us." It was not meant maliciously. It was just a remark. Another, shorter pause was followed by uncomfortable laughter. It was just a remark, but it fingered the reality they felt. And it showed that our supply of seed corn is dangerously low.

Somehow we decided that this is the way it would be. At every stage the decision has been accompanied by rationalizations and delusions, but for all that, no less firmly made. Maybe the chaplain was ineffective and so the ministry was closed, but congregations are seldom closed to get rid of an ineffective rector. Or perhaps the ministry is effective but the diocese cannot afford it. Perhaps the diocese refuses to take a hard look at its priorities and simply finds the most vulnerable ministries expendable. Perhaps the job really belongs to the congregation closest to the campus, although precious few of those congregations have shown either the willingness or the capacity for the job. Maybe we can make the position part-time or half-time or quarter-time or eighth-time; then, when we have made it impossible, we can declare it undoable. Maybe it is not so bad to have a gap in our ministry to young adults, since so many of them take a "vacation" from church anyway, yet we do not propose abandoning ministry to people in their fifties because so many of their generation are also "vacationing" from church. The Episcopal Church decided to take this course. It began as a retrenchment; it accelerated into retreat; it approaches abandonment. Whatever we did, it certainly worked. We lost the baby boomers, which makes it all the easier for us to lose Generation X. If we keep it up, the church will not have to worry about losing the next generation because there will not be any of us left.

There are some exceptions to this whole-scale abandonment. The Trinity Institute, in cooperation with campus ministries, has expanded its videoconferencing network to include many university campuses. The phenomenal success of the "Jesus at 2000" conference and the follow-up discussion on the Internet demonstrates the hunger on campus for deeply thoughtful expressions of Christianity. The Episcopal Church Foundation has funded pilot projects in campus ministry leadership. Seabury-Western Theological Seminary has implemented a curriculum in campus and young adult ministry. The Episcopal Society for Ministry in Higher Education, the Association of Episcopal Colleges, and the office of young adult and higher education ministries have begun collaboration on a churchwide event to reenergize commitment to campus ministry and lay plans for the future. National and provincial student gatherings continue to be life-changing events for many participants. There are pockets of hope in an unraveling fabric.

But now the decade of evangelism is almost over. Since its inception, Episcopal ministries with youth and young adults have continued to recede. Apparently our primary commitment is to proselytizing the already-churched and bringing back the formerly-churched—especially those approaching middle age—and equipping them with naive and mindless spiritualities that steer clear of the intellectual integrity that was once our pride and joy. It has not occurred to us that there are a couple of generations out there that we have forgotten and another that we have lost touch with. By now they are so invisible in the church that we do not even miss them. Given half a chance, they would evangelize their own and invigorate us as well. That would be good news indeed, real evangelism. But we cannot wait until they are fifty and we are dead.

While we abandon our campus ministries, parachurch organizations continue to flood the campuses with resources and staff. The campuses are being evangelized and the gospel preached—just not by us. And it is not the gospel of an overwhelmingly generous God who takes on our human life and limitation, who loves us to death, who will stop at nothing to redeem us, who delights in our bodies and our minds, who insists on justice and demands peace, who fixates on reconciliation and keeps giving and forgiving until we give up and respond. As we withdraw from the campuses we consign the rising generations to an understanding of Christianity that is cramped and confined, unsacramental, non-liturgical, and anti-intellectual. This brand of Christianity has little appreciation of history and tradition and their interplay with reason and experience, and only the most rudimentary understanding of scripture and the diversity of theology represented in the canonical writings. When the Anglican voice is most needed on the campuses, we have silenced it.

Jesus' Bar and Grille

Campus as Eucharistic Community   *Ronald H. Clingenpeel*

> There are three things that last forever: faith, hope, and love.
>
>   (1 Corinthians 13:13a)

It is Sunday evening at the campus chapel. This is the main service of the day. People stand or kneel at the altar, each with a care, a concern, a desire. Jane worries about a chemical engineering exam scheduled for the next morning. Tom and Betsy await their first child, due just before Tom graduates with a master's degree. *The Body of Christ, the bread of heaven....* Samantha, an insurance agent, is here because twenty-five years after her graduation she wants to give something back to the campus ministry. She is the cook tonight. Ralph wonders what to do now that he did not get tenure. *The Blood of Christ, the cup of salvation....* Kate wonders about getting out quickly after the service so she can get to her studies. Bill hopes his date will wait for him. Terry worries about academic probation. *The Body of Christ, the bread of heaven....* Gerald has wandered in because he heard there is free food, and he is hungry. Macy is writing a book. *The Blood of Christ, the cup of salvation....*

They gather here, bound by their common life in the academic community and their journey in Christ. They gather here because on this evening it is where they want to be. They gather here because they search for faith, for hope, and for love. They search for God. Some of them come because they were reared in the church, some because they have heard about the church through friends, and some because they responded to an ad, a poster, or a newsletter. They gather at Christ's table because the church has come to them.

Every week students, faculty, staff, and their families join to celebrate the eucharist and share in fellowship. To some this gathering may look no different from any parish church, but there is a difference. These people come from a common place and share a common outlook. They live what some consider an isolated existence, where the cares and concerns of the world are not real. Often they are told they do not know what the "real world" is like. The university is their village, and the campus ministry is their parish. Here they talk together of common matters just as farmers might do in a rural community, or steel workers in an urban parish. They also share the cares of love and relationship, fear and agony, death and grief, joy and celebration, that are experienced by every human being. They have come to the church for a variety of reasons, but without the church's presence on campus, they would have nowhere to go. Without this presence they would have no place in which to examine their faith, find hope and peace, and experience the fellowship of love.

↵ Faith

Anglicanism has long had a relationship with the academic community. From this community arose Thomas Cranmer and Richard Hooker. It was the academic community that trained scholars and missionaries like William Tyndale, George Herbert, John Henry Hobart, and James Lloyd Breck. Anglicans Dorothy Sayers and C. S. Lewis spent their lives in academia. It was the love of learning of women in religious orders like St. Mary's and St. Helena's that helped establish secondary schools for young women in various parts of the country. Because the Anglican tradition relies on a learned mind and an inquiring heart, Episcopalians also founded Columbia University, Trinity College, the University of the South, Kenyon College, St. Augustine's College, and other institutions of higher learning.

Academic communities are fundamental to the search for truth. Biologists examine the tiniest of living organisms to learn about life in general, while historians look for the truth behind events, movements, and people in ages past. Engineers learn about structures in an attempt to construct better buildings. Each discipline of the academic community seeks to learn about and better understand the world in which we live. This mix of linguistics, physics, mathematics, anthropology, and other disciplines, however, often fails to examine issues of religious faith. Few institutions incorporate it into the curriculum, so the church's involvement in the educational process seems unnatural.

Anglicans bring faith to the academic community, but not an unexamined faith. This faith is tested, questioned, and reviewed. It is a faith deepened through study and prayer. In the Episcopal Church questions are welcome because as people examine their faith and practice, they begin to see more clearly the relationship that is possible with God and with one another. Scripture, tradition, and reason form the foundation for the faith Episcopalians bring to the academic community. The eucharistic feast is the place where people practice this faith. It is a faith grounded in a historical practice that appeals to the contemporary heart. It is not sentimental but addresses everyday issues of pain and grief, joy and celebration, love and disinterest. In the eucharist people find the story of faith, as they hear the words of scripture and the ancient liturgy of the faith community.

Jane, Tom, Betsy and the others are at the eucharist because it becomes the focal point of their faith in God. It allows them to express their deepest passions.

"Cotton-candy religion" is sweet and sticky, and the American brand turns God into a kindly grandfather. Some of us are old enough to remember movies like *Going My Way* and *A Man Called Peter*. In such movies God suffers from an acute case of the "quaints," as Terry Holmes described the image of the church that many bring to college.[1] There are those in the academic community who believe that religion is little more than the sweet stickiness portrayed in movies and on television. The television show *M*A*S*H** confronted the ethical and personal dilemmas faced by doctors and nurses in a war zone, but seldom did it address religious issues. *M*A*S*H** even had a chaplain who, although he did many kind acts and faced a few dilemmas, was a bumbling and exceedingly nice guy more interested in his sister's basketball career than issues of faith and reality. In one episode he finally earns respect after performing a tracheotomy under battle conditions! Even prime-time television shows in the nineties like *ER* and *Chicago Hope* rarely raise religious issues, although they are constantly confronting life and death situations.

With these types of popular images, it is understandable that young people come to college with little regard for faith. They have no experience of it. Some may argue that those reared in the church do have some respect for religion, but we cannot assume that to be true. In *Welcome to the Jungle: The Why Behind "Generation X,"* Geoffrey T. Holtz describes the situations in which the current generation of college students were raised. He blames the baby boomers for the problems of Generation X, because one common child-rearing method was to use television as a companion.[2] If that is true, children have grown up watching television shows that ignore religious issues, present evangelists as shysters, glorify sex and violence, and act as if faith has no place in the stories of society. Students may come to college with no interest in questions of religious faith, but as they confront and investigate their areas of study many find that religion and faith are important. The church's presence on campus is critical as a sign that issues of faith are also serious and worthy of investigation.

⌁ Hope

A hit-and-run accident leaves a campus police officer dead, a student dies in an automobile accident, another student commits suicide, and the university provost resigns. A few years ago these were the front page stories of a single edition of the student newspaper of Tulane University, the *Tulane Hullaboo*. Students are mugged on their way to the local convenience store, or arrested for buying illegal drugs. A student accuses a professor of sexual misconduct. A young man and woman decide to marry, another student wins an award for an architectural design, and a poet has her work published in a major journal. The college campus is not an ivory tower. The campus is a part of the "real world," as much a part of everyday life as anywhere else.

The campus church is a place of hope—a place where people believe that no situation or person is beyond redemption. The fellowship of the campus understands issues of fraternity hazing, tenure, residence hall life, and academic intimidation. The fellowship of the campus church will examine issues of race, gender, sexuality, and social unrest. Christianity does not flinch at these issues, but embraces them as it attempts to understand God's will.

The church on campus deals with the common, everyday things of life that people face, as well as with those things distinctive to academia. The church brings the hope of the resurrection and the grace of God to every moment of campus life. Resurrection points to the hope that Christ redeems all situations and people. Overburdened by classes, exams, social commitments, meetings, and the pressure to produce, members of the campus community can find a place of rest, hope, and understanding in the church. The campus ministry can be a place of calm in the midst of desperation, where people can look for signs of hope. A student at Newcomb College wrote this note to a chaplain: "As a college student who, as most do, usually sleeps in on Sundays and whose Bible has been opened much too infrequently this semester, I greatly appreciate the bit of uplifting and inspiration that your newsletter offers. It is one of those 'little things' that helps make life special." Something as small as a weekly newsletter about campus life was a sign of hope in the midst of her routine.

Students are not the only ones who look for these signs of hope. A sense of desperation and loss often confronts faculty and staff. The daily routine can lead to a loss of purpose and direction. Research can bog down and become unproductive. Faculty can lose the enjoyment and excitement of teaching. It is the place of the church to care about those who feel dispossessed or lost. In a world that may seem hopeless, the church brings the power of the cross to bear, representing hope in the midst of despair and desperation. The church, understanding the ebb and flow of campus life, must address the things that faculty, students, and staff face daily. The cross of Christ speaks to these issues directly, and the church is the place where that interpretation takes place.

↩ Love

A young man sits alone in the cafeteria daily. Soon, he has new friends—friends who belong to a cult. It does not take long for the lonely and dispossessed on campus to be discovered. They are easy prey for cult members. The university can be a large, cold place, where people begin to feel they are nothing more than computer numbers. In the midst of such an impersonal environment, friends of any sort are welcome. Many students are looking for a place to belong, where they can learn and grow. Religious groups can be right or, in some instances, wrong. Cults work college campuses because the pressure of college life can often enhance students' negative feelings. People who are feeling extremely pressured or insecure are easy targets for cults. When there are no alternatives, students searching for fellowship and community may choose the clear answers and sense of belonging that a cult provides.

The church is a safe harbor in the storm of academic and personal turmoil. It is a place of comfort and challenge for those looking for a home. People have a need to belong to something that is larger than themselves; without it the world appears chaotic. The church provides a place for fellowship and love. At the Last Supper, Jesus commanded his disciples to eat the bread and share the cup and to love one another. Such love calls us into community. Love must bind us together to care for one another, learn from one another, and support one another. Love must break down the walls that separate us. Love must endure the shortcomings and foibles we all have. Love must respect the dignity of every human being. The fellowship of the church must reflect this love.

The need to belong is a part of each of us. In the fellowship of the eucharist we find our place. We find the love of Christ in the sacrament of the altar. The students, faculty, and staff who gather at the altar lay upon it the cares of their heart and the life of the academic community. They offer these things to God, seeking love and affirmation. They experience the God who loves them. They experience the God who does not abandon them. Instead of feeling dispossessed, they are accepted. It is too easy to get lost in the hustle of common parish life. In the campus ministry they find the Christ who meets them in the academic community. This is the God and the community of love for them.

Endnotes
1. Urban T. Holmes III, *The Priest in Community: Exploring the Roots of Ministry* (New York: Seabury Press, 1978), 11.
2. Geoffrey T. Holtz, *Welcome to the Jungle: The Why Behind "Generation X"* (New York: St. Martin's Press, 1995), 179ff.

Faith by Example

Evangelism in Secondary Schools   *Ann Gordon*

The purpose of Episcopal schools is best expressed by the late John Verdery, longtime headmaster of Wooster School, in his article, "Why Church Schools?" There Verdery clearly articulates that the one reason Episcopal schools must exist is to deal with religious values and questions of faith. No matter the age group served, all church schools are intended to be spiritual and moral communities where ethical issues are a part of the daily experience and "gospel values are presented in ways that are authentic and relevant."[1]

There are over one thousand Episcopal schools within the United States, including nursery schools, child care centers, elementary schools, middle and high schools, and boarding schools. Some are located adjacent to parish churches and are closely tied to the sponsoring congregation, while others are separately incorporated institutions that operate independently of a sponsoring church body, with the bishop's consent. The student bodies of these schools reflect a broad ethnic and religious diversity. Episcopalians are often the minority, while Christians of other denominations as well as Jews, Hindus, Muslims, and others complete the enrollment figures. Accordingly, one challenge for these schools is to maintain their Episcopal identity and ethos as they attempt to provide an atmosphere in which there is an appreciation for the diversity and values of all religious traditions and beliefs. In order to proclaim the Christian faith in a pluralistic society, it is their responsibility "to listen carefully and learn humbly from those whose perceptions of God's mystery differ from our own."[2]

Most Episcopal schools reflect their Anglican heritage through the conviction that character is formed by respecting tradition and by developing independent thought. These two emphases permeate a school's academic and religious life. There are four principal means by which Episcopal schools flesh out their church identity, the first of which is *living out the faith by example*. Every aspect of school life, including admissions, hiring policies, discipline practices, leadership, and the social, economic, racial and religious mix of the student population, is constantly measured against the standards of a *church* institution—the extent which they take seriously what Jesus took seriously.

A second means of fleshing out church identity is *situating the heart and soul of the school in the chapel.* Whether in a Gothic setting or a multipurpose room, chapel is where foundational religious education occurs in the gathering and healing of real life issues, such as the death of a student, a teacher's AIDS diagnosis, war and terrorism, cheating and fair play. *The Book of Common Prayer* and *The Book of Occasional Services* provide the basis for most of the worship services, which are frequently led and designed by students. Chapel in an Episcopal school today is intended for all students, regardless of their religious background. When gathered for worship, "there may be an African-American third grader boldly singing with an Asian high schooler, a Muslim bowing his head next to a Roman Catholic who is kneeling, a Jewish girl receiving a blessing beside an Episcopalian awaiting communion. All of them striving through their life in Episcopal schools to come to know, each in their own ways, what God looks like."[3]

In *fostering spiritual development and providing religious education,* Episcopal schools take seriously the spiritual life and spiritual formation of students. Through various religious study courses students are encouraged to talk about religious and spiritual experiences in reflective ways, fostering knowledge of a student's own religious heritage, as well as that of others. Religious education and spiritual formation are not isolated aspects of school life but are integrated throughout the curriculum, be it in the classroom, on the playing field, or in the performing arts center. For the nursery-age child stained glass windows and simple prayers provide the medium, while the primary-age child is introduced to scripture, and middle and high school students take courses on world religions and ethics. Children of all ages have an opportunity to explore and reflect upon everyone's spiritual and ethical traditions in the daily life of the school community.

Finally, *community service and outreach* are required of every student. Social ministry is a hallmark of Episcopal schools. Through service and outreach programs students are able to see the application of the moral focus of the gospel to the whole of life. Students learn to serve God by serving others, engaging in hurricane and earthquake relief, food collection and distribution, partnerships with struggling schools throughout the Anglican Communion, and in numerous other ways.

ᴗ· The Nature of Evangelism in Episcopal Schools

Episcopal schools are evangelizing institutions, but with "a ministry of attraction and nurture, not conversion," as one educator writes.[4] Typically, an Episcopal school's student body is approximately twenty-five percent Episcopalian, while the remaining seventy-five percent represents other denominations, other faiths, and the unchurched. It is evident that claiming affiliation with a denomination does not necessarily mean active participation in that church. There are a number of people who send their children to Episcopal schools but do not actually practice a faith, Episcopal or otherwise, nor do they attend church on a regular basis. The school is often the only "church" to which they or their children are exposed. Consequently, the potential for evangelism in Episcopal schools among the unchurched families and those who have lapsed from their own church origins is great. Our singular Anglican heritage of tolerance, inclusion, rigorous scholarship, and social justice obviously has great appeal and is undoubtedly the reason many people choose Episcopal education for their children in the first place. The groundwork has been laid for evangelism.

Parents today want a moral structure for their children so that they may have a sound basis for living a life that is decent and honorable. They want an intellectual foundation for their children that is stimulating and challenging. They want their children to understand and accommodate different points of view—qualities which are inherent in the multicultural society in which we live. Parents also want their children to learn firsthand Marian Wright Edelman's dictum, "Service is the rent we pay for living,"[5] by having their children participate in outreach and community service programs. They want their children exposed to some form of religious tradition, but one which respects their own religious heritage. As one Baha'i parent says of her daughter's parish day school:

> We wanted not only fine academics, but even more, we wanted a tradition and conviction reflected in the school's philosophy which was consonant with the major cornerstones of our own faith: that we are in our most fundamental essence spiritual beings; that we are all members of one human family; that God's love is present, creative, and working in our lives; and that the word of God has a transforming power on humankind, both individually and collectively.[6]

It is often in the context of worship that parents and students fully realize the openness and plurality of Anglican spirituality. Students from many religious traditions volunteer for school or chapel, taking responsibility for planning worship experiences for the school community. This student-centered approach demands the same strong commitment to excellence, tradition, and dignity that we require in parish worship committees. Peter Coman, a retired principal of an Australian Anglican school, sums up the strengths and appeal of church schools in this way:

Why have Anglicans been so successful in establishing good schools? They have always had a delight in intellectual discipline, strong worship and a strong moral framework, which is appealing in a multicultural society. Within them there is a need for gentle, persuasive evangelism; for the retention of sanctity and beauty; intelligent reading of the scriptures and disarming and non-judgmental prayer.[7]

Evangelism from the perspective of the Episcopal Church has three attributes, and they apply to Episcopal schools in the following ways. First of all, *evangelism is community oriented.* Enrolling in an Episcopal school is like joining a new family. The school community is made up of students, parents, faculty, administrators, and trustees, as well as parishioners and vestry members in the case of parish day schools, who create and share a corporate life unique to each school setting. The school family gathers for important occasions in the life of the community, encompassing those events from birth to death, as all families do, seeking God's presence in their lives. "Episcopal schools," according to educator Louise Macatee, "discover their roots deep in a tradition that views compassion as call, not as good deed, and shares such commitments with its students, instructing them in the acts of love.... This is the substance and foundation of Episcopal school community life." Another view of Christian community echoes this thought: "Faith and works go hand in hand. It is through their reciprocal grasp that a school becomes—and remains—that remarkable sort of community that we describe as a Church school."[8]

In the second place, *evangelism is an invitation to worship.* Chapel is the most obvious symbol of what makes an Episcopal school unique, framed by the discipline of community prayer and spiritual reflection about common issues. In Episcopal schools we have been given the space of time and place that we call worship, into which we bring our school community with all of its feelings, and offer them to God. The chaplain serves as teacher, preacher, and storyteller, and has the opportunity "to explain the liturgical year, the history of the Episcopal and the wider Christian church, and the relevance of the Gospel to the great issues of the day."[9] Prayers and hymns from many traditions, scripture readings, homilies, candles, crosses, and banners are important symbols which are integrated into a student's worship life through school chapel services. Through exposure to the rich Anglican liturgy, the school often serves as an instrument of conversion. To many students and their families, we are the only church they know.

Third, *evangelism is essentially pastoral.* The pastoral intention and concern of our school communities are characteristics that differentiate Episcopal schools from their public and private counterparts. In the pastoral atmosphere of a school, there is care and concern for the individual as well as for the whole community. As Louise Macatee writes, "We are drawn together by a God whose healing comes into this world not only through knowledge but also through the power of community."[10] An Episcopal school invites a student to step into a community that cares about them and seeks healing as part of a community animated by Christ's love.

Each school, whether large or small, boarding or day, interprets and refines its mission in light of its own essential character and unique experience. On the one hand, a parish day school, which is located on the same property as its sponsoring church, has more frequent opportunities to involve the church, its clergy, and parishioners in the ongoing life of the school. The school's chapel services are often held in the church and the parish clergy minister to school families in need of pastoral services. This daily interaction between the educational institution and the church becomes the basis for evangelism. As a witness to this process, a young parent, who is now an active communicant and lay minister in an Episcopal congregation in the southwest, tells her story:

> I began attending the chapel services at an Episcopal school soon after our unchurched family had relocated to a new city. My purpose for attending chapel services was straightforward: I wanted to see what kind of propaganda my daughter was receiving. I intended to attend chapel for just a couple of weeks. Instead, I found myself drawn in, as each week yet another element of the chapel service touched my heart. The children's harmonizing, as they sang Isaiah's song, brought unexpected tears. The simple goodness of the school chaplain's homily messages felt like personal invitations to become part of the good news of Christ's church. One day at the monthly chapel eucharist, during the Prayers of the People, I heard, "I ask your prayers for all who seek God, or a deeper knowledge of him. Pray that they may find and be found by him" and I felt that God had found me.

On the other hand, boarding schools provide a different approach. Here the student is the focus, and the family is absent from the day-to-day involvement and influence of the church. The boarding school's own chapel, rather than a parish church, is more likely to be the setting in which worship takes place and where student vestries take on the responsibility for planning the services, supported by the school chaplain or local clergy. During their adolescent years, students question their faith in an effort to determine what they believe. It is often the least suspecting student who, in later years, recognizes the impact and influence of the spiritual formation that can take place in an Episcopal boarding school. An excerpt from a letter written to a northeastern boarding school chaplain from a former student illustrates the point:

> For many years after I left school, I felt a conflicting set of emotions about my experience there. I had been utterly miserable and depressed, yet I always looked back on the school with great fondness. Perhaps it was just memory's "rose-tinted glasses," but I think there was a lot more to it.
>
> In the last two years, I have become a serious and studious Jew. I observe Shabbat on Friday night, attend synagogue on Saturday mornings, and attend a variety of classes on Torah and Hebrew. So what does this have to do with the school and you? A lot, I think. Though the school was to a great degree a forced, painful assimilation process for me, the grandson of an ill-educated Latvian immigrant, it was also a place of serious God-consciousness. You may not think of it in those terms, but compared to public high school and college, the school achieved a marvelous level of moral and ethical debate.
>
> I think my confusion over whether my years there were "good" or "bad" is a result of that tension. I was depressed to be at a school because I did not fit in the most basic ways. I was a Jew at a Christian institution feeling a lot of pressure to buy into something I didn't want. Yet, in retrospect, the profound spirituality I am now exploring was being nurtured back then with your excellent chapel talks.

✧ Successful Evangelism: Reports from the Field

The mission of Episcopal schools, John Verdery writes, is "not to proselytize, but simply confront the young with the importance of deciding what they believe in by letting them know, by our actions more than by our words, what we believe in."[11] Given this viewpoint, are Episcopal schools successful agents of evangelism? Information from two surveys conducted by the National Association of Episcopal Schools (NAES) would suggest an affirmative answer.

In a random sample of two hundred fifty congregations with day schools, NAES received over one hundred replies. While not statistically significant, the responses do paint a valuable picture. Participants were asked to determine how many students, parents, and faculty had entered the congregation from the school through baptism, confirmation, and/or reception over a two-year period. Nearly sixteen percent of reported parish growth was a direct result of the ministry of Episcopal parish day schools, a figure that includes teenagers and young parents and faculty members, as well as younger children.

The data about evangelism of youth and young adults in Episcopal schools are just as positive, but broader and more complex. Another survey, conducted in 1996 in day and boarding schools, while again not statistically significant, indicates there is a lively and active evangelism ministry in church schools where moral and spiritual growth, the development of personal values, and witness to the power of a religious faith are part of the daily fare. In most schools, students are required to attend chapel services, yet they are free to determine the level of their individual participation. Student involvement in chapel includes serving as acolytes, lay readers, ushers, vergers, chalice bearers, and members of the choir, generally functioning in all capacities except for those requiring sacerdotal activities. Several boarding schools of less than two hundred students reported that anywhere from sixty to one hundred students are involved in chapel program in some way.

Furthermore, a focus on the student's spiritual life and spiritual formation seems to have replaced an emphasis on religious or denominational formation, even among schools where between thirty-five and forty percent of the students are Episcopalians. School leadership, especially heads of school and chaplains, work with students to provide school chapel services that are intended for *all* students, yet, as one chaplain remarked, there is a "tremendous force for diversity, most of which is secular. We try to keep religious diversity and resist secularism."

When asked how a school can best handle religious diversity, one school chaplain responded, "by stressing the Anglican respect for all faith traditions and by dealing swiftly and proactively with all breaches of respect." The chaplain continued:

> Many students, whether Episcopal or not, take pride in our chapel services as the primary reason of what [the school] is supposed to be about as a supportive community. We would certainly have to deal harshly with anybody who was intolerant of another person's religious beliefs. I should note that there is a *mezzuzah* on the front doorpost of our chapel; most students know what it stands for and touch it as they depart after services.

The response to religious diversity in worship is varied. Many schools stand firm as Christian schools with a Christian/Episcopal form of worship, and while they may invite religious leaders from other faith traditions to participate in chapel, they do not strive to make chapel a forum for diverse religious beliefs. Others start from the Christian point of reference and include different religious concepts, such as prayers during special holy days, guest speakers from other traditions, emphasis on the commonly held tenets and values of the world's religions, and occasionally recognition and celebration of the religious practices of other faiths. One school states that it acknowledges diversity through preaching and open communion during the eucharist. While the survey sample was small, personal observation would lead to the conclusion that it is representative of most secondary Episcopal schools in fostering an attitude of maintaining the Episcopal nature of worship while making an effort to be open and inclusive of the traditions represented by its students.

Our survey also showed voluntary services, primarily morning eucharists, are held at least once a week in most school settings, and it is common to provide opportunities for students of other denominations and faiths to participate in the worship of their own tradition. This is particularly true for boarding schools where transportation to Saturday or Sunday services is made available. One of the chaplains in a large day school on the west coast is a rabbi who holds monthly Shabbat services for the school's Jewish community.

Confirmation classes are typically held once a year in boarding schools, with the number of confirmands ranging from eight to twelve each year. The survey did not indicate, however, whether these were students who would have been confirmed in their own home settings or whether they were actual converts to the Episcopal Church. Many schools also provide opportunities for informal Bible study and prayer groups, and one school schedules a weekly Torah study.

Episcopal secondary schools use many aspects of school life as avenues for evangelism. Chapel is overwhelmingly considered by the schools as the primary means of evangelizing. Religious study courses and the dialogue they encourage are considered by the chaplains as a major springboard into faith for many young people. Other effective ways are through pastoral care and counseling, strong community service and outreach programs, and the committed Christians within the school community who, by example, witness to God's presence in their lives. One boarding school chaplain voices the sentiment of many others in saying that all aspects of school life can be seen as tools for evangelism. He reminds us that evangelism happens not so much through program as through personal contact and personal example.

It follows, then, that the presence of a school chaplain is a primary source of evangelism in Episcopal schools. The crucial role of their ministry should not be underestimated; it is a ministry of *presence*. They serve as teachers, preachers, counselors, and organizers of community service and outreach. In those roles, chaplains set the standards for moral example, personal integrity, and community life, living by word and example what it means to encounter the gospel and recognize the power of God in their lives. They are a strong support for students who are learning through their own questions about their beliefs, honoring each student's spiritual journey and bearing personal witness to Christian love in action.

The spiritual development of all students is further strengthened by religious studies courses, which are often required. They encourage students to reflect on the meaning of their lives, including their ethical and spiritual values, to appreciate and respect a wide range of religious traditions, and to foster the ability to think about and discuss religious ideas in a critical, rational way. Students are nurtured by the religious faith that permeates the school community and by the way we respect our own tradition even as we include components of others in our celebrations. Issues of faith and religious observance are taken seriously as students encounter the Holy Spirit in real and human terms. Denominational lines are blurred as students put faith into practice. The student-led chapel service in one large urban high school consists of a Jewish head acolyte and a vestry comprised of Roman Catholic, Muslim, Jewish, and Episcopal students. These students are spiritually strengthened in a Christian setting where they are challenged to awake to their faith and use it to govern their behavior, attitude, and actions.

Often the seeds of faith sown in school chapels and religious studies courses do not bear immediate fruit, but sometimes they do. Stories from chaplains in Episcopal schools provide powerful examples of how they have seen students come into greater awareness of the presence of God in their lives:

> This past fall, a student asked to be baptized during chapel. She felt as if God were calling her during chapel and religious studies classes to get more involved. She had been raised outside any faith. She was baptized in a moving service in the middle of weekly chapel service. She will be confirmed in the chapel with six other students on Pentecost.

> This week I met with an alumnus to discuss his decision to seek ordination as a Presbyterian minister. He credits the school with setting him on this course.

> One of our seniors has decided to delay his college entrance for one year. God called him into a year of service with handicapped children. He will work with children who have severe disabilities. He wants to give to others before he continues his own education.

There is ample evidence that Episcopal schools perform an important ministry with young people who struggle with faith issues and who are in need of finding faith. If this is evangelism, then Episcopal schools do it well. As John Verdery comments:

> If we are winsome enough, and if God so wills it, some of our students may grow up to be devout Christians, and some even loyal members of the Episcopal Church. When that happens, so be it. When it does not, so be it.

Before curriculum revision and special sacred studies courses and liturgical reform and even missionary zeal, the word is witness.[12]

Episcopal church schools are growing and expanding at a rate not seen in thirty years. Schools are being started all over the country, from Alaska to Florida, with much of the interest centered around the middle and high school student. Episcopal schools, centers for witness and evangelism, are providing a solid formation for young women and men who will be making choices about what kind of a society we will have in the next millennium. As these schools expand the church's mission, the potential for evangelism has never been greater. The unique relationship between the Episcopal Church and its schools provide many opportunities for mutual support and shared ministry. Evangelism opportunities abound in this partnership.

Endnotes

1. John Verdery, "Why Church Schools" in *Reasons for Being: The Culture and Character of Episcopal Schools* (New York: National Association of Episcopal Schools, 1997), 3-5.

2. Resolution of the General Convention of the Episcopal Church, A060a, *Journal of the General Convention,* 1991.

3. John Merchant, "Preface," in *Worship in Episcopal Schools, (New York: National Association of Episcopal Schools, 1991 et seq.).*

4. Roger Bowen, "Opportunities for Ministry in Episcopal Schools," in *Reasons for Being,* 25.

5. Marian Wright Edelman, *The Measure of Our Success: A Letter to My Children and Yours* (Boston: Houghton Mifflin, 1992), 7.

6. Deborah Bley, "An Abiding Commitment: Reflections of a Non-Episcopal Parent," in *Church/School Relations Workbook* (New York, 1989 et seq.), 1.19

7. Peter Coman, *Values for Living in the Presence of Diversity: An Australian Approach* (Brisbane, 1997), 4.

8. Louise Macatee, "How Do We Live? The Community of Episcopal Schools," in *A Guide for Religious Education in Episcopal Schools,* (New York: National Association of Episcopal Schools, 1992 et seq.), 4.3. Brinton W. Woodward, Jr., "The School as a Christian Community," in *Reasons for Being,* 17.

9. John E. Bellamey, "The Five Senses and Holy Objects," in *Worship in Episcopal Schools,* 1.19.

10. Macatee, "How Do We Live?", in *A Guide for Religious Education,* 4.5-4.6.

11. Verdery, "Why Church Schools?", in *Reasons for Being,* 5.

12. *Ibid.*

part five

Prophetic Witness

Evangelism, Diakonia, and Young Adults

Julia Easley and John Robertson

Evangelism with young people is a privileged subject in the church today for many reasons, including anxiety about the future of the church, a genuine concern for the welfare of young people, and a desire to benefit from the culture's deepening interest in spirituality. While the church's desire to connect with young people is certainly good news, many evangelistic efforts proceed without careful reflection on what the community hopes to accomplish.

Under the heading of "evangelism with youth and young adults" congregations and dioceses seem bent upon hastily planning programs to get more people under the age of thirty to come to church. Equating evangelism with church growth is not new, nor is it without merit. But evangelizing for the primary purpose of recruitment is the result of (and results in) a limited understanding of the ministry of evangelism and of the gospel it seeks, and we seek, to proclaim. While understandable, it cannot and should not be the goal of evangelism, for "the struggle of the Christians to grow in grace is radically different from this struggle of any group of Christians to grow fatter."[1] If growing fatter is not our incentive for evangelizing young people, then what is the motivation? Similarly, what can the church hope to accomplish through its evangelization of young people?

While the concept of evangelism means different things, many of us would agree that to evangelize involves doing two things: proclaiming and inviting. Evangelists proclaim the gospel, the good news of Christ. As Jesus said when he read in the synagogue from the prophet Isaiah:

> The Spirit of the Lord is upon me,
> because he has anointed me
>   to bring good news to the poor.
> He has sent me to proclaim
> release to the captives
>   and recovery of sight to the blind,
>   to let the oppressed go free,
> to proclaim the year of the Lord's favor. (Luke 4:18)

Evangelists proclaim the good news that God loves those who grieve, who are afflicted, who are brokenhearted, who are captive, and who are in prison. It is a promise of consolation, liberation, and abundance. When Jesus proclaimed the good news, those who listened to him were amazed (Luke 4:22). Similarly, the evangelist's proclamation of the gospel must evoke a reaction. Merely showing up, speaking the words, and letting it go at that is not enough. Such evangelism can actually be an evasion, wrote Terry Holmes, if we do not try to persuade our hearers as effectively as we can.[2] The importance of persuasion is not for the sake of increasing membership in one or another denomination, nor is it to uphold a set of doctrines or codes. Rather, evangelistic persuasion endeavors to let the good news capture the listener's imagination. If the hearer of the good news has become involved with the story, even in small ways, the evangelist has the opportunity to perform the second task of inviting the listener to respond to what has been heard.

When Jesus proclaimed the gospel, his invitation was to "repent, and believe in the good news" (Mark 1:15). We usually associate repentance with regret and shame, with feelings of sorrow and remorse for our sins, but the concept is much broader. A more complete and accurate understanding of repentance lies in its synonym, "conversion," which means "to turn around." As such, interpreting the call to repentance as a summons to conversion rightly establishes as the focus of Jesus' invitation the changing of people's hearts and minds. The biblical understanding of conversion means primarily one thing. It is turning to God, a process of living into a new relationship with the Holy One, as Orlando Costas describes:

> This process, which has a distinct although not consciously uniform beginning, implies a constant turning from the self to God. In turning to God…[women and men] are reconciled to the true source of life and are renewed in their vocation.[3]

Jesus' call to repentance, to conversion, therefore, is an offer of reconciliation and renewal. Following his example, the evangelist invites the gospel's listener to join a new creation and be renewed in a new life in the Spirit of Christ (2 Corinthians 5:17).

⌁ A Community of Disciples

The promised new creation in turn entails the creation of a community, in the full sense of the word, of those who believe in the good news. It is therefore the church as community, not the church as institution. As Kortright Davis notes:

We might well be on a better track if we were to think of the church more in terms of a community of response, a community that has accepted a new and special relationship with God through Christ.[4]

This community of believers is gathered with Christ in its midst and serves as a sign of hope in a world preoccupied with despair.

Jesus also sent his followers into the world to make disciples. Making disciples was the mission; baptizing and teaching was the method. In the Great Commission he told his followers,

"Go therefore and make disciples of all nations, baptizing them in the name of the Father and of the Son and of the Holy Spirit, and teaching them to obey everything that I have commanded you" (Matthew 28:19-20). The invitation to conversion, therefore, also calls people into communion with one another with one goal in mind: a new life as disciples in Christ.

The essence of Jesus' teaching is summed up in the two great commandments to love God with all our hearts and to love our neighbors as ourselves. With this he called a new community of believers who were to love God and one another with every part of their being: with their hearts and souls and minds and bodies. By teaching and example, Jesus expected his disciples to love in both word and deed. Loving God and neighbor, therefore, was no abstraction but a mandate for specific action reflecting the kind of love the disciples received from God and knew through Christ.

The primary image for the love Jesus modeled to his followers was that of a servant. "The greatest among you must become like the youngest," he taught them, "and the leader like one who serves. For who is greater, the one who is at the table or the one who serves? Is it not the one who is at the table? But I am among you as one who serves" (Luke 22:26-27). The Greek word for service is *diakonia,* which means to care for and provide for the needs of others. When Jesus commanded his disciples to love, he intended them to engage in a ministry of *diakonia,* loving, caring for, and providing for those in need. The evangelist, as a disciple sent to make disciples, invites the hearers of the gospel to love God and neighbor by becoming a servant: providing food for the hungry, dispensing drink for the thirsty, welcoming the stranger, clothing the naked, and comforting the sick and imprisoned (Matthew 25:31-46).

In most contexts, service is done for some "greater" good. Doing good works provides a benefit. Social workers teach so that clients will learn. Physicians treat so that patients will heal. Agencies get funded so that circumstances will improve. But in the Christian context, service is "complete in itself, the proclaimed message of concrete deeds. *Diakonia* does not need any justification other than that of offering a gift of love for the sake of God's love."[5] Christians live out Jesus' teaching not in order to make a better world, although such is certain to occur, but because living out Christ's commandments is *in itself* valuable and good.

These are the basic principles of evangelism. Evangelists do two things. First, they proclaim the gospel, the good news that God loves the sorrowful, the poor, the persecuted, and the imprisoned. Second, they invite the hearers of the good news to respond by turning to God through repentance as conversion, by gathering in and creating community with others, and by serving those in need. This is the essence of evangelism: the establishment of a community of people who are converted to a new life in the Spirit of Christ and who are committed to serving those in need. We evangelize not to grow fatter, but to serve.

✌ The Lives of Young Adults

Young people today, especially those of college age, are far different from the images with which they are popularly portrayed. In contrast to the pervasive indifference often attributed to Generation X, most young people are quite attuned to the world around them and have a keen desire to contribute to society, with all its problems and challenges. Their hopes and dreams, their fears and anxieties, and their wants and needs mirror those of earlier generations. This is not to say that young adults today are simply less experienced versions of their elders. People in their late teens and twenties encounter a world which is radically different from any encountered before. Their reality is not a repeat of the sixties, nor is it, as some would hope, a nostalgic reincarnation of the mythical fifties.

Instead, the world of today's young adults is one of drastic and constant change and reorientation. Technology, especially information technology, has radically revolutionized the way people communicate and make sense of their lives. A strange economics of scarcity for most and abundance for some permeates the culture, while for the first time in a long while the prospect of finding work that is both a means to survive and to thrive seems increasingly remote. In America, they are the first generation that may fail to improve its standard of living over the previous generation. Meanwhile, the shadow of the HIV/AIDS epidemic leaves many young people to the task of trying to find meaningful relationships without a road map to lead the way. The complexity of social, political, and economic conflict in neighborhoods and nations around the globe threatens their hope for a peaceful world.

Having been bombarded from birth by the sounds and images of a consumer-oriented and heavily marketed capitalistic society dominated by the ethics of power and greed, young people often appear both more cynical toward and more amenable to quick gratification and the promise of escape. Having been constantly exposed to the skills of advertisers and the market, young adults in their twenties often view *any* exhortation as a form of manipulation. Similarly, having been reared with easy access to innumerable theories, criticisms, and interest group rhetoric, young people tend to shut out such discourse in favor of the seemingly more mundane issues of daily life and activity.

There is, however, more good news here than bad. Living in this loud and changing world, young people possess a set of skills many of their elders do not and never will possess. In the presence of competing schools of thought, most young people have the ability to recognize and tolerate differing and mutually exclusive perspectives. Young people also do not easily swallow claims of ultimate truth and authority. When confronted with such notions, they recognize the shaky foundations upon which those kinds of claims often, if not usually, rest. They see these epistemological ideas as necessary uncertainties, and therefore retain a certain kind of humility regarding the issues previous generations could not yield upon. In the face of the pressures and cynicism contemporary society creates and exudes, young people not only retain their openness but also continue to seek answers and meaning.

The religious lives of young adults are also distinguished from those of previous generations. Many young people profess an interest in deepening their spirituality, but few identify with any particular faith community. Some continue to hold Christian beliefs and evidence the values of the gospel, but do not subscribe to any particular doctrine or creed. Many criticize the church for being irrelevant, and some report negative experiences in church. Most who identify themselves as Christians do not regularly attend services. When pressed, they cannot bring together what the world around them accepts as the nature of reality with their religious training. They neither experience the kinds of miracles reported in the Bible or by television evangelists, nor do they believe most of the ontological claims upon which the church traditionally rests.

Whether this is fortunate or unfortunate remains to be seen. It is also beside the point. Any community, gathered for whatever purpose, reflects the realities of its experience. From these experiences arise a community's concerns, skills, needs, and perspectives on life. This is as true now as in the past. Consequently, the young people whom evangelists hope to call to Jesus bring with them an acute awareness of a radically changing world, a sophistication in processing and communicating their experiences, a healthy impatience with simplistic answers to complex issues, and a perspective that church attendance is not the only measure of one's commitment to a deepening spirituality.

∿ Evangelism with Young Adults

The problem for young adults who are being evangelized is that as a group they are too sophisticated and skeptical about overt teaching and preaching. The problem for the church is that it is often too stuck in its own allegiance to God-talk to recognize this. Consequently, the more the church talks about Jesus, the more young adults hear a call to say and perhaps even believe certain words, to deny the dissonance that exists between traditional religious tenets and scientific "reality," and to be good churchgoing Christians at all costs. The result of this is often twofold: the first yields unconverted and unfulfilled young adults continuing to seek spiritual meaning, and the second entails hand-wringing and chest-beating by the church at the failure of the people to truly accept the message of Christ and salvation.

The church's goal for proclaiming the gospel to youth and young adults is not to make little Episcopalians. Its hope ought to be much larger and prophetic: the gathering of young people into a Christian community for the purpose of serving the poor, the persecuted, and those in any need or trouble. "By this everyone will know that you are my disciples, if you have love for one another" (John 13:35). To create such a community requires an approach and sophistication dictated by the social context young adults live within now.

What Jesus expects from us is an evangelism of love. From there the needs of the people are met through the ministries of his disciples. To meet the needs of young adults (or anyone else) who may not at first want to hear the Bible but still desire and require a deepening of their spiritual selves, effective evangelism demands an acceptance of the validity of those individuals as they truly exist in the day-to-day world. By responding to young people's concerns about finding meaning in a radically shifting universe, by attending to their desires for a sense of peace and purpose in a reality where truth is rarely clear, and most important, by demonstrating a deep and open faith that not only countenances but embraces the vast uncertainties of a God-created world approaching its third millennium, effective evangelism can occur and thrive.

Imagine, first, that the Spirit of Christ continues to exist in the contemporary world as much as it did in the first millennium. Imagine, also, that world itself, with all its fluidity and competing realities, is as God-given as the world of Eden. Imagine, finally, that God's magic fills and engenders the reality young adults now possess. If true, then God clearly also continues to call the church to respond effectively in fulfilling Christ's commandment of service in love within such a world.

If the language of the church fails to reach its audience, perhaps God's call nowadays involves less of that kind of talk and more examples of a genuine

Christian life in service *for its own sake*. At least for young adults, this means not worrying for the time being about the Nicene Creed and instead worrying that people are fed and nurtured, served and accepted, valued and acknowledged. The language and activity of Christian service in such a context is not necessarily startling or exciting. It appears, instead, in the creation of a community whose mission is to create both a warm breakfast and a good conversation for the homeless and a few hours each week of work and selflessness for college students seeking an endeavor geared solely toward meeting the needs of others. It appears in the creation of a prayer group that just as easily finds itself chatting about the frustrations of the lack of jobs for art historians as it does reading biblical texts or seeing the film *Jesus of Montreal*. And it appears in a twenty-year-old's realization and acceptance of the fact that she is a lesbian, as well as in the joyful realization that a graduate student determines himself called to the priesthood.

Evangelism as Christian service is demonstrated as effectively in the acceptance that twenty-somethings on a college ministry retreat *will* sneak out of the retreat center and head for the nearest bar as it is in the acceptance that the same group is just as likely to insist upon morning prayer the next day. Evangelism as Christian service is demonstrated as effectively on the back of a Harley-Davidson or the display of a new tattoo as it is in full vestments or a double-breasted suit. Evangelism as Christian service is as effective in the creation of a lay hospital visitation ministry, whose members may only vaguely realize its church connection, as it is in the creation of a eucharistic mission group devoted to incense and sacraments.

If it is the case that God calls us to evangelism in Christian service to young adults, and if those same young adults have less desire for an education about the core doctrines of Christian faith than for living examples of how Christlike people look and act, then effective evangelism accepts reality where it stands. For people in college who are just beginning their adult lives, this is exactly the reality that challenges us today. And, as members of a community that accepts without question the evangelical call to minister to this particular portion of God's creation, we have little choice but to also accept, not only without complaint but with joy, hope, and excitement, the responsibility for making that ministry succeed and thrive. Such an endeavor may or may not fill an empty pew. No matter. The call lies not there, but in the demonstration of Christian love through *diakonia*, which is its own reward.

Endnotes

1. Kortright Davis, "Can Mission and Church Be Integrated?", in *Crossroads are for Meeting: Essays on the Mission and Common Life of the Church in a Global Society*, ed. Philip Turner and Frank Sugeno (New York: The Society for Promoting Christian Knowledge, 1986), 122.

2. Urban T. Holmes III, *Turning to Christ: A Theology of Renewal and Evangelization* (New York: The Seabury Press, 1981), 144.

3. Orlando E. Costas, *Liberating News: A Theology of Contextual Evangelization* (Grand Rapids, Mich.: William B. Eerdmans Publishing Co., 1989), 114.

4. Davis, "Can Mission and Church Be Integrated?", in *Crossroads,* 117.

5. Costas, *Liberating News,* 140-141.

Prophetic Witness and Worship with Students
Steven Charleston

Here is a very simple "true or false" question about college students. Most students attending undergraduate colleges or universities do not attend worship services on a regular basis. True or false?

If you answered "true," you are probably right. I say probably because it is not my intention to offer the results of a scientific survey to support this opinion, but rather to speak to the practical experience of scores of ministers who work in undergraduate communities. The fact that most college students would rather sleep in on a Sunday morning than attend worship is something of a truism, if not a proven sociological fact. Of course, there are exceptions to the rule. There are some colleges that are intentionally identified with a religious community where students are much more likely to attend worship, and there are always core groups of highly motivated students who attend services even in the face of negative peer pressure. But for the majority of young people in both private and public universities or colleges, consistent participation in public worship is uncommon.

If we accept this simple premise, then we can begin to wonder why it is true. For example, we might say that college students do not attend worship because they are exercising a new freedom from parental supervision and expectations. We might also point to negative peer pressure, illustrating how the group dynamic to conform to a secular standard affects even those students who might otherwise define themselves as "religious." We could even analyze those worship opportunities offered to students, especially the ones that students describe as "boring" and "irrelevant." In fact, all three of these approaches offer valuable clues for us to follow. They contain elements of that truism we are investigating. But before we focus on any single clue, it might be worthwhile to examine the larger picture they present to us about worship life among college youth.

✂ Disorganized Religion
Over all, students seem to be voting with their feet. They are not attending public worship because of a variety of factors, but the fundamental point is that public

worship as an experience is not sufficiently persuasive, attractive, or engaging to overcome the desire to stay away. Whatever is lacking in it from the student perspective is lacking to such a degree that the greatest number of young men and women prefer to remain uninvolved.

This reality has prompted some observers to conclude that college students are disinterested in religion, or to be more precise, in *organized* religion. In a way, this has become another truism for our culture: college-age students find traditional, institutional forms of religion completely outdated. The conspicuous absence of these young people during worship is seen as a kind of prooftext for the failure of organized religion to adapt to contemporary realities. The church, synagogue, and mosque are implicitly assumed to be out of step with youth. In response, the attempts to modernize worship and bring it up to speed for the tastes of the "infotainment generation" are characterized as either cutting edge or silly, depending on the bias of the critic.

However, before we accept these truisms about student attitudes and organized religion's responses, we need to consider a separate piece of puzzling evidence that seems to contradict the stereotype of college students as spiritually lazy or materialistically self-absorbed. Consider this: while few students attend formal worship on a regular basis, an increasing number volunteer for community service programs. If our churches, synagogues, and mosques have a dearth of students, our civic action programs have a growing resource of student volunteers. The significance of student volunteerism can be highlighted in comparison to public worship. While students may seem disinclined to make public affirmations of their personal faith in corporate worship settings, they are very inspired to make public commitments to help others. Even more important, they make these commitments at considerable personal sacrifice. Given the demands on their time, not only for academic reasons but also for their own social needs, students seem even more willing to offer their limited time than other segments of the population. In addition, they work in challenging settings, such as children's hospitals and shelters for the homeless, where the emotional engagement of their work can be intense.

If students do distance themselves from organized religion as expressed in public worship, then they embrace *disorganized* religion as embodied in selfless acts of public service. Please understand that my use of the word implies no qualitative value judgment at all. By disorganized I simply mean religious expression that is carried out without reference to specific liturgies or creeds. While serving others as a volunteer is a highly ethical act, there is no intentional identification with a particular liturgy; there is no naming of the sacred as such and no need to make an affirmation of it in front of others; there are no clergy involved except as co-workers on a volunteer basis. This disorganized shape of religion allows participation with a very genuine commitment complete with a rich sense of ethical and moral content, but does not identify the person with a set creed, tradition, or institution. It is a generic form of "religion" open to all persons, even those who would disqualify themselves from any religious community.

When college students are viewed from this perspective, we suddenly find ourselves in a position to make an astonishing claim on their behalf: young men and women undergraduates, who serve so faithfully as volunteers, are clearly among the most "religious" people in the United States. There are not many other members of our society who can match them in sacrificial commitment.

✙ The Prophetic Surprise

As hopeful as this perception of college-going young Americans may seem, there is, of course, a catch. While the term "religious" can be used as a kind of semantic umbrella to cover student participation in community service, it still does so without the student's own permission or acceptance. Some students may be more conscious of exercising a "religious" impulse in their volunteerism than others; most might be surprised to find themselves described as "religious" because they seek to help others. It is much more likely that students would categorize their actions as being humanitarian, ethical, or simply "the right thing to do," rather than as a conscious extension of their faith. Making the connection between worship and witness as twin expressions of a religious faith is what still seems to be missing for the majority of young men and women on campus. Furthermore, I would suggest that making that connection (or, to be even more precise, helping people make it for themselves in their own way) is exactly the job description of the college chaplain.

While admittedly I am using some linguistic shorthand for the sake of space, I do need to be clear about what we mean by *worship* and *witness*. By worship I mean the *public affirmation of a personal faith* in community with others who share the same religious commitment. By witness I mean the *personal affirmation of a public act* in community with others who may or may not share similar religious beliefs.

With these two ideas in mind, we are ready to name the process which connects these two interrelated aspects of a conscious religious life. *Evangelism* is the process of self-discovery by which an individual comes to recognize that both worship and witness are integral parts of a unified whole. When a man or a woman truly integrates both elements into his or her life, then two things occur: worship is seen as an extension of witness, and witness is seen as an extension of worship. Like yin and yang, the two are held in the ethical equilibrium we call religion. The private affirmation of the motivation behind public acts of compassion (which may only be known to the person who does them) becomes the public affirmation of a faith that can be shared, examined, and defined.

The organizational principle of religion, seen in this way, has nothing to do with institutions, but rather with the maturing of faith that only occurs when that faith is open to examination, to definition, and to shared critique. Making the connection, therefore, between worship and witness is crucial. For the self-discovery to occur, some spark of recognition must pass between these two elements. At some moment, the person must become conscious that the motivation for acts of love arises from some source of deeply held conviction. While we may speak of "random acts of kindness," these acts, in reality, do not emerge from a random game of ethical chance. Instead, they are intimately tied to a person's whole matrix of values and traditions. Evangelism is the process (sometimes sudden, sometimes slow) by which the intentional bridge is made between a conscious desire to share love and an equally conscious reflection on the source of that love. And it is my contention that this electric moment, so central to the development of religious faith, is what we need to describe as being truly *prophetic*.

Unfortunately, a great deal of what passes for "prophetic" in the life of the contemporary church is only partisan. There is a big difference. Whenever a religious politician of any cause or special interest proclaims some strident aspect of the party line, he or she is often described as "prophetic." However, what I am trying to disclose in this discussion is something entirely different. If evangelism is a process of self-discovery, then what is discovered is the prophetic connection between what a person believes and what a person does. The prophetic is the moment of that discovery, of that recognition. It is when the linkage is revealed and two things that were thought to be separate are suddenly found to be intimately related. The prophetic surprise that embodies true evangelism is the joyous awareness that life is not disjointed between worship and witness, but rather an active balance between the two that energizes life and gives it a sense of purpose.

⌀ Prophetic Worship

The fundamental issue for ministry with college students is this: without the balance of a regular worship experience, these young men and women are being denied the prophetic possibility of making vital connections between what they believe and what they do. One-half of the equation is missing. Consequently, as Christian ministers, we cannot be cavalier about the absence of students from participation in worship. We cannot merely dismiss this situation as a harmless given, a cultural "truism" for their age and interest level. To do so not only would denigrate the central value of worship itself in human development and intellectual growth, but it would acquiesce to consigning a generation of adults to a stunted religious life.

Worship, the public affirmation of personal faith in community, is the reflective action that completes the circle of witness, the equally public act of commitment to the ideal of community. If the circle is broken, then worship becomes a meaningless ritual and witness becomes a diminished form of charity. Restoring worship, therefore, to its proper balance with witness is the great opportunity in campus ministry. The good news is students are already upholding their side of the equation through increased participation in community service. They are clearly making a witness. The fact that this witness is *disorganized* religious expression is no cause for concern unless we abrogate our responsibility as agents of organized religion in giving them a meaningful opportunity to reflect on their actions in community with others who share the same values or traditions. That is our job.

The question, of course, is how we fulfill that job. How do we help students enter into the process of self-discovery through worship that genuinely invites them to make prophetic connections for themselves? Answering that question is the task of chaplaincies in conversation with the communities they serve. Consequently, the answers are likely to take many forms, depending on the nature of the school, the makeup of the student body, the context of the local environment, and the variety of religious traditions involved. Even so, we can offer one general principle that can establish a guideline for the future of worship on our campuses: to be effective and to be a catalyst, the worship experience must be prophetic in the way in which we have been using that word.

Prophetic does not mean partisan. Consequently, prophetic worship is not automatically worship with an agenda. It does not have to be aimed only at social issues of the day in order to appear relevant to students. Nor does it necessarily have to be contemporary in form; very traditional elements may serve the prophetic process far better than the newer inventions of postmodern culture. In addition, truly prophetic worship may be grounded in one form of organized religion, specific to one tradition, but it can be just as effective by being grounded in disorganized religion, inclusive of all traditions. The shape of the liturgy can be dictated by circumstance and purpose, as long as the result is designed to promote the prophetic response.

In the end, the goal must be to confront students with the prophetic challenge of life. Worship, in this style, is not comfortable or even predictable. In fact, it may be unsettling and emotional. It may just as easily be comforting and supportive. The demand of the worship experience upon the conscience, the expectations, and the emotions of the participants will shift along the spectrum already laid out by their own actions and commitments in service to some ideal and some community outside themselves. For students who have made these commitments to a broad degree, worship may offer a wide range of prophetic possibilities. For other students with more limited encounters or a more narrow vision of community, worship may simply be an introduction to broader horizons of thought and action. It may affirm the witness already being made by the first type of student, while challenging the witness that is still being formed by the second. There really is no need to expect worship to be regimented in its effects on the persons involved; the important thing is for the prophetic process to begin under their ownership.

To be authentic, the prophetic process has to originate spontaneously within the human spirit. Furthermore, the catalyst must be the kind of experience that draws deeply on a person's own core beliefs in order to connect them consciously to the world around them. Worship and witness must be set in motion as a dynamic process of self-discovery under the direction of the human spirit. Then there is a real chance for someone to find a pattern of action and response that not only makes sense, but that can be sustained through a lifetime. When this is achieved, life ceases to be a series of random acts, even random acts of kindness, and starts to become a conscious relationship between the believer and the believed, the giver and the recipient, the lover and the beloved. A connection is made, a process is begun, and a human life is both defined and enriched.

✧ Conclusions

I believe there are three conclusions we can reach from this brief discussion of college students and worship. First, we have to take this situation seriously and not just assume that it is a "truism" that college students do not go to worship. The reasons they may not participate are varied, but the results are the same: these young men and women are being denied the opportunity to make some of the most important connections in their whole lives.

Second, we ought to see student activism and volunteerism for what they are: clear signals of a deeper religious impulse that is sincere but unfocused. The goal is not to "organize" religion for students, but rather, to invite them to organize reality for themselves as a conscious process of action-reflection. This process is not evangelism for the sake of recruiting students into a denomination, but evangelism in the true sense of that word: the critical moments of self-discovery that mature, enrich, and sustain the human spirit, whatever denomination or tradition the person chooses to embrace.

Finally, we must make liturgical renewal and reform a priority for ministry with young people. It is time to put as much energy into the creation of prophetic worship as we do into the maintenance of parish worship.

Beyond Traditional Models of Youth Ministry

Charles Virga

Recently someone told me about the theory put forth by a biblical scholar that Jesus had a twin brother named Judas (not Judas Iscariot). Both Jesus and his brother were involved in ministry together and often were mistaken for each other. I thought it was an interesting and amusing idea, but I forgot all about it until I heard a story told by a Baptist minister at a local clergy association meeting in the town where I live in Massachusetts. He read aloud the story in Luke 2:1-20 of the angels appearing to the shepherds, announcing the birth of Jesus, and commented that the shepherds acted "out of character" when they left their flocks and went out to announce what they had been told by the angels. The pastor went on to connect this biblical account to a news story about a school district in the United States that will not permit its school bus drivers to wish their student riders a Merry Christmas.

"How outrageous!" my colleague exclaimed. "What has this country come to when we cannot announce the coming of Jesus Christ to everyone with the same pride and joy as the shepherds did two thousand years ago?" I sat back and thought, "Maybe the guy who told me the other story was right. Jesus did have a twin brother: We just worship and believe in two different brothers. How else could we think so differently?"

After the minister shared his reflection, I told my colleague that I disagreed with him and thought the school district was correct. He responded that he was amazed that a Christian and a priest of a Christian church could take such a position. Uncomfortable with the rising tension in the room, the chairperson of the association stepped in and said that since we come from various perspectives in our approaches to our theological positions, it is natural that we will disagree sometimes. Certainly this is true, but there is another question to be considered. The real difference is in our priorities. What matters more, the needs of the institutional church or the needs of the children on the bus? This distinction in priorities, I believe, is at the very core of the distinction between our two theological perspectives and an important consideration when reflecting on ministry with young people.

The Jesus Christ I worship and want to share and invite others to know is the Jesus Christ who is more concerned with the life and pain of humanity than with the glorification of the church. Only one Jesus was crucified by putting others first. He is my God and Savior. He is the one who gives me through his example a theology and a way of constructing that theology that begins with concern for the needs of people most at risk. This theological construction of whose needs come first has enormous implications for the way that we, as ministers of the gospel, minister and evangelize. When we put the needs of the church first, we inevitably construct a personal christology that runs the enormous risk of taking our narrow views and recruiting others into the service of our own personal or institutional agendas. When the "other" comes first, at least we have a built-in corrective: first we have to listen to what the other needs and has to say, and then expand our own vision of life and faith in order to incorporate that reality into our lives.

↶ The Traditional Model of Youth Ministry

Let me begin by stating that, as one who has done "traditional" youth ministry for many years, I know that this form of youth ministry can be very effective and important in the lives of many young people. Traditional youth ministry has four essential components: invitation, community, pedagogy, and action. I will describe each one briefly in turn.

> ↶ *Invitation.* Here we address the basic needs of young people, including their need for love, security, skills, well-being, enlightenment, power, justice, and respect.

> ↶ *Community.* We develop a community of other adults and friends to meet these needs, since no one person can or should meet the needs of all young people. This is the basis for a thriving Christian community and a good core for evangelism.

> ↶ *Pedagogy.* This includes instruction in faith and teaching about Jesus Christ and the gospel. Before young people can understand the love of God or God's forgiveness and caring, they must experience it first. Only then can they understand what the gospel really means. It is here in the context of the community, built on caring for each other's needs, that young people start to understand the gospel in new ways.

> ↶ *Action.* Here we call young people to live out this faith in action. Social service allows young people and the community that they have developed to grow in their understanding of Christ's teachings and move beyond themselves and their own needs into meaningful encounter with others.

None of the four components in this traditional model exists independently of the others. Meeting basic needs without the development of community or the development of community without social service will only fail. Each component of youth ministry requires attention to the other three. It does not matter so much where the youth minister begins, but if a youth program is to succeed, it requires the development of all four components.

If this model of youth ministry really works, and we can establish a context in which young people can hear and accept Christ, why is that not enough? Why would we want to change anything? These are the appropriate questions to ask only when institutional needs come first. When the needs of young people come first, however, then we must ask a different set of questions. The absence of many young people from our congregations, and the pain of millions of young people not served by our youth ministry programs becomes our priority. You may ask, wouldn't we have the same result if we did put the church first, since Christ is the source of our commitment? By way of reply I would say that experience has demonstrated that the results of such a theology are limited and do not work to the benefit of many young people at risk.

✌ The Status of Young People in the United States
In a report prepared for the 1994 General Convention of the Episcopal Church by the Standing Commission on Human Affairs, the commission reported on the condition of youth in our society.[1] The commission, drawing upon statistics from the Children's Defense Fund and the Carnegie Counsel on Adolescent Development, stated that young people today face obstacles that place them at risk in ways that young people never had to confront in the history of our country. These obstacles include:

> ✌ *Family:* The breakdown of household units because of divorce and birth out of wedlock.

> ✌ *Sexuality:* Statistics demonstrate that a million teenagers between the ages of eighteen and nineteen get pregnant each year, indicating a high incidence of sexual activity and the risk of HIV/AIDS and other STDs when young people are engaging in unprotected sexual activity. The latest growing age group of those being diagnosed with AIDS is twenty- to twenty-nine-years-old.

> ✌ *Homosexuality and Suicide:* The condemnation of homosexuality and subsequent alienation from home and parents causes high rates of attempted suicide among gay and lesbian youth. The report states that thirty percent of youth suicides are committed by gay and lesbian youth annually.

> ✌ *Poverty:* One in five young adolescents age ten to fifteen lives in poverty. As estimated, twenty-five million children are among the homeless in the

United States, with an added twelve million children without health insurance.

∽ *"Isms":* Racism, classism, and sexism are underlying factors in the circumstances that place youth at risk. Poor education, low paying jobs, and outright discrimination contribute to poverty, homophobia, and internalized racism that are such a part of the lives of youth of color. Youth in the lower economic classes, young women, gay men, and lesbian women are doubly and triply at risk.

Youth ministers from all denominations are aware of the issues and dangers confronting youth today in the United States. Yet, when asked in a recent Search Institute poll "What are the most important goals of your youth ministry?" nearly ninety percent of respondents listed, "To nurture faith in the daily decisions of young people" and "To keep youth involved in their congregation." Even the goal "To provide a safe place" was restricted to members of their own congregation or immediate neighborhoods. These goals ranked at the top of the list, while the goal of "reaching out to youth at risk" ranked in the lower half of the list.[2]

In addition, the Carnegie Study on Adolescent Development further confirmed that while youth ministry specialists generally agree that reaching at-risk youth should move up as a priority, for the most part religious organizations are not undertaking that work with any seriousness. The report states that the failure of many denominations to reach youth at risk is particularly compelling in the light of research indicating that religious participation and values often serve as protective factors against high risk behavior. Religious organizations have both the facilities and volunteers needed to provide more extensive youth programs, but they do not do so. The challenge then, states the report, is that religious organizations need to reach low-income urban adolescents, adolescents of color, and adolescents living in high risk environments.[3]

While the Carnegie Institute recognizes this failure of religious organizations to address and include the needs of youth at risk, their challenge is quite naive. For example, if we return to the Search Institute poll of the youth ministers who did name "serving youth at risk" as a goal, only nine percent of these youth ministers felt that they were adequately trained in doing a good job meeting this goal. But much more telling is that when they were later asked what kind of training they felt they needed most, ninety-three percent put "nurturing spiritual growth of youth" as their chief priority and placed the goal of "increasing the congregation's involvement in the community on behalf of youth" next to last.[4]

I believe that youth ministry in the United States is in captivity to the very forces that work against youth in this country in general—that is, racism, sexism, classism, homophobia, and other forms of oppression. If religious organizations and their youth ministry programs are to address the physical and spiritual needs of young people, including youth at risk, it will require a transformation of will and priorities. The forces that work against young people are so overwhelming that youth ministers no longer have the luxury of placing spiritual development as their number one priority without its being understood and undertaken beneath the larger umbrella of social justice. Goals that address the needs of youth at risk can no longer be a last priority, but must be woven into the fabric of all the goals of our ministry. They should hold all other goals accountable to this standard.

✓ Moving Beyond the Traditional Model

Consequently, those committed to moving beyond the traditional four-part model of youth ministry described above to one that responds to the needs of young people at risk will have to do some hard work. They will have to take seriously the structures of society and the importance of social analysis. They must ask and respond to questions that help transform this model if they are to be congruent with the message of Jesus Christ, who died on the cross that the marginalized and the oppressed would come first. Jesus was interested in everyone, loved young people in a special way, and despised the abuse of power in all of its manifestations.

To cooperate with this vision for youth ministry we will need to *extend* our traditional model by adding some new elements to the four components discussed earlier.

- ✓ In the *invitation* to address all the basic needs of young people, we must add the following question: *Who is invited? Who is not, and why?*
- ✓ In the building of *community*, we must constantly ask: *Who is in power? Who is powerless?* And we must constantly analyze: *What kind of power relationships are developing?*
- ✓ In our *pedagogy* we must ask: *Whose experience is valued? Who comes first? Whose experience is ignored and devalued?*
- ✓ In taking *action*, we need to move beyond social service to social action, all the while asking: *What kind of change are we striving for? Who benefits? Who gains and who loses from this change?*

The addition of these transformational questions to youth ministry's four traditional components will hold it accountable to the demands of social justice and ensure that all needs of all young people are addressed. It will also help prevent youth ministry from becoming captive to the status quo. Moreover, this transformational approach can offer us the possibility of creating a new vision and action plan for youth ministry that is more consistent with the prophetic tradition.

To pay attention and incorporate transformational questions and responses into our work with young people offers exciting and liberating possibilities for doing youth ministry in the twenty-first century. In the first place, youth ministry now has the potential of being truly *inclusive*. When we address the basic needs of those who are absent, we are reminded that we have before us an incomplete image of the whole, like holding up a broken mirror. These questions inspire in us a certain restlessness that drives us to complete the picture rather settling for limited success.

Second, in the building of community, ministry that confronts the issue of *power and empowerment* can move between faith and politics. It can create sacred space that helps fund the vision of the reign of God on earth.

Third, in our pedagogy, our teaching and instruction in faith will begin at a new starting point and have a different agenda: we will move from a model of personal conversion to a model of *social conversion*. This model develops an understanding that I cannot have a relationship with the Christ of justice without solidarity with my brothers and sisters with whom I am in community. We can move beyond a youth ministry in which the more privilege one has, the more one's experience is valued toward a youth ministry that analyzes what corrupts the prophetic nature of Christ's divinity and reclaims the power of Christ's call for young and old to build a new heaven and a new earth.

Fourth, in order to meet the basic needs of all young people, to restructure power relationships, and to understand what God calls us to be and do, our *action* must be directed toward *social and structural change* at the very core of our institutional life. Our failure to work toward change of structures runs the risk of making everything else we do a mere academic exercise.

✓ A New Curriculum for Youth Ministry

The change I have described from traditional practices to a transformational model of youth ministry will not come without tension and conflict. This movement will disrupt business as usual, disturb unequal power relationships, and endanger the status quo. But our failure to do so denies the youth we serve the opportunity to witness and understand the true prophetic nature of our faith and to experience a relationship with the Christ who loves them so much that he puts them first.

Movement from traditional ways of youth ministry to transformational ministry will require new education and training of youth ministers. Traditional curricula are not adequate or capable of visioning or of making the change of commitment necessary to undertake this new form of youth ministry. Creative approaches and environments for training and education will need to be established in addition to the traditional academic curricula on adolescence and faith development. This expanded curricula will be developed according to the following pedagogical assumptions:

- ⌣ In the realm of basic needs, we must expand our *needs assessment* theory to include young people as participants in defining their own needs.
- ⌣ In our building of community, we must include *anti-oppression training* through which youth ministers can confront their own prejudices and see the relationship between prejudice and power. They will also gain experience in consensus decision-making and become comfortable with the mutual sharing of power, particularly their own.
- ⌣ In the area of pedagogy, the focus will change from personal spirituality and conversion to *social reflection*. Youth ministers will learn the nature of power relationships and how to use the tools of social analysis in their work.
- ⌣ The focus of service will change from direct care and relief to the means of broad scale structural change. Youth ministers and the young people they serve will learn the skills of *strategic planning* and *community organizing*.
- ⌣ Finally, I would like to add a fifth component to my model, that of *spirituality*. Youth ministries will learn to place theological reflection under the umbrella of social justice. New models of theological reflection that start with the experience of oppressed youth will be used as the basis for all that justifies and inspires this new way of doing youth ministry.

It is after all these initial steps are undertaken that I believe we can, with confidence, be more comfortable with the distinction in our priorities between who comes first: the needs of an adult church or the needs of young people. Remember that the shepherds of Luke's gospel with which I began had first to go see what they had been told by the angels. And so there is no doubt in my mind that the real power of our evangelism and ministry is in the living out of the gospel with young people.

Endnotes

1. For the full report see the Standing Commission on Human Affairs, *The Blue Book,* 71st General Convention, held in Indianapolis, Indiana (August 1994), 306-331.

2. Peter Scales, et al., *The Attitudes and Needs of Religious Youth Workers: Perspectives from the Field* (Minneapolis: Search Institute, 1995), 14-19.

3. Carnegie Corporation of New York, *A Matter of Time: Risk and Opportunity in the Nonschool Hours* (New York: Carnegie Corporation, 1992), 52-54.

4. Scales, *Attitudes and Needs,* 14-19.

"Dearer to God are the Prayers of the Poor"

Ministry and Evangelism From Poor Youth

Richard L. Harris

In a religious culture that allows us to assume the gospel is good news for the rich, or at least the educated middle class, it takes considerable effort of will to think of the good news as being for the poor. We are so conditioned by our political debates and our inherited model of religion that we instinctively think of the gospel as being for the churchgoer—the tax paying, mostly law-abiding, pledging churchgoer. As an act of generosity, we may be able to accept that the good news may *also* be for the poor, but to think that the gospel is *primarily* or even *solely* good news for the poor is difficult. If we read the gospels and listen to what Christ is saying and doing, however, then we may have to admit that, for him at least, the good news had its focus on the poor. And if for him, why not for us also?

What emerges from our reading of the gospels and our encounter with Christ, however, is that while the good news may be for the poor, it is not doled out to them like a meal at a soup kitchen. The gospel is lived out not *to* the poor but *with* the poor, as proclamation and celebration. Christ ate and drank with the poor; he enjoyed their company. They were his friends and his family—his loved ones. Thus the gospel accounts of Jesus begin to reveal to us a different and even more unsettling idea: the gospel may not only be good news *for* the poor, it may also be good news *from* the poor. Given that the vast majority of the world's poor are young people, this would include *from* young people as well. Through their struggle God has chosen to show his creative love for the world. This understanding of God working in us has brought me to new understanding of how I hear and see God in my daily life.

Jesus offered a succinct summary of the law of God: "You shall love the Lord your God with all your heart, and with all your soul, and with all your mind" and "You shall love your neighbor as yourself" (Matthew 22:37). These are known as the two great commandments but actually they are one. They are inseparable. Our love for God is given substance in the love we have for others and the manner in which we serve their need. To pray "Our Father in heaven" implies a relationship of love we have for and with our brothers and sisters on earth.

It would be difficult to read the four gospels of the life of Jesus without coming to the conclusion that he was just as interested in the practicalities of life as in the so-called spiritualities. Indeed, he did not seem to draw a such distinction. For Jesus there was a wholeness about life and he refused to break it up into separate compartments. For instance, it was entirely natural for him to include, at the very core of the prayer he taught his disciples, a petition for daily bread. Bread took its rightful place alongside what some would consider weightier matters like forgiveness and temptation. Ordinary, everyday, practical matters to do with our life in the world are part of his concern—and if we are serious about his example then they must become ours as well.

Young people are not "souls with ears" into which we are required to pour either our good news or our good advice. They are our brothers and sisters. Like us, they are made in the image of God. Wherever circumstances threaten to deny or to diminish that image we, as partners with God, are not simply to discredit such things, to preach sermons at special times of the year or to allocated token funds. We are to challenge and confront them in the name of Jesus Christ and, whenever possible, convey practical help to those who are in need of it. Obedience to the Lord's command to love our neighbor involves us in serving them, not saving them!

Jesus taught by example and, through his words and actions, left little room for us to evade the challenge. As we face this moral imperative it is not good enough for us to view poor young people as objects of our charity. We must see them as sharers in our humanity who possess the same potential we do. Any concept of development therefore must be integral and holistic, incorporating the conditions and needs of the poor. The process must be "bottom up" and not "top down." In a real sense there must be a new evangelism of development arising out of the experiences of the poor. Instead of the tendency to pity and patronize the poor, we must allow the poor space in our analysis, conceptualization, and planning. It is not sufficient to conduct an examination of poverty without considering how the poor themselves help to shape and direct an inquiry about their own condition. Through this process of learning from the poor, those who are in more dominant positions in our society can be re-evangelized, and their perspectives and values revised. It is fundamental to any analysis of poverty to grasp fully the pain of the poor and the reasons why they are made poor. Poverty is not a question of fate, nor is it the result of ignorance, but the result of structures and systems. The experiences of poor young people must therefore inform our consciences, attitudes, and actions.

Liberation theologians have called our attention to an "option for the poor"—a clear recognition of the systemic relationship between wealth and poverty. Due to the persistence of an unequal system, a significant group of people in our cities, our rural areas, and around the world can only reap the benefits of a poverty-stricken underclass. Our battle then is to understand the political and economic demands put upon us as co-creators with God. At our baptism we promised to do God's work for justice, freedom, and peace. In a real sense we must allow the poor to evangelize us and call our attention to the claims of the gospel.

This gospel of the poor promises peace and reconciliation—it rejoices in forgiveness—but it firmly announces that these have nothing to do with friendly relationships that leave unfair and oppressive social orders unchanged, nor with cooperation rather than confrontation in the face of injustice. Forgiveness goes with repentance, reconciliation goes with justice. It is not peace-keepers who are blessed but those who hunger and thirst after what is right. This gospel, like ours, promises to teach us the truth that will make us free, but truth will not be readily discovered in the realm of ideas where we argue over doctrines and abstractions and give or withhold our agreements until we "believe" them.

If we allow poor young people to evangelize us we will experience the great reversal that the gospel is not only *for* the poor, but also *from* the poor. We will discover that God has the inclination to speak the liberating word through the powerless. Indeed, the powerful need to hear this word from the lips of those they have rejected in their society, so that there may be mutual liberation. If we can become aware of the social, political, and economic systems that control our lives, we may then find ourselves on the same side of the struggle as those who are the outcasts of those systems. We can find ourselves learning about such struggles from those whom we charitably tried to help before. They can become our teachers, rather that we theirs. Within its life the church must create opportunities for this conversation to take place. We must work to convert relationships of powerlessness, privilege, and disadvantage to relationships of mutuality, participation, and solidarity.

⌁ The Church and Poor Youth

A growing number of young people in the United States are growing up in circumstances that limit the development of their potential, compromise their health, impair their sense of self, and restrict their chances for a successful life. For those who are poor and for people of color who must face racism day after day, their everyday lives fail to provide the resources, supports, and opportunities essential to healthy development and reasonable preparation for adulthood. The settings in which many young people find themselves have deteriorated dramatically, and many cannot even step outside their doors for fear of violence. Many neighborhoods provide little or no opportunity for healthy stimulation or recreation. At the same time, support systems offered by churches, community sports and arts programs, and tutoring programs have all but disappeared. Under such circumstances, the risk of experiences that compromise their health and life (such as school failure or dropout, trouble with the law, or heavy substance abuse) becomes substantially greater.

Schools in urban areas where poor families are concentrated do not have the resources needed to sustain their mission, while their buildings are in disrepair and the threat of violence hangs over their classrooms and corridors. Neighborhoods have disintegrated, buildings are more dilapidated, and streets are often physically dangerous. Families are frequently headed by single parents, often a working mother unable to obtain competent child care, or by two working parents with less time for childrearing because they are striving to maintain their standard of living despite a general decline in wages. These are the settings that are shaping today's young people.

The response of the church has often been too little and too late. We find ourselves providing program models that are inappropriate for the challenges that many of our young people face today. A monthly or even weekly recreation program for fun and fellowship is the model, but it lacks the depth needed to serve young people who find themselves on the edge. Programs that provide a holistic approach by supporting both young people and their families have a better chance of meeting the needs.

∿ A Different Model

In 1990, Camp St. Augustine, a small summer camp for boys in Boston, took on an added challenge by deciding not to abandon the campers after the summer was over, but to find a way to work with these boys year round. What follows is my account of this ministry, both where it is going and what its leaders, through trial and error, have found to be effective.

Saint Augustine Ministries provides year-round emotional and practical support to boys of diverse ethnic backgrounds growing up in the violence and anonymity of Boston's inner city. Most of the families we serve have incomes well below the poverty level and some live in homeless shelters. These boys are referred to us by congregations, social service agencies, mental health agencies, and neighborhood organizations.

Through advocacy, mentor and afterschool programs, and a residential summer camp, we help boys ranging in ages from seven to seventeen to stay in school, with their families, and away from drugs and gangs. In the summer, the program sponsors Camp St. Augustine and hosts two three-week sessions at its site in Foxboro, Massachusetts. During the year the camp provides support and advocacy for all the boys in the summer program through home visitations, retreats, and health, psychological, and social service referrals. A mentor program provides thirty of the boys with a college student from Boston College to help with their homework, offer friendship, and provide a positive role model. In addition, Saint Augustine Ministries runs a "homework-based" afterschool program during the school year to support the boys in their efforts to get an education. It tracks their health, their progress in school, and their family lives through services and programs that create an intentional community comprised of African-American, Anglo, and Hispanic young people. Most important, it provides a support system that follows them all year long, striving to be a *presence* in their lives, not just a *program*.

The core of the agency's program continues to be the summer camp. Located on thirty acres of forest about thirty miles south of Boston, the camp has eight rustic cabins, a swimming pool, a central lodge, a dining room, a peaceful chapel, and, since it adjoins a state forest, miles of woods in which to camp, hike, and explore. Daily activities include reading and creative writing, arts and crafts, camping skills, sports, and swimming. In a peace and justice class that meets one hour each day, campers study famous peacemakers, explore models and methods of resolving conflict, learn to cooperate instead of compete, build a sense of self-esteem, and learn that they can make a difference in their communities. The class is an opportunity for these boys to contemplate the issues of racism, HIV/AIDS, parent-child relationships, drugs, and violence.

Every effort is made to recruit boys starting in the summer after the second grade, and ninety percent of our boys return to camp year after year. We ask for that commitment from their families at the outset, because the only way we can provide the stability our campers lack is through deliberate continuity. They attend the program every year as campers until they graduate in the summer after eighth grade. At that point, they have the option of continuing on as Counselors in Training (CIT), a three-year leadership training program designed to give these young men skills to succeed not only at Camp St. Augustine but in their home communities as well. Developing boys who not only survive their lot but are also willing and able to take on leadership roles at home is a crucial element of the camp's program, especially as the boys get older. Here they get a taste of what it takes to make good decisions, and to see what it is like to rely on others and have others rely on them. Each session of the leadership program ends with a one-week backpacking trip on the wilderness trails of New England, where the boys can test out what they have learned and develop communities of their own.

Those who work in the program believe that it serves the boys in several ways. First, it provides them with a community that stays with them year after year. In the city things are always changing: kids move, their parents get divorced, their schools are huge and anonymous. Ideally, the camp is a community on which they can rely.

Second, Saint Augustine Ministries provides them with numerous chances to succeed. We want to give a chance to the kid who has bad grades, who always gets chosen last for teams, who does not have many friends. We want to praise him for learning to swim, for making something beautiful in arts and crafts, for writing a terrific story in reading class. We want him to leave the program with new confidence.

One of the most important things the program does is give them a space in which to deal with the issues that haunt their daily lives. At camp they can discuss racism, the burdens of poverty and wealth, how hard it is to deal with parents, and how afraid they sometimes are. It is a special time for them when they know there are people who care about them and really listen. As they address these issues one by one for themselves, they have the chance to become instruments of change in their own lives, families, and communities.

Finally, the program provides them an opportunity to be away from their homes and the roles they play within their families, a chance to be who they have always wanted be. They can have fun at the camp doing extraordinary things, things they would not ordinarily get a chance to do.

From September through June, the offices of Saint Augustine Ministries in Boston provide space for an afterschool program for doing homework. Monday through Friday, from two in the afternoon until six, with the help of volunteers from Boston College we provide some recreation time, tutoring in school work, opportunities for enrichment, and people who will listen and counsel. Small groups help provide an atmosphere of intimacy where young people can share their joys as well as their frustrations, their successes as well as their failures. Staff, both paid and volunteer, provide a level of care that would be impossible with larger programs. Enrichment programs include swimming instruction, Tae Kwon Do lessons, and field trips to museums and other areas of interest; these opportunities give young people a chance to broaden their horizons beyond their own neighborhoods.

Often the program is asked by families, agencies, or the school system to act as advocate for that child in the school system. In a large city like Boston, families can often find the school system unresponsive to their needs. In many cases, because of the lack of preschool education or home stimulation, students enter school already behind and have a hard time ever catching up. Many children pass from grade to grade without learning even basic skills in reading and mathematics. Challenging the school system can be a daunting task, one that most families are afraid to take on. With some local resources, Saint Augustine Ministries will help a family make its case for their child.

The last few decades have seen the dismantling of systems that assisted many children through their growing years and into adulthood. The disappearance of extended families in neighborhoods and even church systems have created a void for many children. Once guided through the difficult years by many adults, children are now left to figure out life's lessons for themselves. Raised mostly in single-parent homes, living in neighborhoods with few working males, and educated in impersonal schools, these young people cannot count on day-to-day adult guidance. Parents, of course, are the best source of support, but for many adolescents parents are not involved in their lives in a positive manner. In some cases, parents are absent or abusive; in many more cases, parents strive to be good parents but lack the capacity or opportunity to learn how.

In response, a number of communities have discovered that mentoring can address a very real need for children who are not receiving enough personal attention from adults. The belief that mentoring leads to improved outcomes for young people is supported by social scientists studying resilient youth, those who grow up in economically disadvantaged circumstances but somehow manage to survive and succeed. Our mentoring program matches boys one-on-one with Boston College students who serve as "big brothers" and "big sisters," spending at least one afternoon per week with them as friends, tutors, and emotional supports for the family. Every three weeks they plan a special weekend outing, such as going to the zoo or the science museum, or spending a night at Boston College. Each mentor has weekly contact with a supervisor as well as a mid-year evaluation.

Mentor programs like these are time-consuming services. They require a great deal of work to provide education and support for the mentors and to keep families who participate aware of their child's progress. Mentor programs should not be seen as substitutes for adequately funded schools and social services, nor should they hide the need for more schools that function as communities where students can get help from their counselors more than once or twice a year. Mentors provide what most experiences do not: personal attention and support.

This kind of holistic ministry requires constant assessment of the needs of young people and their families. Focus groups of young people, parent support group meetings, and collaboration with other community-based agencies help to ensure that those agencies do not continue to provide programs or services that are no longer needed. As this is being written, plans are underway to expand the afterschool program, find additional mentors who will make a minimum two-year commitment, fund a part-time education consultant/case worker, and develop several coed programs.

⌁ A Gospel *from* the Poor

What has become clearer in the development of Saint Augustine Ministries is that in order to meet the needs of young people at risk the church will need to respond in new and challenging ways. We will have to address the needs of young people in the community, not just the needs of adults in the pews. We will have to venture much closer to the pain that scares us and walk hand in hand with those who are often outcasts in our faith communities. It takes courage but, at least at Saint Augustine Ministries, the rewards have been returned sevenfold. The lives of young people have been touched, in some cases saved from death, because someone actually cared.

It is interesting to note the liberating power of the gospel when we place the poor at the center of our interpretation and proclamation. The rereading of God's word with the eyes and experience of those who are marginalized and oppressed will yield fresh insights into the meaning of scripture. As poor and powerless young people come to inherit the power given to them from God, they have shared with us their excitement of God's word as it is revealed to them. These often-forgotten young people dare to voice the liberating power of the gospel even in their condition of struggle and suffering.

Perhaps it is in the area of spirituality that the poor witness most powerfully to the gospel. When one removes poverty from a purely materialistic perspective, important as this is, one is challenged by the spiritual wealth of the poor as they drink from their own wells, keep faith and hope alive, and celebrate in song, music, and dance. Their worship is marked by thanksgiving, praise, and celebration, all infused and inspired by the scriptures read and proclaimed, by spontaneous prayers and testimonies, and by the empowerment of the Spirit. This has been repeatedly demonstrated in black churches across the United States and in the churches of Latin America and Africa. African spirituality is filled with communal praise and thanksgiving, hope in the struggle, and faith that God will right wrong and exalt the humble and meek. God is not an abstraction, conceived by ideas and ideology, liberal or conservative; but is dynamically present within the contradictions of life, actively liberating those who are downtrodden and deprived.

Evangelism from poor young people also challenges our notion of God. God is not one who bolsters power and guarantees wealth and success. The true God is the living God who fosters life, and stands with those who struggle for food, freedom, dignity, and community. The faith of the Hebrew people was shaped by their struggle to survive hardship and oppression and become the people of God. Jesus was conscious of his ministry of liberation (Luke 4:16-21) and identified as good religious practice whatever was done for the least of our brothers and sisters (Matthew 25:31-40). He related all of life to God. Religious laws were declared ineffectual if they did not relate to human needs and issue in the celebration of life (Mark 2:15-28; 7:1-13). The Spirit of the living God indeed anoints for liberation and empowerment. God calls us into community with all our neighbors and pushes us to work for the participation of everyone in that community. This call commits us both to the practical ministries of service and the prophetic ministries as we share and serve, and also to witness against injustice.

There are basic needs to be met if life for poor young people as human beings is to flourish. In a civil society there is the need for advocacy on behalf of those who have no voice, and the need also for institutions to be shaped and motivated by justice. Indeed, evangelism from the poor calls into question the idolatrous pursuit of wealth for wealth's sake that leaves victims in its trail. It also bring us face to face with our covenanted humanity that erases the line between "us" and "them." We come to know and practice neighborliness, and appreciate the discipleship, worship, spirituality, and theology that are shaped by struggle. We desperately need a gospel from the poor.

> Brother let me be your servant,
> Let me be as Christ in you.
> Pray that I may have the grace
> To let you be my servant too.

Afterword

Disorganized Religion

Sheryl A. Kujawa

The concept of "disorganized religion" in relation to the evangelization of young people was first brought to my attention by Steven Charleston, former bishop of Alaska and now chaplain of Trinity College in Hartford. The concept rang true to my experience of the myriad ways the church is called today to respond in bringing the gospel in a meaningful way to youth and young adults, to schools and college campuses. If indeed the evangelization of young people means the beginning of a continuous, lifelong process of moving toward an ever-deepening sense of personal and social conversion to Christ and the gospel, and a commitment to the continuation of his mission in bringing about the reign of God, then "disorganized religion" is an appropriate response to this challenge to the church to take a deeper look at our common life and reflect on how it does or does not support young people in the evangelization process. How do we welcome young people? Are we aware of their cultures, needs, and concerns? Within the context of our life and ministry do we "seek and serve Christ" as we experience him in our younger sisters and brothers, at the same time respecting their dignity as human beings?

Unfortunately, despite all the recent verbiage over the Decade of Evangelism, not much has been done within the Episcopal Church to improve our level of support for ministries with young people or to better appreciate the richness that young people bring to the church. If the church continues the status quo, we run the risk of losing generations of young people. The nominal Episcopalian of the future is not going to be someone who is still angry about a statement made by a church leader or an action of the General Convention. No, nominal Episcopalians will be today's young people, who are bored with an increasingly aging church that is not even vaguely aware of their needs or beliefs. For many young people, attending their local church is a cross-cultural experience.

Conversely, young people, too, need to be challenged to contribute to evangelization efforts. These efforts should be supported not because we fear our demise as an institution, but because young people are among the joyful and the needy of the church now. They have a baptismal right to excellent ministry—to receive it and to share in it and to give it to each other and to the larger church. Whether we emotionally and financially invest in young people has, and will continue to have, a profound impact on the quality of our communal life. Similar concerns were voiced decades ago by Martin Luther King, Jr.:

> The contemporary church is often a weak, ineffectual voice with an uncertain sound. It is so often the arch-supporter of the status quo. Far from being disturbed by the presence of the church, the power structure of the average community is consoled by the church's silent and often vocal sanction of things as they are. But the judgement of God is upon the church as never before. If the church today does not recapture the sacrificial spirit of the early church, it will lose its authentic ring, forfeit the loyalty of millions, and be dismissed as an irrelevant social club with no meaning for the twentieth century. I am meeting young people every day whose disappointment with the church has risen to outright disgust.[1]

Many young people want to live a committed Christian life, yet we often have a hard time coping with them when they do. Once converted, young people will form their own opinions of the gospel message. "Every evangelist runs the risk that the seed of the gospel, once planted in the life of a new believer, may grow into a dynamic force which threatens to overthrow the very status quo in which the evangelist finds comfort and rest," writes one evangelist. Furthermore, a recent article on "millennial" young people argues that the church is often run by "control freaks" who diminish young people to a subplot in the overall life of the church in spite of data suggesting that the majority of persons who make faith commitments do so during their teenage years.[2] Gone are the days when guilt and obligation were strong motivations for church attendance. Beginning with the current young adult population, people will vote with their feet; they will go where they are spiritually nourished and supported in their vocation.

✢ Our Anglican and Episcopal Context

As we have discovered, there is certainly no shortage of approaches to ministries with youth and young adults and in higher education within the Episcopal Church; our diversity as a church allows for considerable flexibility in both theology and programming. There is no one "Episcopal" way to evangelize young people, any more than there is one way to evangelize persons of any other age group. No single program will meet the needs of all young people within our denomination, nor is it realistic for us to assume that, even if we had a single program designed to meet the needs of all Episcopalians, all our congregations and dioceses would use it.

There is no one theology for ministries with young people in the Episcopal Church—rather, ministry is to be found within the total life of our congregations and dioceses, and, increasingly, beyond the confines of institutional life itself.

Historically, Episcopalians who work with young people have in common the same characteristics of our ethos as do those who work in other ministries. The diocese headed by a resident bishop is the central unit of our church structure. We have in common our worship and form of governance, rather than our theology. The Anglican Communion, of which we are a part, is by definition global and interdependent, meaning that we are inextricably linked with others within our own church and beyond. We share an understanding of the threefold nature of authority as it is found in scripture, tradition, and reason. These characteristics of what it means to be an Episcopalian inform, in process and in content, what it means to minister with young people within our church. The comprehensiveness of the Anglican tradition is a great gift that allows us to respond to young people in a variety of contexts, just as our denominational tolerance for religious questioning can assist us in dealing with the religious questions of youth in developmentally appropriate ways.[3]

One of the phrases used frequently by George Carey, the current Archbishop of Canterbury, when discussing the evangelization of young people is "a theology of the church as home." Carey reminds us that it is often young people themselves who serve as the most effective evangelists among their peers, and that it is the vocation of the church to give them a spiritual home for their pilgrimage. Archbishop Carey is also concerned with the spiritual needs of young people who have no regular experience of church life, so there is an urgency in his message to the members of the Anglican Communion to address the need for the evangelization of young people. "We must recall that the church is always 'one generation from extinction,'" reasons Carey. "If all church members, young and old alike, do not hand on the incomparable riches of Christ then we shall be failing our Lord....We are called upon, as a church, to proclaim the gospel afresh in each generation."[4]

Under the best circumstances, the church is called to maintain a balance between the need to pass along our Anglican heritage and ancient traditions to young people, while at the same time remaining open to their contributions and influences. Though often met with fear, the diversity and change required when young people challenge the church are integral if we are to remain faithful to the message of the gospel in our own age.

The Episcopal Church has long been involved with youth and young adults, particularly through ministries in higher education, though this level of commitment has ebbed and flowed throughout the generations. In the last twenty-five years, Episcopalians have tried to formulate the evangelization of youth within the larger context of relational ministry. Relational youth ministry places evangelism as an inherent part of congregational ministry, where segregated youth programs are not expected to carry the gospel alone. Within the context of relational youth ministry, interpersonal relationships are channels of grace and a primary vehicle for sharing, transmitting, discovering, and testing the Christian faith. The diversity of persons, culture, ideas, and theology within the church are affirmed, as is the sacramental life of the Episcopal Church. Within a relational approach to the evangelization of youth there is an openness to various sources of revelation and to the continuing action of the Holy Spirit; questioning and struggle in life and faith are affirmed, and dogmatism and "canned answers" are distrusted. The Incarnation is a sign that all of life can be taken seriously, discussed, and celebrated by a Christian; there is not a sharp distinction between sacred and secular.

Relational ministry with young people recognizes the possibilities and limits of what it means to be human, created in the image of God. It pays attention to the related issues and concerns of identity, such as meaning, alienation, brokenness, reconciliation, sexuality, values, decision-making, failure, accomplishment, development, and faith. Such an approach recognizes the common mission and ministry of all baptized persons, regardless of age. This means that "program" grows out of our encounter with that mission and ministry and is therefore determined by the lives of young people where they "live and move and have their being." It is in the midst of our living and relating to one another that we come to face what it means to share and participate in the mission and ministry of the baptized. The life and ministry of Jesus presents a radical example of being in honest relationship with self and others, openly seeking the truth, and by being with others in the full range of life's joys and sorrows, questions and conflicts.

At a time when our presence on college and university campuses is diminishing at an alarming rate, it is important to remember that our Anglican belief in the importance of reason in the life of faith has contributed to an approach to the academy unique among other Christian denominations. Comparing the role of the Episcopal chaplain on campus with the English parson and village life, Alda Marsh Morgan has argued that Episcopalians are more likely to accept the university community, whereas other denominations are more likely to operate as outsiders.[5]

Recent studies also suggest the importance of ministries in higher education in the task of the evangelization of young people. Gallup polls have confirmed that young people begin leaving the church between the ages of twelve and sixteen. Though young people tend to make faith commitments in their teenage and young adult years, the Alban Institute has determined that they do not automatically return to the church once they have left, "unless room is made for them and invitation extended in that period between the ages of eighteen and twenty-nine when the urge to commitment comes." Moreover, other statistics suggest that over fifty percent of those who affiliate with the Episcopal Church in adulthood do so through the ministry of higher education.[6]

Episcopal efforts in higher education are aimed directly at students, as well as at faculty and staff who have a long-term impact on students and the quality of student life. It is necessarily a ministry in the workplace, more like hospital and military chaplaincy and prison ministry than traditional parish ministry. The question of vocation and God's calling to ministry (in whatever arena) is a crucial one here. The variety of styles of campus ministries have necessarily expanded, as the demand continues to outstrip our church's resources to meet students, faculty, and staff on campus. Some campuses have diocesan-funded ministries, some are served regionally, some are reached by congregations who see their ministry area as one that includes a campus. Our commitment to ministry in higher education is also one that includes engagement in some of the most crucial and exciting conversations emerging in our society. The church must continue to offer a voice from a faith perspective on such questions as ethical decision-making in medicine, the appropriate use of technology, and whether God is dead or alive. Our ministers in higher education continue to play an evangelical role in connecting religion and the intellectual life.

Less formal in approach, the Episcopal Church's outreach and evangelism to young adults outside the student population has had a much more sporadic history than our efforts in higher education ministries. The generation coming of age in this and the next decade, sometimes called Generation X or 13th Generation, constitutes a substantial gap in our church's reach. Whether one accepts or challenges these labels, there are some core experiences and trends that affect all those were born in the United States in the period roughly between 1961 and 1981. These include: the dramatically rising cost of higher education (with diminishing economic returns); the transition from a primarily industrial economy to one that is driven by services and symbolic knowledge; the postponement of life decisions such as marriage and career; decreased expectations about owning one's home; and generally reduced social mobility. These factors greatly affect our approach to reaching young adults.

Just as campus ministries are concerned with retaining and making new young Christians, the Episcopal Church needs to have a strategy for reaching those who have left campus life or have never been to college. Much of our church's work with this particular group of young adults has only recently begun, and much remains to be done in sharing methods, learnings, experiments, and mistakes in this formational stage in what is for many a newly identified area of ministry.

As in our ministries in higher education, some young adult work will be done by dioceses in convening young adults and young adult leaders, some networking of learnings will be facilitated on the national and regional level, and much work will be done by local congregations in mission, whether individually or in groups. The approaches will be generated primarily by constituents themselves, the values focusing on honoring individuals' life situations and experiences and offering faith understandings in a language that they resonate with. Unlike ministry with children, for instance, young adults can take primary responsibility for shaping programming and offering leadership.

Campus and young adult ministries offer young adults a safe place for exploring the possibilities of a new future—not in a vacuum, but in community with their peers as well as across generations. As we test some of the learnings from the faith development arena, we find that mentoring intergenerational relationships are some of the most formative and in-formative for young adults. Young adult ministries and higher education ministries are related, but neither is merely a subset of the other. With a broad age range of eighteen to thirty, young adult ministries comprise at least two subgroups arranged by age: eighteen to twenty-five and twenty-five to thirty. The area of higher education ministries, of course, includes some young adults, but also those who make the campus a focus of their life and work. If congregations and dioceses set one of these areas of ministry against the other, our holistic vision of reaching every generation with the message of Jesus Christ will be seriously compromised.

While there is a long history of ministries with young people in many corners of the Episcopal Church, the time has come to face the reality that all our efforts combined only reach a fraction of the young people within our communities. There young people and the issues that affect them and the world are a most profound challenge for the church. Though many within the church have and continue to make honest attempts to be inclusive of young people, their relative absence from many of our congregations points to the reality that we might not, in effect, be as open has we claim to be. Rather than making the false assumption that young people are already an integral part of our common life, a commitment to evangelization suggests the desire to incorporate the needs of young people within the church's mission. Moreover, evangelization needs to be incorporated into our ministries with young people, as is program, pastoral care, worship, spirituality, and social action.

We are mistaken in thinking that it is a natural for young people to leave the congregation or that we are simply to await their return following this phase of rebellion. These assumptions prevent us from looking seriously at the issues of belonging for young people in faith communities. There are no mysterious reasons why young people so often fail to participate in congregational life. For the most part, they are not welcome, and in many instances there are no opportunities for meaningful participation. Perhaps there is no room in the liturgical life of the congregation for the contributions of young people, or the language itself seems irrelevant, or the concepts do not apply to daily life. This pattern will be reversed only when our congregations take seriously the evangelization of young people in all aspects of its life.

Until the late 1960s, campus ministries and church-related camps played an important role in retaining and identifying young adult leaders for the church, many to ordained ministry. Currently, however, the median age of Episcopal Church seminarians is thirty-nine and is in no danger of falling. Because younger people in their twenties with vocations to the ordained ministry are not welcome in many of our dioceses, they go elsewhere to exercise their leadership skills. Though many young people are deeply attracted to the richness of the Anglican tradition, "brand" loyalties are a thing of the past, and if we refuse to take their vocation seriously they will find other communities that will offer them a context to live out their vocation. Moreover, with the projected rise in clergy retirements over the next decades, congregations and commissions of the church must pay attention to nurturing and identifying commitments by young adults to membership and ministry. More opportunities for service and reflection geared toward lay young adults also have to be created, and varied approaches to worship and community must be offered. If local congregations more closely reflected the demography of their surrounding areas, they would have many more young adults than they do now.

History teaches us that not all the "good news" proclaimed by the church is the Christian gospel, nor does every manner of spreading the faith do it justice. Evangelization is not a proclamation of sublime realities with no accompanying effort to make those realities concrete. Evangelization, as the proclamation of the gospel in deeds and actions, is the vocation of the church. It is the place where faith and justice meet.

✣ Challenges of the Postmodern Era

At the beginning of this century the ecumenical movement called for "the evangelization of the world in this generation."[7] As we stand on the threshold of the twenty-first century, it appears that our forebears failed to meet their goal, and we are left wondering what to do next. For young people, the century ahead is likely to be filled with stark realities not even considered a century ago, presenting difficult challenges for the Christian church. The Christian hegemony of our ancestors is now called into question within our own country and in many places throughout the world. From within a society that has marginalized religion to a greater extent, we need to begin to ask ourselves if we are prepared to go beyond merely replacing our decreasing numbers and to reform and revitalize our vocation to reflect the gospel anew.

Lately, much is made by writers on youth culture of the impact of postmodern culture. Simply put, our society is in the throes of a major transition, or the movement from modernity to postmodernity. Postmodernism is characterized by the breakdown in order as established by cultural, scientific, and religious traditions. In the postmodern world, people have rejected the Enlightenment ideals of optimism and progress, replacing them with a gnawing pessimism. For the first time in generations, young people no longer believe that progress is inevitable and that we can solve the world's problems. Their world is constantly changing, their internal life is often fragmented, and perhaps the most sobering reality is that they have adjusted to life in a state of chaos. As they confront their own downward mobility, they are critical of the competitive lifestyles of those of us in the generations before them. Experience has taught them the fragility of the human condition and the need for cooperation for our survival.

It would be tragic if the Episcopal Church ended up being among the last defenders of a dying modernity rather than looking seriously at what the advent of the postmodern era means for us. Though few suggest that we go back to the pre-scientific age, we need to come to terms with the fact that our culture is no longer distinctively Christian. In *The Culture of Disbelief,* Stephen Carter describes the person who believes in God today as a "cultural minority." Though this cultural minority factor is not numerical—ninety-six percent profess to believe in God—it is a minority nonetheless because it operates silently within our culture.[8] The legacy of this disbelief for young people is that they become adults in a culture that refuses to take religion and personal faith seriously. A major part of the challenge in communicating the faith in the postmodern world is that it is but one more piece of information available to young people already overloaded with information.

Adults who work with young people are frequently asked, "How do we get young people involved in the church?" when the real question should be, "How can the *church* can be more involved with young people?" Ministries with youth and young adults should not be about nurturing potential adult believers, but rather about enabling the continued growth of young believers. The shift toward lifelong learning communities is perhaps the key to changing the mentality that sees the main motivation behind ministries with young people as providing instruction which can be drawn on in later years.

Those concerned with the evangelization of young people differ about whether the proclamation of the gospel should be explicit or implicit. Regardless of this difference, however, it can be said that the most effective evangelists with young people are those who take seriously their lives, their culture, and their concerns. While many approach the evangelization of young people almost solely in terms of their absence from our congregations, perhaps a more helpful entry point would be to start out with the needs and concerns of young people themselves. Instead of asking why young people do not come to our churches, we should begin to concentrate on the question, "How can we as a church better respond to their needs?"

Effective evangelization of young people means being alert to their personal experience of God's active presence. It does not mean that we abandon the tradition of the faith community. Rather, we need to make an effort to connect the young people's experience with the community's understanding of God and the church as a supportive community. The most powerful human influence on the forming faith of young people is that exerted by families and peers who are living and expressing their own. To a large extent, they make their moral judgments in keeping with what is expected of them by family, peers, and significant others in their lives.

Young people are seeking personal commitment. Commitment includes reaching out toward people, ideas, beliefs, causes, and work choices. The church can assist young people as they begin this formation process of building commitment and purpose in their lives. Participation in the life of the church provides an outlet for the curiosity, idealism, and desire for accomplishment that is characteristic of youth. Involvement in worship and community service can be a source of affiliation when they are actively involved in planning and decision-making.

Young people are engaged in the search for and establishing of their own identities. Their commitment to the search for personal identity springs from the key existential questions confronting all humankind. Who am I? What is the meaning of my life? What happens after I die? Responding to these questions is necessary to the discovery of ourselves as beings created by God who are called to a unique vocation during our lifetime. Young people are at an ideal stage for this search, with their energy and open-mindedness for capturing Christian meaning and living out the gospel with intensity, but too frequently they hear the gospel as a series of prohibitions rather than the invitation to a new way of being in Christ. Authentic Christian spirituality springs from our discipleship and our attempts to live out a Christian praxis. The evangelization of young people requires the development of profound spiritualities, not superficial slogans. They want and expect more from us. They are looking for signs of transformation in those who would evangelize them.

Many unchurched young people are painfully aware that they want something more. They yearn for mentors in the faith. They yearn for a community with integrity. In a sense, they call our congregations into account. They would like our communities to be something better, to be places where a commitment to freedom, mutual direction, and action are the norm. It is the work of evangelism to help young people see themselves as the protagonists of their own lives, claim their personal and collective stories in the present and in the future, and then learn to recognize the presence of God in their lives and in the lives of others.

One of the reasons meaningful liturgy is so important to young people today is that it is both a sign of community transformation and a vehicle for their own transformation. Young people are seeking a connection with the rites of a community. The problem is that many of our communities have isolated liturgy from Christian social action, resulting in what is perceived by young people to be empty ritual and formalism. Who can take seriously a God who is detached from poverty, violence, and oppression? Liturgy that responds to young people opens up the liturgical assembly so that they become more than spectators. Worship is offered not out of guilt or obligation, but out of one's inner life and calling to a greater sense of engagement with the world.

In a recent article, "The Gospel for Generation X: Making Room in the Church for Busters," author Dieter Zander comments: "Perhaps no other generation has needed the church so much, yet sought it so little." Zander is writing about "baby busters"—those now in their teens, twenties, and early thirties. From about 1965 through 1980, the number of births across the United States went "bust," giving a name to a new generation with a substantially different mindset from the baby boomers who preceded them. Though everyone born between 1965 and 1980 is technically qualified for the "buster" category, the distinction between a buster and the preceding generation is more profoundly evident in attitude than age. A key distinction between the attitudes of baby boomers and baby busters is around the ability to achieve the "American dream." Though this dream has been achieved by many baby boomers—the suburban home, the high income, and the successful career—it is considered unobtainable, perhaps even undesirable, to many of the busters. Busters "believe that the traditional American dream is beyond their grasp," writes Zander. "Plus they have watched boomers destroy their families and relationships while climbing the corporate ladder....Busters are fashioning a new American dream: to be whole, and to live in harmony with others and their surroundings. They would rather work to live than live to work."⁹ Zander's sentiments are confirmed by one young woman in her mid-twenties as she writes:

I, for one, had a hard time trusting anything: Love is forever (my parents divorced when I was four). Uncle Sam is your friend (if you're American, and sometimes not even then). Technology will solve the world's problems (just turn off the TV, dear, and take your Prozac)....I had no mentors in the faith. There are no Christians within climbing distance of my family tree. When I came to God, I came out of desperation.[10]

Another sobering postmodern reality for a church less than comfortable with young people is that we now live in a society in which adolescence has been extended, for some even into the late twenties. Robert Bly in *The Sibling Society* writes about what he sees as a phenomenon of extended adolescence now occurring throughout American culture. According to Bly, young people today have no effective rituals of initiation, and no real way to show when they have reached adulthood. Instead, he argues, young men and women go around in circles. Rejecting what Bly calls "the paternal society" for a "sibling society," today's young people live in a culture which prizes a state of "half adulthood":

> The parents regress to become more like children, and the children, through abandonment, are forced to become adults too soon and don't quite make it....What the young need—stability, presence, attention, advice, good psychic food, unpolluted stories—is exactly what the sibling society won't give them.[11]

A similar view is voiced by a commentator on grunge music. "It's as if kids don't know who to blame: their parents, the media, the schools—or themselves," she writes. "Instead, grunge expresses this generation's almost willful refusal to reach for large truths."[12]

Obviously, not all young people between the ages of eighteen and thirty share these attitudes, yet current studies of generations of young people suggest some common characteristics important for consideration in evangelizing young people. These characteristics include:

- ✓ *Pain.* Close to fifty percent of young people between the ages of eighteen and thirty come from divorced and blended families. Many lacked reliable adult role models while growing up. The pain experienced in family life has contributed to feelings of loneliness and isolation. For many, friends are more family than family. The search for intimacy is a driving force in their lives. Young people in this age group place a high value on community—meaning open, secure, and inclusive relationships.
- ✓ *Distrust of authority.* It is hard to think of a form of authority that has not in some way failed the young people in our culture—the government, the

family, the educational system, our health and welfare system, as well as the church. Consequently, many youth have a profound distrust of traditional forms of authority, including the church. Young people often place a higher value on personal relationships than on institutions, on authenticity than on excellence.

✌ *Fear.* Though young people want to find a sense of hope on a local scale and want their lives to make a difference, many live in fear of the future. Limited economic potential, sex in the age of HIV/AIDS, and a ruined environment are only a few of the negative realities they are facing.

✌ *Grassroots orientation.* With few entry level jobs available, and without the potential to make it "big" as had the previous generation, many young people seek to do good when it is achievable, in relationships or in local causes, and believe in the power of the personal.

✌ *Spiritual hunger.* Though often ignored and feared by organized religion, many young people are looking for a transcendent meaning. Not tied to denominational loyalties, young people will be open to religious experiences that meet their personal needs for intimacy and community and that contribute to global needs.[13]

At times it seems we in the church have naively built our ministries with young people on the premise that all young people are the same. Yet when we read the gospels we find that part of the radical nature of Jesus' ministry was that he ministered directly to people's cultural and social—as well as psychological and spiritual—needs. If we examine the actual extent of diversity in the world today, the critical nature of building understanding between groups remains obvious, and increased cultural competence becomes an essential ingredient to our survival and participation in our own communities and the world. For example:

✌ The United States is becoming the most multicultural country on earth. In a recent census, the overall population in the U. S. increased by eleven percent, the Asian population doubled, the percentage of African-Americans increased by seventeen percent, the percentage of Hispanic-Americans increased by sixty-one percent, and the percentage of American Indians by seventy-one percent.

✌ In a recent United States census, the most frequently named ethnic groups identified by Americans were: English, German, Irish, African-American, French, Italian, Scottish, Polish, Mexican, American Indian, and Dutch.

✌ In the year 2000, seventy-five percent of the people entering the work force in the United States will be people of color.[14]

Rather than hold onto the outdated vision of the American melting pot, we are called into the new vision of a rainbow, salad bowl, symphony, or mosaic. These days, even our smallest schools and colleges have fairly diverse students populations. Increasing mobility through international travel and higher education has opened the way to an increased sense of cultural diversity in many areas of the United States. As members of the Anglican Communion, we are called to a vision of being together that is by definition global and interdependent. Young people today will be better prepared to live into this reality if they are equipped from an early age with the skills to live within a diverse society. While some educational systems have taken on the work of diversity education, it is important for those of us who work with young people within a church context, and/or who live with young people within families, to look to the task of building cultural competence as well.

The vast majority of our approaches to the evangelization of young people use models formed within a European-American, middle-class cultural context; it is hardly surprising that we reach primarily European-American, middle-class young people. Church leaders among people of color bemoan the lack of culturally appropriate efforts to evangelize youth of color within the Episcopal Church, who are pressured to sacrifice their cultural heritage and personal identity to "fit in" with a predominately white church. It is a primary task of evangelization for young people to learn to recognize and appreciate their own cultural backgrounds. The effort to transform the church in this regard is a *learned* skill, not simply part of our standard outreach. We have a long way to go before the evangelization of young people of color is seen as an imperative to the mission of the whole church.

◡: The Challenge of Conversion

What does this analysis tell us about the evangelization of youth and young adults within the Episcopal Church? It suggests the need for a major transformation—a *conversion* of sorts—in the way we carry out our mission and ministry. I use the word conversion deliberately, for in a basic sense it refers to a change from one lifestyle to another. Conversion requires an abandonment of an unsatisfying perspective in favor of a renewed sense of a more meaningful life. While we have accomplished successful programs for young people in the past, the evidence shows that we are still a long way from creating a faith community where they feel valued for who they are, even if that identity may threaten institutional life.

Moreover, even stronger evidence suggests that we contribute little to the evangelization of young people who are not our own children, or who are significantly endangered. While it could be argued that we are a product of a society which devalues the young, the gospel suggests that something more should be expected of the followers of Jesus joined together in a covenanted community. Are we willing to face the fears that prevent us from becoming the kind of covenanted community that would be more meaningful for young people, and perhaps for ourselves? Do we even want to hear what God has revealed to the young people in our midst?

Although many places within the Episcopal Church claim that young people are a priority, a look at the way we actually spend our time and resources show that this is true in very few locations. How then do we begin to live into the conversion process necessary for more effective evangelization with young people? In order to begin, I propose that we carefully consider three interrelated processes: *relationship*, *repentance*, and *renewal*.

Relationship

Jesus Christ calls each of us into relationship with each other as Christians, and the mission and ministry resulting from this relationship is not defined by age. Young people have made the same baptismal commitments as adults have, and are equally called to ministry. Yet many adults within the church and society are fearful and threatened by young people. Recent articles claim adolescence is a "disease" and refer to the "age war" within American society as a result of the last fifteen years of public and private dislike for and fear of teenagers on the part of adults. The National Association of Private Psychiatric Hospitals has even begun to recommend more hospitalizations of young people to treat the "severe psychological problems of adolescents."[15]

To a large degree the church has abandoned young people. While we are usually concerned with young people who are our own, we neglect the rest, even those living in close proximity. Comparatively few church leaders offer concrete solutions for this omission, or advocate for the inclusion of ministries with young people as a mission imperative for the whole church. Still, some young people do remain active in the church, and while it is difficult to give easy answers about why they remain a part of a community that is not always interested in them, their own voices give us some clues:

> The church has been helpful in discerning what God wants me to do with my life. More specifically, what area of study I should go into. (Grace, age 19)

> Sunday worship is designed to provide people with the resources needed to carry out a ministry that really matters in their daily lives. (Paul, age 18)

> Far and away, the appeal of the Episcopal Church is the loving way it accepts people with no discrimination. We are a church equally for lovers of tradition and ritual, for progressive minds, and for activists of all kinds. (Susie, age 21)

It provides me with a sense of balance. I can deal with the hard times because I know I have a community that supports me no matter what. (Ethan, age 29)

I believe that the Episcopal Church encourages dialogue. That in itself is one of the greatest lessons I have learned. (LaTonya, age 25)[16]

While there is no one factor preventing genuine, healthy relationships between young people and adults, we cannot ignore the possibility that young people represent to us the inevitability of change and chaos. We cannot be in relationship with young people until we heal our own demons, resolve our own adolescence, and develop compassion for our younger sisters and brothers. We need to develop a sense of compassion for young people that is based on a common sense of humanity that bridges the gulf of even many years, and that is built on the sense that our salvation is dependent upon one another.

Some would like to evangelize young people by fiat. Personally, I believe that this way of proceeding is long past. The only way to evangelize young people in our times is to move among them, listen deeply to what they have to say, and establish bonds of caring. Only then can we begin to speak the truth credibly among them and only then can we move with them into the mystery of Jesus. Part of the reason so many religious youth programs for young people fail is that many adults want to teach young people religion, but few are willing to enter their lives with the kind of patient walking along exemplified by Jesus in his own ministry. Young people are interested in knowing more about Jesus. They are looking for identity, purpose, affirmation, healing, authenticity, and community from the church. They want to know what the church has to say about issues that concern them—spirituality, sexuality, family, economics, violence. The problem is that we have to be willing to engage those topics with them, sometimes admitting our own ignorance in the face of the world's problems.

Repentance

As part of our process of conversion in the evangelization of young people we are called to start the grief and healing necessary to begin life anew in the Spirit. Such a process would lead us to "refound" the church around the pastoral strategies needed to effect good evangelization. This concept has little to do with acquiring greater numbers of people. Rather, it is a radical call to gospel living, to personal and social conversion, and to moving into the world with a sense of mission. Part of this repentance, in regard to young people, is the recognition that young people are who they are because they have inherited an adult world where they have known neglect, abuse, racism, sexism, addiction, and other forms of oppression. As

Christian adults we need to repent for our complicity in the factors that devalue young people in our church and society.

The sad reality is that young people at every economic level are often neglected by the adults who should care for them, or get lost in large institutions that undermine their healthy development. Many young people attend schools that ignore their needs and capacities. For those young people who fail to complete high school, and even for those who do, there are few or no job opportunities. Living under these conditions, and with few or no role models, it is becoming particularly hard for many young people to look ahead with any confidence.

More than ever before, national, community, and religious leadership must be held responsible for helping this generation of young people enter a society that offers genuine equality and opportunity for all people, including young people of color and young women. The failure of today's youth to grow into physically, mentally, and spiritually healthy adults will ultimately turn a substantial number of them into adults who are without humane values and a sense of what is right and wrong. Rich or poor, young people are in danger of turning to drugs, alcohol, or suicide in an attempt to escape from the depression, self-doubt, and anxiety that haunt them when the future seems so frightening. Gay and lesbian young people, who often feel alienated and judged by the church, have an even higher rate of suicide than do heterosexual young people. Yet many of our congregations see these endangered young people as *outside* their membership. Faithful adults concerned with the evangelization of young people are called to a greater sense of accountability for all young people.

Renewal

Lastly, what would an Episcopal Church renewed with a mission for the evangelization of young people look like? As we look toward the new millennium, how are we called to live as a covenanted community? Some of the most critical challenges facing the Episcopal Church involve our collective ability or inability to provide the kind of community that is real and attractive to this generation of young people. Living in an age when denominational loyalties are receding into the background, we must set denominational priorities that are real and relevant to people who are reticent to affiliate with a religious institution often plagued by divisions. Once again, we are called to stretch the boundaries of what we mean by relational youth ministries, demonstrating our commitment to support people of faith, and living a lifestyle that promotes healing, the responsible stewardship of resources and talents, and a genuine sense of intimacy and connectedness.

How might we make the Episcopal Church a place of genuine hospitality for young people—socially, culturally, liturgically, spiritually? Though there is no one way to support the evangelization of young people, some important factors include:

- ✌ A willingness to embrace a variety of liturgical and musical styles on a flexible schedule, thus encouraging youth participation.
- ✌ An openness and appreciation of new forms of technology and their contribution to reaching young people.
- ✌ A commitment to the development of leaders who can relate to young people, and to the lay and ordained vocations for young people themselves.
- ✌ An attitude suggesting that change and conflict are healthy, along with an ability to discuss controversial issues.
- ✌ A commitment to intercultural awareness and eradication of all forms of oppression.
- ✌ Training in pastoral strategies for evangelization for lay and ordained leaders, including young people themselves.
- ✌ Renewed support for programs and resources relating to ministries with youth and young adults and in higher education across the church, as an integral part of the church's mission.
- ✌ Decision-making and planning styles that include young people on all levels of the church's life and ministry.
- ✌ A proactive strategy to seek out relationships with young people traditionally considered outside church boundaries.
- ✌ A deepened understanding of the human developmental process, and a renewed appreciation for persons at all stages of life.
- ✌ A willingness to work more collaboratively, sharing ministry across generations, with the realization that no generation possesses all truth.
- ✌ Support for families in stress and crisis.
- ✌ A fresh understanding of age-old biblical truths in light of contemporary life.
- ✌ More contact and cooperation with other denominations and faith groups.
- ✌ Programming that includes the elements of a deeper spirituality, small group Bible study, and social action activities.

For the church to be converted to the evangelization of young people we will need to meet the challenges of a prophetic ministry that incarnates community, practices a stewardship of care, honors the politics of diversity and inclusion, and reverences mystery with a profound sense of servant ministry. Just as the story of the early church was not limited to the congregation, so we are now called to look beyond our institutional boundaries to young people in remote places who are separated from one another, to become for them a sustaining image of life in Christ. We owe it to the church to pass on her richness to young people, and we owe it to young people to enable them to become active participants in bringing forth the reign of God. Hopefully the church of the twenty-first century will be one where young people are called to minister and flourish in a community based on ancient traditions and steeped in innovative expressions of the gospel of Christ.

Endnotes

1. Martin Luther King, Jr., *Letter from Birmingham City Jail,* copyright 1986 by Coretta Scott King.

2. Jim Wallis, *Agenda for Biblical People* (London: Triangle, 1986), quoted in *Youth A Part: Young People and the Church* (London: National Society/Church House Publishing), 1996, 12. Wendy Murray Zoba, "The Class of 00," *Christianity Today* 41, no. 2 (February 3, 1997), 28.

3. For a discussion on the "The Anglican Way: Catechetical Ethos," see *Called to Teach and Learn: A Catechetical Guide for the Episcopal Church* (New York: The Domestic and Foreign Missionary Society [PECUSA], 1994, 1996), 63-75.

4. George Carey, quoted in *Youth Apart,* ix.

5. Alda Marsh Morgan, "Matter Made Articulate in the Divine Praise," in *Invitation to Dialogue: The Theology of College Chaplaincy and Campus Ministry* (New York: Education in Society, NCCC USA, 1986), 61-62. See also Donald P. Owens, Jr., *Disciples: An Outline for an In-Depth Journey in Faith* (unpublished manuscript, 1996),

6. Sam Portaro, "The Task Force on Campus Ministry: A Response," in *Task Force on Campus Ministry* (Chicago: Diocese of Chicago, 1990), 3; Owens, *Disciples,* 40.

7. David Devadas, *Ecumenism and Youth* (Geneva: World Council of Churches, 1995), 1-2.

8. Stephen Carter, *The Culture of Disbelief* (New York: Basic Books, 1993), 279.

9. Dieter Zander, "The Gospel for Generation X: Making Room in the Church for Busters," *Leadership* (Spring 1995), 37.

10. Piper Lowell, "Out of Desperation," *Sojourners* (November 1994), 20.

11. Robert Bly, "A World of Half-Adults," *Utne Reader* (May-June 1996), 52-54. See also Robert Bly, *The Sibling Society* (Reading, Mass.: Addison Wesley, 1996).

12. Sarah Ferguson, "Feel the Pain: Meet the Lost Souls of a Damaged Generation," *Leadership* (Spring 1995), 44.

13. Adapted and expanded from Zander, "The Gospel for Generation X," 37-39.

14. These examples were adapted from Michigan Metro Girl Scout Council, *Diversity Awareness* (Detroit: Michigan Metro Girl Scout Council, 1992), 41-42.

15. Douglas Foster, "The Disease *IS* Adolescence...Symptoms are Violence, Suicide, Drugs, Alcohol, Car Wrecks, and Poverty," *Utne Reader* (July/August 1994), 50-56. Mike A. Males, *The Scapegoat Generation: America's War on Adolescents* (Monroe, Maine: Common Courage Press, 1996), 243, 283-284.

16. Responses gleaned from a questionnaire developed by Lisa Kimball and David Selzer in 1996 and circulated to youth and young adults for the Ministries with Young People Cluster, Episcopal Church Center.

Questions for Discussion

These discussion questions are designed to help congregational leaders bridge the gap between the theology and theories outlines in *Disorganized Religion* and their home context. They are designed to assist leaders in a series of group sessions, or to establish a course of independent study and reading for an individual. For group study, four or five sessions are ideal, but you will need to find a schedule that best fits your situation. Choose the areas that seem most important to you, and use the questions as a way to provoke discussion on the issues presented in the text. Afterward, look at specific ways the ideas presented could be acted upon within your context.

Disorganized Religion is not intended to be a how-to manual or a formal course of study. Rather, it is designed to offer a variety of perspectives and ideas related to the evangelization of youth and young adults. Those seeking concrete program outlines should consult the selected reading list at the back of the book.

✓ Part One: Sharing the Good News

The articles in this section discuss both the challenges and the opportunities of the evangelization of youth and young adults. Clearly, individuals and congregations interested in the evangelization of young people must look toward deepening relationships as a first step in gaining understanding between generations.

Reflect on the life of your own congregation as you consider the following questions.

✓ In what ways are young people a part of community life? In what areas of your corporate life are young people conspicuously absent?

✓ What are some of the ways your congregation could more fully respond to young people? What changes and commitments would your congregation need to make in order more fully to recognize the gifts, skills, and talents of young people?

∿ How might you reach beyond your own families to young adults and students in the congregation?

∿ Part Two: Identity and Culture

The underlying theme of the articles in this section is the importance of culture in the identity formation of young people, as well as the importance of cultural factors in the evangelization process. The church's work with young people must relate directly to their stage of life and their cultural context. This requires the church to be faithful in passing on the unchanging elements of Christian belief, while at the same time empowering young people to live out the application of those elements within their own cultural context.

Take a few moments to reflect on your own adolescence and young adult years.

∿ What issues were of most concern to you during that time of your life? What did you think about the church during those years? How best did you experience God?

∿ Who were the persons you most admired? Who were your mentors in the faith? How do you think young people today might respond to these same questions?

∿ What message do young people today have for the church? What is the role of the church in relation to young people in a society that devalues and depersonalizes them?

∿ Part Three: Evangelism and Liturgy

Spiritual development takes place in communities, and is not just an individual occupation. Young people yearn for religious rituals that authentically communicate the gospel and provide opportunities for them to reflect on their own lives in light of scripture. One of the challenges for the church is to enable experimentation within worship which is more meaningful to young people, while at the same time remaining part of the whole mission of the church.

∿ What are some of the traditional roles of young people within the worshiping community? How might those roles be expanded to include young people in other dimensions of worship life?

⌁ How might worship in a congregation become part of an outreach ministry to young people?

⌁ What is your own experience of Christian initiation? How might our rites better respond to the needs of young people?

⌁ **Part Four: Church and Academy**

This section focuses on the importance of the church's ministries in education in regard to the evangelization of young people. While diminishing at an alarming rate, Episcopal campus ministries continue to carry out important ministries of Christian formation and outreach. Though young vocations to the ordained ministry are on the decline, in the past campus ministries have played an important role in vocational discernment and recruitment of ordained leadership. Similarly, Episcopal primary and secondary schools provide important religious education for young people from many religious backgrounds.

⌁ In what ways does your congregation or diocese work with local educational institutions? In addition to inviting students to participate in worship, what are some other ways your congregation might make itself available to students?

⌁ If you are in a college or university town, how is your congregation perceived by people on campus?

⌁ What are some concrete ways the church can support young people in their vocations?

⌁ **Part Five: Prophetic Witness**

Young people are marginalized and discriminated against in both church and society. Racism, sexism, classism, homophobia, and other forms of oppression seriously affect the spiritual health of young people within and beyond the church. A church that takes the evangelization of young people seriously sees the connections between the devalued status of young people and its own prophetic ministry. Further, the church's evangelization efforts should include education and training for young people that enable them to become partners with adults working for justice in church and society.

⌁ How do you feel the Episcopal Church is living out its prophetic ministry to young people?

↜ In your experience, what are the connections between evangelism and service?

↜ How are young people marginalized or discriminated against within your own community? What are some concrete ways that the church could advocate for young people within your community?

↜ How might young people become more engaged in local service and social action efforts in your community?

Selected Reading List

This list is not intended to be exhaustive, but provides information about some of the works pertaining to the evangelization of youth and young adults available today.

Atkinson, Harley. *Handbook of Young Adult Religious Education.* Birmingham: Religious Education Press, 1995.

Brennan, Patrick. *Full Cycle Youth Evangelization: A Resource for Youth Ministries.* Allen, Texas: Tabor, 1993.

Caddy, Barbara B., T. William Hall, and Robert J. Marzano. *School Wars: Resolving Our Conflicts Over Religion and Values.* New York: Simon & Schuster, 1997.

Called to Teach and Learn: A Catechetical Guide for the Episcopal Church. New York: The Episcopal Church Center, 1994.

Carey, George. *Spiritual Journey: 1,000 Young Adults Share the Reconciling Experience of Taizé with the Archbishop of Canterbury.* Harrisburg: Morehouse Publishing, 1994.

Carmody, Denise Lardner. *Organizing a Christian Mind: A Theology of Higher Education.* Valley Forge: Trinity Press International, 1996.

Chu, Thomas K., Sheryl A. Kajawa and Anne Rowthorn. *Godworks: Youth and Young Adult Ministry Models...Evangelism at Work With Young People* Harrisburg: Morehouse, 1997.

Clement, Shirley F., and Thomas L. Salsgiver. *Youth Ministry and Evangelism: New Wine for a New Day.* Nashville: Discipleship Resources, 1991.

Daloz, Laurent A., et al. *Common Fire: Lives of Commitment in a Complex World.* Boston: Beacon Press, 1996.

Francis, Leslie, and William Kay. *Teenage Religion and Values.* Herefordshire, England: Gracewing, 1995.

Garber, Julie, ed. *Ministry with Young Adults: The Search for Intimacy.* Elgin: Faith Quest, Brethren Press, 1992.

Gribbon, Robert. *Developing Faith in Young Adults.* Washington, D. C.: The Alban Institute, 1992.

Gribbon, Robert. *Students, Churches, and Higher Education: Congregational Ministry in a Learning Society.* Charlotte: United Ministries in Higher Education, 1996.

Gura, Carol, and Carol Koch. *Ministering to Young Adults: A Resource Manual.* Winona: St. Mary's Press, 1987.

Harris, Maria. *Proclaim Jubilee: A Spirituality for the Twenty-First Century.* Louisville: Westminster/John Knox Press, 1996.

Heath, Shirley Brice, and Milbrey W. McLaughlin, eds. *Identity and Inner City Youth: Beyond Ethnicity and Gender.* New York: Teachers College Press, 1993.

Howe, Neil, and William Strauss. *The Fourth Turning.* New York: Broadway Books, 1997.

Howe, Neil, and William Strauss. *13th Gen: Abort, Retry, Ignore, Fail?* New York: Vintage, 1993.

Hughes, Amanda Millay, and David E. Crean. *The Journey to Adulthood: A Parish Program of Spiritual Formation for Young People.* LeaderResources, 38 Mulberry Street, Box 302, Leeds, MA 01053-0302.

Jones, Reginald L., ed. *Black Adolescents.* Berkeley: Cobb and Henry Publishers, 1989.

Kew, Richard, and Roger White. *Toward 2015: A Church Odyssey.* Cambridge, Mass.: Cowley Publications, 1997.

Kujawa, Sheryl A., and Lois Sibley, eds. *Resource Book for Ministries with Youth and Young Adults in the Episcopal Church.* New York: The Episcopal Church Center, 1995.

Loeb, Paul Rogat. *Generation at the Crossroads: Apathy and Action on the American Campus.* New Brunswick: Rutgers University Press, 1994.

Mahedy, William, and Janet Bernardi. *A Generation Alone.* Downer's Grove: InterVarsity Press, 1994.

Males, Mike A. *The Scapegoat Generation: America's War on Adolescents.* Monroe: Common Courage Press, 1996.

Matthaei, Sondra Higgins. *Faith Matters: Faith-Mentoring in the Faith Community.* Valley Forge: Trinity International, 1996.

Miller, Craig Kennet. *Post Moderns: The Beliefs, Hopes, and Fears of Young Americans, 1965–1981.* Alpharetta, Georgia: Discipleship Resources, 1997.

Mitchell, Susan. *The Official Guide to the Generations.* Ithaca: New Strategist Publications, 1995.

Office of Evangelism Ministries. *The Catechumenal Process: Adult Initiation and Formation for Christian Life and Ministry.* New York: The Church Hymnal Corporation, 1990.

Palladino, Grace. *Teenagers: An American History.* New York: Basic Books, 1996.

Parks, Sharon. *The Critical Years: Young Adults and the Search for Meaning, Faith and Commitment.* New York: HarperCollins, 1986.

Peters-Pries, Pam. *Living Unplugged: Young Adults, Faith and the Uncommon Life.* Newton: Faith and Life Press, 1996.

Plumbline: A Journal of Ministry in Higher Education. The Episcopal Church at Northwestern University, 2010 Orrington Avenue, Evanston, IL 60201-2912.

Portaro, Sam. *Conflict and a Christian Life.* Harrisburg: Morehouse Publishing, 1996.

Portaro, Sam, and Gary Peluso. *Inquiring and Discerning Hearts: Vocation and Ministry with Young Adults on Campus.* Alpharetta, Georgia: Scholars Press, 1993.

Prophets of Hope Editorial Team. *Evangelization of Hispanic Young People.* Winona: St. Mary's Press, 1995. (Available in Spanish and English.)

Prophets of Hope Editorial Team. *Hispanic Young People and the Church's Pastoral Response.* Winona: St. Mary's Press, 1994. (Available in Spanish and English.)

Shelton, Charles. *Adolescent Spirituality: Pastoral Ministry for High School and College Youth.* New York: Crossroad, 1989.

Ward, Pete. *Worship and Youth Culture: A Guide to Alternative Worship.* London: Marshall Pickering/HarperCollins, 1993.

Ward, Pete. *Youth Culture and the Gospel.* London: Marshall Pickering/HarperCollins, 1992.

Ward, Pete. *Youth Work and the Mission of God.* London: SPCK, 1997.

Warren, Michael, ed. *Readings and Resources in Youth Ministry.* Winona: St. Mary's Press, 1987.

Winter, Gibson. *America in Search of Its Soul.* Harrisburg: Morehouse Publishing, 1996.

Youth A Part: Young People and the Church. London: National Society/Church House Publishing, 1996.

Youthworkers' Encyclopedia. Center for Youth Studies, 130 Essex Street, South Hamilton, MA 01982; (978) 468-7111, ext. 573; e-mail: cys@gcts.edu.

Cowley Publications is a ministry of the Society of St. John the Evangelist, a religious community for men in the Episcopal Church. Emerging from the Society's tradition of prayer, theological reflection, and diversity of mission, the press is centered in the rich heritage of the Anglican Communion.

Cowley Publications seeks to provide books, audio cassettes, and other resources for the ongoing theological exploration and spiritual development of the Episcopal Church and others in the body of Christ. To this end, it is dedicated to developing a new generation of theological writers, encouraging them to produce timely, creative, and stimulating publications of excellence, and making these publications available widely, reaching both clergy and lay persons.